KU-572-484

Contents

FOR THE JUDYS

11 JAN 1979

WITHDRAWN

040215

DRURY LANE

The Rotunda. *Peter Abbey*

DRURY
LANE

Three Centuries of the Theatre Royal
1663–1971

BRIAN DOBBS

LIBRARY
ACC. No.   DEPT
060215
CLASS No.
792.0942 DOB
UNIVERSITY
OF CHESTER

PADGATE
COLLEGE OF EDUCATION
LIBRARY
ACC. NO. 75, 980

CASSELL · LONDON

CASSELL & COMPANY LTD
35 Red Lion Square, London WC1R 4SJ
Sydney, Auckland
Toronto, Johannesburg

© Brian Dobbs 1972

All rights reserved. No part of this publication
may be reproduced, stored in a retrieval system,
or transmitted, in any form or by any means,
electronic, mechanical, photocopying, recording
or otherwise, without the prior permission of
Cassell and Company Ltd.

First published 1972

I.S.B.N. 0 304 93859 9

22407

Printed in Great Britain by
Unwin Brothers Limited
Woking and London
F. 472

Illustrations

Preface

IF the Adelphi theatre or the Strand theatre had never existed, it would be possible to conclude that the history of drama would have been changed little. If the Theatre Royal Drury Lane had never existed, the whole course of dramatic history would have changed radically. Theatre, of all the arts, is the one which tends to mirror the taste and social history of its times. It can show the habits, attitudes and concerns of a people as accurately as a novel or a painting. Drury Lane had a monopoly of legitimate drama awarded under less than honourable circumstances, which was used, abused, shared and avoided but which lasted from 1663 to 1843, so the very existence of the house had a profound effect on writing, acting and staging.

On its boards have stepped fops, charlatans, prostitutes, murderers and highwaymen; alongside actors and actresses of genius. It has seen almost every manifestation of public entertainment, from Shakespearean tragedy and Restoration comedy, to melodrama, opera, pantomime and performing animals. The common view of the Lane as an example of a great literary showpiece descending to an off-shoot of show business, has carefully to be qualified. Without an audience, there can be no theatre. A theatre which attracts an audience is a commercial theatre. To attract an audience, a theatre has to give that audience what it wants. What makes the history of Drury Lane so fascinating is what audiences wanted at different periods of history, and its uncanny sense of providing it at the right time. This is why it can boast a longer survival than any other theatre in the world.

It would be impossible in a book of this size to write a comprehensive history. The architecture of four separate buildings and the financial structure of successive managements have been well covered in Volume **XXXV** of the *Survey of London*, so I have selected only those highlights which seemed to be the most important. Equally, the litigation which has surrounded changes of ownership of the Patent rights, of the lease and of the house, would justify a fat volume of its own. So would a literary history of the plays performed at Drury Lane.

This book is intended rather for the general reader who is aware in a general sense of the house's importance, and wishes to have an account of over 300 years in the life of a theatre unique in world history. To this end, I have dispensed with the scholarly apparatus of footnotes, and included major references in the text. The scholar or theatre historian who wishes to pursue any topic in greater detail will find a long bibliography at the back of the book, which, without claiming to be comprehensive, will give most of the major sources for research. In the quotations from contemporary documents, etc., I have retained the often bizarre spellings and punctuation to give the flavour of the period.

Those only familiar with the previous history of Drury Lane by W. Macqueen Pope will find that I have departed radically from his facts and his interpretation of events. This is because I was forced very early to the conclusion that Raymond Mander and Joe Mitchenson reached in their book *Musical Comedy*, that 'the books of W. Macqueen Pope are clothed with an Edwardian nostalgia and a romantic aura in which research and truth have little place'.

Because this book is not written in terms of 'heroes' and 'great men', I hope it will have the compensating virtue that it is about real people, honest and dishonest, honourable and outrageous, who whatever their times, their dress and their period language, come alive because they have, underneath the inessentials, all the emotions and obsessions that we have today. That Drury Lane attracted some of the most fascinating male and female personalities who ever drew breath meant that its story was a joy to research and write. If only part of my own enthusiasm reaches the reader, I will be content. An unperformed play is no play at all. Equally a book is nothing without a reader.

In addition to the people mentioned in the acknowledgements I would like to express my personal thanks to some individuals without whose help this book would have been impossible. To Alfred Anderson for his assistance with the manuscript, to Dorothea Alexander for opening my eyes to many aspects of theatre I would otherwise have missed, to George Hoare, the manager of Drury Lane, for allowing me to tour the house, to Wendon Dobbs for many invaluable suggestions, to Anthony Latham of the Enthoven collection for his unfailing courtesy, to Peter Abbey for his photographs of the modern Drury Lane specially taken for this book and particularly to Judy Smith for sharing her extensive knowledge of Victorian and Edwardian theatre and for gathering illustrations, I am extremely grateful. Most virtues will be theirs, the faults are solely mine.

In my journey over more than three centuries, I am sure there will inevitably be errors and wrong-headed conclusions. In justification I can only adopt the words that a distinguished predecessor John Genest used on the title page of his 1832 ten volume *Some Account of the English Stage*:

> If any thing be overlooked, or not accurately inserted . . . take into consideration that this history is compiled from all quarters.

October 1971   BRIAN DOBBS

Acknowledgements

NO researcher into theatre history can fail to be in debt to those who have ventured into the field before. With the exception of Mr Macqueen Pope, no-one has attempted the full history of the Drury Lane theatre before but I would like to express my gratitude to those who have taken a close look at certain aspects of London theatre, and on whose discoveries I have been glad to lean.

In addition to the long list of authors in the bibliography, my particular thanks are due to Joseph Q. Adams for his invaluable compilation *The Dramatic Records of Sir Henry Herbert*; to John Leslie Hotson for his incredible search through legal records for *The Commonwealth and Restoration Stage*; to Richard Hindry Barker for the best book on Cibber, *Mr Cibber of Drury Lane*; and to Alwin Thaler and E. B. Watson for two companion volumes, *Shakespeare to Sheridan* and *Sheridan to Robertson* which, although written nearly fifty years ago, remain excellent outlines of important periods of the history of the drama.

Credit is also due to the staffs of the British Museum, the Public Record Office, the Westminster Library, the Enthoven Collection and the British Drama League for help in many different ways; to Raymond Mander and Joe Mitchenson for assistance with illustrations; to John Simmons of Cassell's for guiding this book through its various stages of production; and to J. C. Trewin for not only granting me permission to quote from his biography of Macready, but for providing ample proof in his many books that to be accurate and scholarly is not the same thing as being dull and obscurantist.

PART I

The
Seventeenth
Century

CHAPTER ONE

Royal Favours

1660–3

ON 7 May 1663, eager members of a gowned and periwigged audience stepped from their chairs and coaches and fought their way into a new London theatre. Some were there to see themselves; some were there to see a revival of Beaumont and Fletcher's *The Humorous Lieutenant*, a play written some half a century before; some were there merely to register their presence at so important an event in London's theatre history.

None possessed the foresight to know that more than three centuries later, a thriving theatre would still be operating on the same site and that the name Drury Lane would become synonymous with a lion's share of the history of the drama. Between that first performance of *The Humorous Lieutenant* and Drury Lane's recent musicals like *The Great Waltz*, lies a chequered history as eventful as the plot of any play, a history successively full of real life tragedy and comedy and one which has not infrequently strayed into sheer farce.

Most of that first audience represented a narrowly defined section of the community—the Court and the other satellites orbiting around the restored King Charles II. If they could not be aware of the long history to come, most of them would have known that 7 May 1663 was not only a beginning but also an end—the culmination of a power struggle as ruthless as any delineated in a television soap opera.

Because we tend today to conduct financial and business affairs in an ethical fashion, it takes a conscious effort to recapture the spirit of times when it was taken for granted that men operated from self-interest. What one had, depended either upon an inherited fortune or upon what one could acquire in a shark-infested market place.

The freedom of private enterprise included the freedom to break agreements if it became necessary, the freedom to borrow money on the strength of extravagant promises and the freedom to double-cross one's fellow man whenever it became propitious. In the early days of the Restoration theatre, such freedoms were amply indulged.

For one thing, there was every reason to believe that money invested in a theatre would pay ample dividends. Not only did the Restoration restore a monarchy, a Parliament and a Church of England; it also restored an officially sanctioned audience. To any speculator trying to anticipate demand and, at a profit, provide the necessary supply, theatre was an obvious field for his activities.

Appetites for plays had been sharpened by the eighteen-year fast since 1642 when Cromwell's Puritans closed down every playhouse and imposed legal penalties, even imprisonments, upon those rash enough to bring a little histrionic colour into a grey Puritan world. Thanks to the researches of Leslie Hotson and others, we now know that the eighteen years was not quite the desert that it once appeared. Plays continued to be published, and performances were given in private or even, surreptitiously, in public.

Whether the target is prostitution, drink or drama; good intentions, penal legislation and official disapproval may deter, but not ultimately abolish; and theatre became something of an underground activity. Like Chicago speak-easies, Commonwealth theatres were prone to raids. Evidence exists to show that audiences were seized by troops and fined on the spot or imprisoned. Actors naturally suffered the same fate if their illegal activities were known.

To the majority of the profession, the outbreak of Civil War in 1642 was a disaster. Actors, dramatists and theatre managers suddenly saw their livelihoods snatched away by the victory of the Puritans, leaving their hopes rolling in the dust like the head of Charles I. Many served on the King's side in the war, and the restoration of Charles II must have seemed the answer to two decades of hopeful prayer.

The courtiers who had attended Charles at his court in exile and returned with him were all men familiar with French drama, and were men to whom theatre was a necessary and pleasant part of the civilized and leisurely life. Here then, was an audience, but who was going to satisfy them and reap the rewards for so doing?

Unsurprisingly, there was more than one claimant. How many and who they were and the sequence of events that was to leave two major London companies in existence by the end of 1660 is a subject which has long exercised the ingenuity of every theatre historian. The subject remains clouded in a fog of conflicting evidence and closely argued academic theories, and will undoubtedly be disputed for a long time to come. My own version which follows has been influenced by John

Freehafer, whose article *The formation of the London patent companies in 1660*, published in *Theatre Notebook* in Autumn 1965, seems to me, on the basis of my own researches into the documents and records of the time, to be the most logical explanation of events, and the only one to make adequate allowance for the sort of men involved. As we shall see, this is an important consideration.

On 29 May 1660, King Charles II, with years of poverty and vicissitudes behind him, entered London to claim the throne of England. One doubts that he took the opportunity to say with Shakespeare's Richard II that he wept for joy to stand upon his kingdom once again, but the sentiments cannot have been far from his mind. Unlike that lachrymose monarch, 'Old Rowley' (a nickname for Charles adopted from an exceptionally potent stallion of the day) was well in touch with reality. He was, in addition, as accessible a king as any and leant his ear to innumerable petitions, requests and pleas from his newly acquired subjects. He was now in the position to wield enormous patronage and preferment, and most of his followers were eager to queue up for the largesse being distributed. Chests were bared to display wounds acquired in the King's cause, with the tacit assumption that an annuity, or an office would be forthcoming as a belated reward for services rendered. Even if a job was not freely given, there was always the chance it might be bought. The King is unreliably reported to have advertised on one occasion for his lost dog, adding sardonically that the dog's was the only place at Court that no one seemed to wish to purchase.

Even before the King actually arrived, London was not without theatre companies. A Parliamentary investigation in Richard Cromwell's time found that regular stage performances and interludes had been given as early as 1659. In all probability, Charles came to a London which already had three troupes of actors.

Over at Drury Lane, there was the Cockpit. This, as its name suggests, was originally used for cock-fights but in 1616 it had been converted into a roofed theatre by Christopher Beeston. There, in 1649, an audience had been fined on the spot by Parliamentary soldiers for attending an illicit performance. Now it housed a company of actors under John Rhodes, a bookseller turned manager.

Another venue which stemmed from about 1605, was the Red Bull playhouse in Clerkenwell, which may have been an open theatre or possibly partly roofed. Here surreptitious performances and puppet plays had been given during the Commonwealth and now it provided a temporary home for a troupe under Michael Mohun, an actor who had been a major in the King's Civil War army.

The third theatre, and the last to be built in London before the Civil War, was the Salisbury Court theatre situated where Salisbury Square is today. Here, William Beeston was the manager and there is reason to believe that he staged a performance of a play by John Tatham called *The Rump*. This political satire, in which Puritan generals Lambert and Fleetwood are thinly veiled as Bertlam and Woodfleet, leans toward the temporary government of General Monk, rather than Charles's restoration, suggesting that it may well have been performed as early as February 1660, particularly as the Rump Parliament itself had been dissolved by 16 March and there would be little point in sending it up after that date. Beeston and his actors would be the third company in existence when Charles arrived.

Any of the three managers, Rhodes, Mohun and Beeston, could have been forgiven an air of complacency as they viewed their immediate prospects. Presumably the penal legislation imposed by the Puritan enemies of the drama would soon be lifted, they could go through the formality of applying for licences to perform plays and in return for a small fee, they could open their doors without concealment to cash in on what promised to be a theatrical and financial bonanza. What they did not know was that others, more ruthless than they, were eagerly anticipating getting in on the act. Rhodes, Mohun and Beeston were close to the theatre; they were not close to the Court and consequently not close to the King's ear. Their enemies were.

The first of these was a man whose fortunes were to be closely, and at times disastrously, linked with the early fortunes of the first theatre on the Drury Lane site. His name was Thomas Killigrew. Killigrew, and this is a recurring tendency among the personalities who figure in this book, seems a little larger than life to twentieth-century eyes. It is worth tracing his career before the Restoration to know something of his character. There were so many members of his family around at the time that even the *Dictionary of National Biography* manages to confuse them. The many sins of his son by his first marriage, Henry Killigrew, have been visited upon the father by some historians, which is a pity because Thomas had a full catalogue of his own to answer for.

Thomas was born in 1612, the son of Sir Robert Killigrew, a man closely implicated in the mysterious death of Overbury in the Tower of London. His mother was Mary Woodhouse, niece of Sir Francis Bacon. She was to be described in years to come as 'a cunning old woman who had been herself too much, and was too long versed in amours'.

Thomas himself was to tell Pepys that his first connection with the theatre was as a child, one of the small boys who turned up at the Red

Bull playhouse and were given free admission in return for their services in impersonating pocket-sized devils when the play demanded it.

He was semi-illiterate, not the strongest recommendation for a future playwright. In his family bible, he solemnly recorded his marriage to Cecilia, daughter of Sir John Crofts, who becomes 'Cissillia Croftes'. This was on '29 Juene 1636', and in 'Aprill 1637', his 'suenne Harrey' was born.

The young Thomas secured a place at Court in 1633 as a page to Charles I, presumably on the strength of his father's connections. This gave him the opportunity to do what he was best fitted for, living on his wits. One of the Court's more unpleasant practices was estate-begging. This open invitation to informing and witch-hunting worked like this. If one could initiate, or even finance as an investment, the arrest and conviction of some luckless transgressor, bribing a few professional informers if the evidence was too flimsy, it was then possible to claim the estates and possessions of the victim. Before Thomas had been at the Court a year, he and another courtier reaped the benefits from the prosecution of a Jesuit called Francis Smith. Smith cannot have been much of an adversary; he was in his eighties. Thomas also collected from a similar case against a Francis Lockwood, who 'died a Popish priest'.

The source of these windfalls mattered far less to Killigrew than the ready money. He needed every penny. And for every one he received, he spent two. His fee as page often went direct from the Treasury to some of his creditors. Thomas, particularly after the death of his first wife in 1638, was a gay liver. His first attempt at dramatic writing, *The Parson's Wedding*, a play considered indecent even in a libertarian age, could well have been an attempt to earn cash, as much as a bid to acquire a literary reputation.

He was also acquiring enemies. Hollar published an engraving of Killigrew showing him slumped on his elbow looking woebegone. A monkey sits on his shoulder, and the pattern on his gown is made up of twenty-four women's faces, most of them clearly recognizable portraits. In case anyone should miss the point of where Killigrew's money was being spent, Hollar adds some scurrilous verses.

> Foole that I was, who had so faire a State,
> Fower or five thousant by the yeare at least,
> And wast it so as I have done, of late,
> On Whores and Bawdes, and like a filthie beast
> Caught fowle diseases, which consume mee Sore,
> And all proceedes from loving everie whore . . . .

That would seem to put it fairly plainly.

With the outbreak of the Civil War, Killigrew and his fellow courtiers were in trouble. He himself was arrested on the order of the House of Commons although they were partly doing him a favour inasmuch as they protected him from his eager creditors. In July 1643, he was released in exchange for another prisoner. What war service he saw, we do not know, unless we can believe the testimony of another of his enemies, Richard Flecknoe, who wrote a *Life of Thomaso* to denigrate our hero. Perhaps it is true that

> All the Employment he had during the Warrs, was now and then to bring up a Convoy of Wenches to the Camp . . . whence he gain'd the honourable Title of Pimp-Master General of the Army. . . .

On his release from custody, Killigrew disappeared to the Continent. Abroad he travelled, wrote and found another wife Charlotte, one of whose attractions was a dowry of £10,000. He also found a kindred soul in the future Charles II. One can see why the two got on. At the Court in exile in France, one can see the two exchanging stories of past sexual conquests, planning fresh ones and contriving schemes to raise badly needed finances. Thomas undertook at least two journeys to Italy to raise credit on Charles's behalf.

One of these Italian sorties kept Thomas in Venice for about two years as Resident for the exiled King. He was duly expelled in 1633 for 'vicious behaviour' though this could have been a dark Venetian political plot to win favour with Cromwell.

When Charles was restored to the throne, Killigrew saw every reason to remind him of his past services and glean any crumbs dropping from the royal table. From Cromwell's plate to the Keepership of the Armoury at Greenwich, if it meant money, Thomas put in a claim for it. In three years, his name appears in the Treasury Books nearly fifty times. Flecknoe unkindly suggested:

> He was so ill-Natur'd, as he car'd not in whose light he stood. . . . He thought all the World made for him, and he for none; and that all wisdom consisted in keeping his own, and getting as much as he could of another Man's.

However rapacious Killigrew seemed to his enemies, Charles found him congenial company. Killigrew had built up a reputation for ready wit and made himself a sort of unofficial jester at Old Rowley's elbow.

His humour might not get many laughs today but Pepys gives us a nice eye-witness report of Killigrew's arrival from France with the restored King:

> Walking upon the Decks, where persons of Honour all the afternoon— among others, Thom Killigrew (a merry droll, but a gentleman of great esteem with the King): among many merry stories, he told one how he writ a letter three or four days ago to the Princess Royall about a Queen Dowager of Judaea and Palestine that was in The Hague incognita, that made love to the King, & c; which was Mr. Cary (a Courtiers) wife that had been a Nun, who are all married to Jesus.

No, I am not sure I see it either.

On an earlier occasion, Thomas is supposed to have been shown around Louis XIV's private chapel where a prominent feature was a triptych with a Crucifixion panel in the centre and side panels depicting the Pope and Louis himself. 'Well,' said Thomas, 'I was told Christ was crucified between two thieves but I didn't believe it till now.'

Another equally apocryphal story had him threatening Charles that he will resuscitate the remains of Protector Cromwell because 'no-one else is taking care of the kingdom'.

Quite apart from the opportunity to deliver similar *bons mots*, Killigrew knew that the King's indulgence might well give him the chance to move in to the realms of the theatre. At this point the plot decidedly thickens and it is time to introduce another major protagonist—Sir William D'Avenant.

D'Avenant's career before 1660 had been no less chequered than Killigrew's. He was born in 1606 as the second son of an Oxford vintner. His father became Mayor of Oxford and whether civic duties took him away from the hearth once too often or not, there is a persistent legend that the true father of young William was a not infrequent visitor at the D'Avenant household—William Shakespeare. This legend gained much currency and Sir William himself in later life was at no pains to deny it. In view of the fact that he became so closely involved in the theatre himself, such a suspected lineage can have done his image no harm.

At some time in the 1620s he became one of the minor hangers-on at Court and began to write plays. These were extremely popular and when the Poet Laureate, the great Ben Jonson, died in 1637, the Queen herself put forward Sir William D'Avenant's name as successor. Armed with this prestigious title, he went on from strength to strength and in addition

9

to acquiring a patent under the Great Seal in 1639 to erect a theatre of his own, he was appointed the Governor of the King and Queen's Company of actors performing in the Cockpit theatre at Drury Lane.

His sexual proclivities were in a similar category to Killigrew's but he was less fortunate than Thomas in that his pleasures cost him a considerable disfigurement, one which the wits of the day found an appropriate target for their barbs. Syphilis cost him his nose.

John Evelyn the diarist helpfully recorded the source—'He gott a terrible clap of a Black handsome wench that lay in Acre-yard, Westminster. . . .' (How did Evelyn know?)

It has been said that once when Sir William strode down a street an old lady called after him, 'God bless your eyesight sir, God bless your eyesight'. When he asked the reason for such an unlikely benediction, she pointed out that in the event of his vision failing he would have nothing on which to perch a pair of spectacles.

When the Civil War broke out, D'Avenant did his best to preserve his livelihood as a theatre manager by attempting to raise forces for the King's side, for which offence he was arrested twice but managed to escape both times. The second time he decided that discretion was the better part of valour and fled to France.

On the Queen's behalf, he returned to England with stores for the Earl of Newcastle. Newcastle made him Lieutenant General of Ordnance and however little he knew of strategy and ballistics, he distinguished himself sufficiently at the siege of Gloucester to be thought worthy of a knighthood for valour. When the Royalist cause collapsed he again returned to France until 1643 when the Queen sent him to Virginia. It proved not to be a lucky mission because his ship was captured *en route* by a boarding party of Parliamentary supporters, and Sir William finished up in the Tower of London. Surprisingly enough, he was well treated during his two-year imprisonment and allowed the rare privilege of writing and publishing poetry.

When he got out of prison, he had no visible source of income and unless he could find a way of evading the restrictions on theatrical activity, starvation loomed. Assiduously he began to cultivate what few friends he had in positions of power. One of these was Whitelocke, his latter-day jailer as Lord Keeper of the Tower. Somehow, and it is a testimony to his powers of persuasion that he did so, he obtained permission to stage some quasi-dramatic entertainments in private. The privacy of the performances did not preclude taking money at the door.

The first of them was *The First Day's Entertainment at Rutland House, by Declamations and Musick* in November 1656. The 'Musick' was an important factor in evading the fate which would have befallen a performance of a play. Encouraged by this success, his next venture was *The Siege of Rhodes*, an opera written by himself. There are reasons for believing this to be the first opera performed in England, and Sir William added two other innovations to make *The Siege of Rhodes* a notable landmark in theatre annals. He used a rudimentary form of scenery and cast a woman in one of the roles, both startling departures from the general practices of Elizabethan and Jacobean staging.

Having got away with this, D'Avenant began to sail closer and closer to the wind. In 1658 he opened the Cockpit at Drury Lane to stage another hybrid entertainment *The Cruelty of the Spaniards in Peru*. The choice of subject was not entirely accidental in view of Cromwell's well-known antipathy to Spain, and presumably it suited the authorities to condone so blatant a piece of propaganda. However, when it came to a sequel, *The History of Sir Francis Drake*, even its patriotic content of Spaniard-bashing failed to avert official attention and we know from the *Publick Intelligence* that Richard Cromwell was asking awkward questions as to who had authorized such a performance.

As with every man of the theatre, the only real answer to Sir William's problems was the return to a government prepared to sanction the drama, but when he tried to accelerate the process by lending assistance to Sir George Booth's rising in Cheshire in 1659, another term of imprisonment was the inevitable outcome. At least this did not last long and soon after his release return to monarchy became inevitable.

Showing a little more political awareness than Beeston, Mohun and Rhodes, he took a lease on Lisle's Tennis Court to convert it into a theatre, went to France, and we can reasonably surmise that he visited Charles to put in a plea for his future status in the London theatre. It is at least conceivable that he and Killigrew came to some private agreement in France that once Charles was on the throne of England, they would run theatrical affairs between them.

I have digressed on the careers of Killigrew and D'Avenant during the Commonwealth at some length because their actions from May to November 1660 stem largely from what sort of men they were. Either independently or in unofficial conjunction, they planned a monopoly of London theatre and if anyone got in their way, he would be ruthlessly suppressed.

A mere six weeks after the May Restoration, a royal warrant was drawn up requiring the issue of a patent under the Great Seal of England to Thomas Killigrew. Obviously, Charles had succumbed to Killigrew's claims that he, in tandem with Sir William, was the man to run the

A modern copy of the Killigrew Patent—one of history's most controversial
documents. *Peter Abbey*

theatre. The document recognized that D'Avenant's patent of 1639 still had legal force and granted Killigrew authority to set up a company of actors and to build a playhouse. Sounding an ominous knell for Mohun, Beeston and Rhodes, it also said that he and D'Avenant would be allowed a monopoly of London theatre. D'Avenant himself was shrewd enough to realize that although this order, if it went through, gave him a measure of authority, he was, to a certain extent, dependent upon Killigrew's good will. Far better, therefore, to try and obtain another even stronger order. Consequently, he drafted one himself and submitted it ten days after Killigrew's.

It starts:

Our will and pleasure is that you prepare a Bill for our signature to passe our Great Seale of England, containing a Grant unto our trusty and well beloved Thomas Killigrew Esq., one of the Groomes of our Bed Chamber and Sir William Davenant Knight, to give them full power and authoritie to erect Two Companys of Players consisting respectively of such persons as they shall chuse and appoint, and to purchase or build and erect at their charge as they shall thinke fitt Two Houses or Theaters . . . for the representations of Tragedys, Comedys, Playes, Operas . . . .

Later on the document gives us one clue as to the line of persuasion Killigrew had been pursuing—the emergence of Killigrew and D'Avenant as guardians of public morality which, in the light of future developments in Restoration comedies, can only be greeted with hollow laughter. Nevertheless, it helped to show the existing companies in a bad light:

. . . in regard of the extraordinary lisence that hath bin lately used in things of this Nature our pleasure is that there shall be no more places of Representations or Companys of Actors or Representers of sceanes in the Cittys of London or Westminster or in the liberties of them then the Two to be now erected by virtue of this Authoritie, but that *all others shall be absolutely suppressed.* . . .

[My italics]

It is doubtful that the King realized the legal implications of this all-embracing monopoly placing such widespread powers into the courtiers' hands. One man, at least, did. This was the Attorney General, Sir Jeffrey Palmer. Although he was unwilling directly to challenge a Royal request, he took the lawyer's usual escape route, procrastination, and delayed putting the order through. His official line was that such a matter was too unimportant to justify such sweeping legislation.

Killigrew and D'Avenant meanwhile pestered the King for immediate action and Palmer mildly acquiesced on 12 August, writing to Charles

> May it please yor Matie: the humble representation wch I made to yor highness concerning the provided grant to Mr Killigrewe and Sr Wm. Davenant was onlie that the matter was more proper for A tolleration; then A Grant under the greate Seale of England; and did not interpose any other obstacle; nor doe find cause to object against the twoo warrants they haue now produced.

The warrant duly passed the privy signet on 21 August, by which time a clause had been added making Killigrew and D'Avenant official censors 'to peruse all playes that haue been formerly written, and to expunge all prophanenesse and scurrility from the same, before they be represented or acted . . . .'

Traditionally, the responsibility for censorship rested with a Court official known as the Master of the Revels. One could anticipate a protest at part of his duties being usurped but without some knowledge of the contemporary incumbent it would be difficult to anticipate its nature. It came, not so much as a protest, more as the angry cry of a wounded buffalo, with lurid curses and bloodthirsty imprecations to match. Someone had trespassed on the territory of Sir Henry Herbert, and someone was going to pay for such effrontery. No one, least of all a jester or a Cromwellian collaborationist, was going to take money out of Sir Henry's pocket.

He had succeeded to the office as early as 1623, and an adroit operation that had been. He approached the then Master, Sir John Astley, and showed himself to be concerned at Sir John's health under the wearisome burden of administrative duties. Not only would he like to help out, he would pay a token £150 a year for the privilege. Sir John stepped down, naïvely imagining that he had struck a reasonable bargain, and Sir Henry stepped up. In no time at all, the investment of the £150 paid handsome dividends to the tune of £4,000 a year. Sir Henry worked on the assumption that if you make a big enough noise and demand a say in enough different fields, there comes a point when not only do people take you at your face value, they do not dream of questioning your authority. He insisted upon issuing annual licences for just about any activity known to man, and then pocketed the proceeds. Licensing fees for plays became the mere tip of the iceberg. Sir Henry demanded, and got, fees from such varied activities as rope-dancing, showing an elephant, parading a camel and two dromedaries, displaying a live beaver, playing a musical organ 'with divers motions in it', and staging an exhibition of pictures in wax.

By 1628, he hit on the brilliant notion that not only should he receive a fee for licensing a play, he should be given a fee for reading it to see if he would license it for a fee. Just before the Civil War, he recorded self-righteously: 'Received from Kirke for a new play which I burnte for the ribaldry and offence that was in it, £2.' Presumably the match came free.

It soon became known to men of the theatre that the only way round the formidable obstacle of Sir Henry, was to drop him a little sweetener in terms of a lump sum, after which his moral objections disappeared, and he became very amenable. On one occasion the King's company paid him £5 and he forbade the Red Bull actors to perform Shakespeare.

At the Restoration, Sir Henry was anxious to resume his collection of sundry fees, suspended for the last eighteen years by the political events of the Commonwealth. He did his best—for the first time feasts, billiards, ninepins and cockfighting came under the Master of the Revels and more fees rolled in. If Killigrew and D'Avenant had been really astute, they would have come to an arrangement with Sir Henry. In return for a percentage of the profits which they could reasonably anticipate, they could have won a powerful and convenient ally. Instead, they made an implacable and noisy enemy.

On 9 July, Killigrew's warrant was passed, and before D'Avenant's draft went through on 21 August, Sir Henry moved on to the attack. He protested directly to the King about the usurpers. D'Avenant was probably the main target for his wrath, because Sir William had been the cause of Sir Henry's losing face during the reign of Charles I. Sir Henry had treated a play of D'Avenant's called *The Witts* with an excessive amount of blue pencil and, on D'Avenant's appeal to the monarch, Charles I himself had ordered the offending lines to be reinstated. Sir Henry's appeal started:

That whereas your petitioner by vertue of seuerall graunts vnder the great seale of England hath executed the said Office as Master of the Revells, for about 40 yeares, in the times of King James, and of King Charles, both of blessed memory, with excepcion only to the time of the late horrid rebellion . . . .

He goes on to say that no one had ever been allowed to play or to build a theatre without his permission, that is, except

Sir William Davenant, Knight, who obtained Leaue of Oliver and Richard Cromwell to vent his Operas, in a time when your petitioner owned not their Authority.

Angrily, and no doubt accurately, he points out that Killigrew and D'Avenant lied when making their application that they had already spoken to him on the subject:

And whereas your petitioner hath been represented to your Maiesty as a person consenting to the said powers expressed in the said Warrant, your petitioner vtterly denies the least Consent or foreknowledge thereof, but looke vpon it as an vniust surprize, and distructiue to the powers graunted vnder the said great seale to your petitioner . . . .

Goodness knows what would happen if their application went through:

It may bee of very ill consequence, as your petitioner is advised, by a new graunt to take away and cut off a braunch of the antient powers graunted to the said Office vnder the great seale . . . .

He forbore to add that it would also cost him a great deal of money.

This was a very piquant situation. Over the next few months there were two people determined to close down the existing companies and set up companies themselves, and another who had a vested interest in preserving a large number of companies and collecting fees from them all. The irony was that both parties claimed royal authority for their actions, while the King himself, whose inconsistencies had led to the conflict, either delegated the necessary decisions to officials like Palmer, or let them take their natural course in the law courts.

Killigrew and D'Avenant, acting under the first warrant, began to silence the existing companies at the end of July. This suppression cannot have been wholly effective because they were dealing with men with a great tradition for defying authority. It had to be repeated about a month later on the basis of the 21 August warrants, and, according to evidence collected by John Freehafer, a third and final attempt at suppression came at about 1 October. The last one was successful.

Meanwhile, Sir Henry had been licensing the Rhodes, Mohun and Beeston companies and promising them protection from Killigrew and D'Avenant. They began to pay him but when the persecution continued, and it is possible that this included short terms of imprisonment for the most recalcitrant of the players, they began to withhold their fees. This brought a series of orders, warrants and summonings from the Master of the Revels Office down on their heads. The unlucky actors had been caught in the crossfire of the power struggle going on around them. It was an unenviable situation; either they succumbed to the power of Killigrew and D'Avenant hell-bent on reducing their ranks to two hand-picked companies and leaving those not selected without the chance of finding employment elsewhere, or they threw in their lot with the irascible and ultimately powerless Sir Henry.

Victory for the courtiers on at least a temporary basis was probably inevitable. Of the two, Killigrew was the more powerful. When it came to a choice of actors and plays, D'Avenant emerged as the subordinate partner in whatever agreement had been reached between them. He was however, more experienced in the ways of the theatre and a shrewder man. He was prepared to bide his time and pick up the pieces that Killigrew left him.

An important piece of documentary evidence must be mentioned at this stage. There is a list, dated 6 October 1660 in the Lord Chamberlain's papers of the time, of 'His Majesty's Comedians'. It provides an invaluable guide to the actors who were caught up in the struggle. The names on the list are Mohun, Burt, Hart, Robert and Edward Shatterell, Cartwright, Clun, Wintershall, Lacy, Baxter, Loveday, Betterton and Kynaston. This list is most commonly accepted as evidence for the existence of a company formed by Killigrew and D'Avenant who opened up in early October with a united company under themselves until they saw fit to split up and form their own individual companies as originally envisaged in the warrants.

As William Van Lennep puts it in the first volume of the monumental *The London Stage 1660–1800*:

. . . the two men pooled their resources into a united company, which, possibly by 8 Oct 1660, opened at the Cockpit in Drury Lane. This temporary union lasted until early November 1660. By 5 Nov 1660 Killigrew's Company, known as the King's, split off to act, first, at the Red Bull and then, on 8 Nov 1660, at Gibbons' Tennis Court in Vere St, where it remained for some time. . . . After the dissolution of the united company, D'Avenant's actors, known as the Duke's Company, presumably opened at the Salisbury Court Theatre, possibly by 5 November 1660.

This has long been the generally accepted view of events. However, given that Killigrew was the more influential figure, I agree with John

Freehafer in doubting the existence of a united company. I think it far more likely that the list of His Majesty's Comedians quoted above is just what it says, a King's company of actors who operated as such from the very first as a company formed under Killigrew.

Not only would it have been a pointless exercise to set up a company for about three weeks and then dissolve it, a subterfuge which would have fooled no one, but also it fits in with the operations of Killigrew as we know him. Without any of D'Avenant's managerial experience, once he had the reins of power, all he was concerned with was getting a play on, any play, staged any old how, as soon as possible. Why should he worry himself that whatever was staged would be an old repertory piece, and that his company of the older actors might face sterling competition later from a rival company of youth and spirit with the added advantage of D'Avenant's unique experience? The major consideration was to get the doors open immediately and cash in on the novelty of legally permitted plays.

To develop the theory further, I would now like to look at the doings of Sir Henry Herbert while the new company was being set up. On their very first day of operations he sent off one of his curt missives to Rhodes at the 'Cockpitt':

> . . . to require you to attende mee concerning your Playhouse called the Cockpitt Playhouse in Drury Lane, And to bring with you such Authority As you haue for Errecting of the said house Into a Playhouse, at your perill.

Two days later, back came the document with an answer from Rhodes— 'That the Kinge did authorize Him'. I think we can be justified in believing from this that Sir Henry was enquiring about Rhodes's authority for leasing the house to a new company, and take it that Rhodes, in his reply, is pointing out that to lease to the King's own company is surely going to be in accord with royal pleasure. Not that Sir Henry let such minor considerations deter him when his blood was up as undoubtedly it was by now. He decided to attack the players directly, and with a nice disregard for Killigrew's authority over them, suggested that it was at Killigrew's and D'Avenant's behest. He sent a warrant to the Cockpit players which said:

> Whereas severall complaints have been made against you, to the Kings most excellent Majesty by Mr Killigrew and Sir William D'Avenant, concerning the unusuall and unreasonable rates taken at

your playhouse doors . . . And the said complaints made use of by the said Mr Killigrew and Sir William Davenant as part of their suggestions for their pretended power and your late restrainte . . . .

The last phrase suggests that Sir Henry thought it opportune to remind Mohun and Co. that it was none other than their new master who had been responsible for having them placed in prison.

The warrant had one effect—a despairing petition direct to the King from the actors themselves. Entitled 'The humble Petition of Michael Mohun, Robert Shatterell, Charles Hart, Nich. Burt, Wm. Cartwright, Walter Clun, and William Wintersell', it goes:

. . . having been suprest by a warrant from your Majestie, Sir Henry Herbert informed us it was Mr Killigrew had caused it, and if wee would give him so much a weeke, he would protect them against Mr Killigrew and all powers. The complaint against us was, scandalous plays, raising the price, and acknowledging noe authority; all which ended in soe much per weeke to him; for which wee had leave to play, and promise of his protection: the which your Majesty knows he was not able to performe, since Mr Killigrew, having your Majesties former grante, suprest us, until wee had by covenant obliged ourselves to act with woemen, a new theatre, and habitts according to our sceanes. And according to your Majesties approbation, *from all the companies we made election of one company*; and so farre Sir Henry Herbert hath bene from protecting us, he hath been a continual disturbance unto us, who were united by your Majesties commande *under Mr Killigrew, as Master of your Majesties Comedians* . . . .

[My italics]

If we read between the lines this tells us a great deal. The choice of the term 'from *all* the companies', rather than from *both* companies, suggests that there were indeed three companies in existence at the time of the suppressions. The document also confirms my suspicions that the new company was under Killigrew, and that, from the outset, it was a King's company of players. I further suspect, since the petition concentrates so hard on the nuisance value of Sir Henry, that not only was Killigrew aware that the petition was to be sent, but that he probably had a hand in its composition. To Killigrew himself, Sir Henry was to be 'a continual disturbance'. And he had not finished yet.

Before the week was out Sir Henry had filed a law suit against the Mohun company for £300 damages when they failed to keep up payments under his original licensing agreement with them. Actually at most they

19

owed him £50 and although the courts eventually found for Sir Henry, he got only £48. On the same day, he brought suits against D'Avenant and Killigrew accusing them of usurping the authority of his office and depriving him of his fees and profits. Because the results of this litigation were dependent upon the time-consuming channels of the courts, we can leave them for a moment to look more closely at what has already happened.

The list of actors quoted above has often been interpreted as an amalgam of only two companies—Rhodes and Mohun. Leslie Hotson, for example, argued that Mohun, Hart, Burt, Robert Shatterell, Edward Shatterell, Cartwright, Clun, Wintershall, Lacy, Baxter and Loveday were all from the Mohun company and that Betterton and Kynaston were from the Rhodes company. I can find only eight names included in other documents to confirm that they were indeed Mohun men, those of Burt, Hart, Mohun himself, the Shatterells, Wintershall, Clun and Cartwright. Kynaston and Betterton were Rhodes men which leaves Lacy, Baxter and Loveday unaccounted for. Surely this is because they came from Beeston's company, and even if we are unable to confirm this, it would further explain why the term 'all the companies' was used in the petition.

We then come to early November. The new company had been playing at the Cockpit since 8 October, and on 5 November the dissolution into two separate companies is supposed to have taken place. Certainly D'Avenant reached an agreement with a number of actors on 5 November. The document is too long to be given in full but it is a businesslike arrangement whereby D'Avenant contracts to supply a new theatre and set up a new company under himself as 'alone . . . Master and Superior'. The actors concerned are Thomas Sheppey, Robert Nokes, James Nokes, Thomas Lovell, John Moseley, Cave Underhill, Robert Turner, Thomas Lilleston and *Thomas Betterton*. That the last-named should be contracting with D'Avenant is extremely interesting. It suggests to me that whereas the others were people that Killigrew had been content to leave out of his company, Betterton had been lured away by D'Avenant with the offer of leading parts (in the King's Company he would be playing only the roles left after his seniors Hart, Mohun and Burt had taken their pick) and the prospect of becoming a full partner in the enterprise. As if in confirmation that there had been something of a poaching operation in Betterton's case, the Lord Chamberlain issued a prohibition, dated 12 December, forbidding actors to change from one company to another.

There is no direct evidence that the new D'Avenant company, who would be known as the Duke's company, did actually play until 29 January 1661, when Pepys visited the 'Blackfryars' theatre which one can assume is a Pepysian slip for Whitefriars, i.e. Salisbury Court theatre, which the diarist also visited on 9 and 23 February 1661. Obviously the company gave some performances prior to those recorded by Pepys but I doubt that they gave many, and I see it far more as a period in which D'Avenant rehearsed, trained and planned for the day (actually in June 1661) when his new theatre at Lisle's Tennis Court in Lincoln's Inn Fields would be ready, and he could resume the experiments with scenic effects which he had started in the Commonwealth. Killigrew had been allowed first choice of plays, and it must have taken some time to build an adequate repertory. On 12 December, D'Avenant had to obtain special permission to perform nine Shakespeare plays, six other plays from the repertory of the old Rhodes company, and rights in his own plays.

Although Killigrew was the more powerful of the two, if we examine his new status carefully he was not all-powerful. In the agreement between D'Avenant and his actors, provision was made for Thomas to get a free box in the new theatre when it was ready, which is more than D'Avenant had been allowed by the King's company, but one wonders how free a choice Killigrew had really had. Some of his actors would probably have picked themselves because they were favourites of the King anyway, and once in Killigrew's company they naturally demanded some say in the running of it. Whereas D'Avenant was able to secure ten shares for himself in his company and a free hand artistically, the inexperienced Killigrew had to be content with fewer shares in his own company, and to leave the day to day running of it in the hands of Hart, Mohun and Lacy.

Furthermore, the much feared monopoly of D'Avenant and Killigrew was not yet an actuality, but existed only on paper. Although their activities had met with a large measure of success another claimant for theatrical favours appeared before the end of the year and, with an abandon which must have infuriated the two, the King allowed the Lord Chamberlain to license George Jolly, an actor-manager who had spent much time in Germany, to set up a company. (Because it lies outside the main theme of this history, I will just mention here that Jolly was eventually cheated out of his licence by the two, but the fact that he got one at all is symptomatic of the limited nature of the power of the warrants the two had been acting under.)

The two companies under D'Avenant and Killigrew continued to enjoy a measure of royal favour. Not only did Charles attend public performances and make payment to them accordingly, he invited them to the Court theatre at Whitehall from time to time to perform in private. The Lord Chamberlain's warrant books, preserved in the Public Record Office, have frequent entries recording such payments. For example, there is an entry dated 14 April 1662 requesting a payment to Killigrew of £160 at £10 a play for each time the King attended at the King's company's performances at Vere Street, and £700 at £20 a play for plays performed at Court.

One cloud on the horizon was Sir Henry and his outstanding law suits against the pair. He also continued to press for payment of fees for the performances of plays. His particular target was the D'Avenant company. On 6 May 1662, he took out a writ against Betterton and the other actors claiming arrears in fees for ten new and one hundred revived plays performed by the company between November 1660 and May 1662. It had little effect particularly when his suits against the masters of the companies produced totally varying results. One hearing in Westminster on 26 May 1662 found for Killigrew and D'Avenant and awarded them £25 costs. The other, heard at the Guildhall a month later, found for Herbert and awarded £25 damages to him. When the King himself produced confusing and contrary orders, it was only to be expected that his courts could do little to clarify the situation.

On 4 July 1662, Sir Henry sent one of his officials around to the theatre to restrain Betterton and his fellow players from acting. It was as well he did not go himself as the unfortunate lackey, Edward Thomas, was confronted by an angry band who '. . . riotously assembled together and assaulted (him) . . . beat and maltreated him, and held him their prisoner for the space of two hours'. It cost the actors a fine of 3s 4d each at the Middlesex sessions a fortnight later, but as a retaliatory blow against Herbert by proxy, they must have thought the money well spent.

Before the law courts produced their conflicting judgements in May and June 1662, Killigrew had continued to exploit the back stairs route to royal favour and on 25 April 1662 obtained from Charles a further indulgence—a Letter Patent which not only confirmed the powers granted under the warrant of 1660, but further, and less ambiguously, proclaimed that Killigrew could both enjoy his new privileges without interference (that is, including Herbert's) and that all other London playhouses, with the noted exception of D'Avenant's, were to be firmly suppressed. This was, to say the least, an invaluable document, and like every other seventeenth century property of any note could be bought, sold, divided, shared or mortgaged. The subsequent history of this new piece of paper was to be marked by interminable disputes and multiple changes of ownership, but for the moment let us just note that it placed Killigrew more firmly in the seat of theatrical power.

D'Avenant had not been idle in unofficial canvassing either, but although he eventually obtained another equally powerful Patent, it took him longer. He first got a sign manual warrant for a separate licence in August 1662, which duly passed the privy seal in November, a Patent was ordered in December, but only on 15 January 1663 was the D'Avenant Patent finally issued.

Behind these bare facts, there lies another development, on the surface completely unexpected. Knowing, however, that we are considering men to whom gain was a prime mover and loyalty a sentiment to be followed only as long as it proved convenient, it was not entirely unpredictable that Killigrew would at some stage throw his erstwhile colleague to the wolves, or more specifically, to the wolf himself, Big Bad Sir Henry Herbert.

At the beginning of June 1662, Killigrew came to a secret agreement with Sir Henry. Perhaps in return for Herbert's support in securing the new patent, he signed a paper to the effect that

> . . . a firme Amity be concluded for life betweene the said Sir Henry Herbert and the said Thomas Killigrew . . . .

In the document Killigrew agrees to pay fees for every play performed by the King's company at 40s for new plays and 20s for revivals, to pay up for the fees outstanding on the same basis since August 1660, to pay Sir Henry's costs incurred in the two actions against the Mohun company, and to force Mohun and the other actors to pay Sir Henry £50 'As a noble present from them, for His [Sir Henry's not God's] great damages susteyned from them and by their means'. The real sell-out was that he also agreed

> to be aydinge and Assistinge unto the said sir Henry Herbert . . . and neither directly nor Indirectly to Ayde or Assiste Sir William Dauenante, Knight . . . .

Just to make sure that Killigrew should not slide out of complying with any of the clauses, Sir Henry had him sign a further paper on 14 July in which

> I, Thomas Killigrew, doe by this presentes obleige myselfe to paey to Sir Henry Herbert all the costes and charges he shall ap, othe make apear, to be expendded in the sute betwixt him and the Kinges companye of acters . . . .

Some historians have found it puzzling that Killigrew should make so abject a surrender to his former enemy. Montague Summers, with his twin penchants for seeing witches under every bed, and coining techni-colour phrases to match the occasion, speaks of the one-sided nature of the agreement in favour of Herbert, a 'pitiless bloodsucker and oppressor'.

If, like D'Avenant, Killigrew had continued to contest Herbert's challenges to their monopoly, the chances are that he would have been at least as successful in so doing as was D'Avenant. My own theory is that in return for Killigrew's 'aydinge and Assistinge', which meant that Herbert could concentrate on his old enemy D'Avenant, Herbert made a guarantee which does not appear on paper. Sir Henry was undoubtedly a force to be reckoned with at a negotiating table but I cannot believe that Killigrew received nothing in return but Sir Henry's general blessings. I would suggest, backed by circumstantial evidence, that Sir Henry promised Killigrew that Thomas should be the next Master of the Revels. Thomas did eventually succeed Sir Henry in 1673 and on 29 March 1664 we know that Herbert sent him a note outlining some of the sources of revenue the holder of the office could tap. If such an offer was made, one can believe that Killigrew would have found it attractive. It provided a ready source of income without the inconvenience of managing a company of actors not renowned for their willing acceptance of authority. And, in the meantime, he could call upon Sir Henry's support if the King's company rebelled against him.

Whatever the true nature of the bargain struck between Herbert and Killigrew, it certainly placed D'Avenant in the firing line. In June, he despairingly petitioned the King for some guidance as to the justice of Herbert's demands upon him and his company. As he said himself, he

. . . has bin molested by Sir Henry Herbert with severall prosecutions at Law . . . has bin enforc'd to answer him in Two Tryals at Law . . . (Two verdicts having pass'd at Common Law contradicting each other) . . . .

In a reply to D'Avenant's charges, Sir Henry naturally put it somewhat differently. It was a great indignity

. . . to bee ousted of his just possession, rightes and profittes, by Sir William Dauenant, a person who exercised the office of the Master of the Reuells to Oliuer the Tyrant, and wrote the First and Seconde Part of Peru, acted at the Cockpitt, in Oliuers tyme, and soly in his fauour; wherin hee sett of the justice of Oliuers actinges, by com-

24

Thomas Killigrew—founder of the Drury Lane theatre and cause of many early problems. *Enthoven Collection*

parison with the Spaniards, and endeavoured therebye to make Oliuers crueltyes appeare mercyes, in respect of the Spanish crueltyes; but the mercyes of the wicked are cruell.

There is no record of the eventual outcome of the dispute but as D'Avenant continued to flourish with his company, it was probably some compromise on fees to save Herbert's face. As D'Avenant succeeded in getting a Patent himself similar to Killigrew's, Herbert's continuing enmity and disparaging references to his Commonwealth activities cannot have done him too much harm. That D'Avenant suffered little for defying Herbert also makes Killigrew's supposed surrender even more unlikely, unless there was another hidden clause to the agreement.

From June 1661, D'Avenant and his company gave performances at the converted Lisle's Tennis Court in Lincoln's Inn Fields on the basis of Sir William's lease taken even before the Restoration. After the brief sojourn at the Cockpit and three intervening days at the Red Bull, Killigrew and his King's company had to be temporarily content with a theatre in Vere Street, another 'tennis court' theatre and one in which they had no facilities for staging plays with scenery. They could, however, claim considerable prestige as members of the King's own company. They were not only actors but sworn servants as well. In the Lord Chamberlain's warrant books there is an entry for 6 October 1660:

> Which are to certifie that Nicholas Burt, Charles Hart, Michaell Mohun, Robert Shatterell, John Lacey, William Wintersell, Walter Clunne, William Cartwright, Edward Shatterell, Edward Kinnaston, Richard Baxter, Thomas Loveday, and Thomas Baterton are his Maties sworne servants as Groomes of the Chamber to his Matie in ordinary without ffee in the quality and playe of his Maties Actors or Comedians in ordinary and are therebye to have and enjoy all rights and privileges thereunto belonging and all persons are required to take notice thereof that they infringe not their freedome and privileges at their perill . . . .

In the warrant books there appear various orders over the next few years to supply this privileged company with 'foure yards of Bastard Scarlett for a Cloake and to each of them a quarter of a yard of crymson Velvett for the Cape'. Sartorially at least Killigrew's men could compete with anyone.

Until, however, they could move into a new theatre they could not rival D'Avenant's scenes and machines. We have, though, plenty of indication from that inveterate playgoer Samuel Pepys that they could still provide some very satisfactory dramatic entertainment.

On 20 November 1660, the diarist went

> . . . to the new Play-house near Lincolnes Inn Fields (which was formerly Gibbon's tennis-court) where the play of *Beggers' Bush* was newly begun . . . . It was well acted (and here I saw the first time one Moone, who is said to be the best actor in the world, lately come over with the King); and ended it is the finest play-house, I believe, that ever was in England.

If one reads Mohun for 'Moone' and company for 'playhouse' (for I doubt that Pepys was referring to the building) one gets the general idea that the fare was more than adequate. His diary is full of equally potted notices, generally enthusiastic. On 7 January 1661 it was a trip

> . . . to the Theatre and there was *The Silent Woman*, the first time that ever did I see it and it is an excellent play. Among other things here, Kinaston the boy hath the good turn to appear in three shapes: 1., as a poor woman in ordinary clothes to please Morose, then in fine clothes as a gallant, and in them was clearly the prettiest woman in the whole house—and lastly as a man; and then likewise did appear the handsomest man in the house.

This is particularly interesting because it demonstrates not only the versatility of Edward Kynaston, but the continuance of the Elizabethan practice of youths playing female roles despite the fact that the Restoration brought actresses to the stage. The two practices must have gone along side by side for a while until the female impersonator died a natural death in the face of the new competition. I would not be unduly surprised if some of the players of women's roles were too overtly suggestive of homosexuality and, lacking Kynaston's subtlety, tended to 'camp' things up too much for the heterosexual Royal taste. I say this because of a clause which appears in both Killigrew's and D'Avenant's respective patents. It says,

> And forasmuch as many plays formerly acted do contain several profane, obscene and scurrilous passages, and *the women parts therein have been acted by men in the habits of women, at which some have taken offence* . . . .
>
> [My italics]

If I am correct, no doubt Killigrew and D'Avenant sold the King on their monopoly at least partly by their promise to supply actresses for women's roles. Doubtless the notion of a supply of actresses did not need much selling in that regal quarter.

To return to our eye witness for a moment, Pepys would duly endorse such a view, for on 12 February 1661 he saw

> *The Scorneful Lady*, now done by a woman, which makes the play appear much better than it ever did to me.

If Pepys liked to see women on the stage, he could also be tolerant of the ones in the audience, providing they were physically appealing. For example, on 28 January 1661,

> . . . I saw again *The Lost Lady*, which doth now please me better than before. And here, I sitting behind in a dark place, a lady spat backward upon me by a mistake, not seeing me. But after seeing her to be a very pretty lady, I was not troubled at it at all.

Pepys alternated between performances by Killigrew's company and those by the Duke's company under D'Avenant. Once D'Avenant's men got underway properly they must have provided some sterling competition. On 2 March 1661, Pepys went

> . . . to the Theatre, where I find so few people (which is strange, and the reason I do not know) that I went out again . . . .

The reason was probably that a lot of people were doing exactly what Pepys did then:

> . . . and so to Salisbury Court—where the house as full as could be. . . .

Having settled with Herbert, Killigrew's next problem was to fulfil the promise made in the Patent and to obtain or build a theatre handsome enough to match the prestige of his King's men, and, more important, to challenge D'Avenant in spectacular scenery. He settled on a site between Brydges Street (which today is Catherine Street) and Drury Lane. Negotiating through two men, William Hewett and Robert Clayton who acted as trustees for Killigrew and his actors, he obtained a ground lease from the owner of the site, William, fifth Earl of Bedford.

Hewett and Clayton reached agreement with the Earl on 20 December 1661. They were given a lease for forty-one years from Christmas 1661 at an annual rent of £50, having to promise in return that they would spend £1,500 on erecting a new playhouse by Christmas 1662. On 28 January 1662, Hewett and Clayton made the lease over to a group known as the building shareholders. This group was Killigrew and Co. in another guise. I realize that this sounds complicated, but only because it was so. As a recipe for future wrangles, the original formula of owner-ship and management of the new theatre was well nigh perfect.

Putting it as simply as possible, there were three elements involved. Firstly, there were the owners of the Patent—Killigrew originally but in the future his heirs, and anyone with ready cash that he or they chose to enter partnership with.

Secondly came the building shareholders, i.e. the men who were to provide the £1,500 for the building of the theatre. This very necessary capital—it eventually cost them £2,400 when, as always, the actual costs rose above the original estimate—was to be raised by selling thirty-six separate shares to private subscribers. The thirty-six shares went as follows: nine each to Killigrew and Sir Robert Howard the playwright, four to Lacy the actor, and two each to the other major actors, Burt, Cartwright, Clun, Hart, Mohun, Shatterell and Wintershall. In return for providing 1/36th of the capital on each share, they could then demand 1/36th of the income gained by renting out their new theatre to the actual users—the third group to concern us.

Thirteen of the actors in the company entered into an agreement to pay £3 10s to the second group for every night they performed at the theatre. This income was to be divided thirty-six ways to go to the holders of the building shares in proportion to their holding. Killigrew, for example, with nine shares, was to get 17s 6d of the £3 10s.

In the early stages the financial arrangements worked moderately well. The Earl got his ground rent, the building shareholders recouped on their investments and the actors took enough at the doors to meet their commitments, pay their own wages and amass some profits from what was left over. We know that Clun in November 1663 sold his two building shares to a London barber and got £215 each for them, a price which would hardly have been possible unless the theatre was making money.

The snag was that the system was geared to a cosy domestic arrangement between friends with common interests in the affairs of the theatre. Once strangers like the barber got their hands on any of the shares in the ground lease, or the building or the box office takings, matters might get more complicated. Inevitably they did.

As we have seen, any piece of paper which proved the owner's right to something or other was a valuable piece of property, and as such, could be sold, shared, mortgaged or bequeathed. The tripartite system gave rise to a multitude of litigation between fathers and sons, widows and creditors, managers and actors which to do full justice would require a legal textbook. Until Garrick's day, as yet eighty years away, when Garrick and his partner obtained both Patent, ground lease and ownership for themselves, the system brought nothing but trouble.

Apart from potential trouble, what did the investors get for their money? We know very little about the site except that it was in a riding

The foyer board showing (inaccurately) the managers and Patent holders of over 300 years. *Peter Abbey*

yard and that it measured 112 feet from east to west and was about sixty feet wide. It was a small oasis surrounded by buildings and could only be approached through two narrow passages barely ten feet wide, one from the west and one from Drury Lane at the east side. There was probably a narrow entrance court in front of the west façade.

The details of the theatre building itself are equally sketchy but the £2,400 had been spent partly to Pepys' liking. Visiting the house the night after the opening, he went home to record in his diary that

The house is made with extraordinary good contrivance, and yet hath some faults, as the narrowness of the passages in and out of the

30

pits, and the distance from the stage to the boxes, which I am confident cannot hear . . . .

Was the narrowness of the passages a miscalculation, or a stroke of inspiration on Killigrew's part that having got the audience in their seats, he wanted to make it as difficult as possible for them to leave?

Another eyewitness who recorded his impressions during the first month was a M. Monconys who thought it the most proper and most beautiful he had seen, being particularly impressed with the green baize linings and the bands of gilt leather decorating the boxes. More practically, he notes that the benches in the pit were ranged in the form of an amphitheatre, each higher than the one in front—the raking being for the benefit of the people of quality who here 'resorted'.

There has been speculation that these descriptions can be matched to an unsigned and undated Wren drawing of an otherwise unidentified theatre. The verdict must be not proven for Wren may have been just trying an idea on paper, but the drawing itself gives some indication of what the new theatre would have looked like. The pit has seven rows of semi-circular benches raked at an angle of fifteen degrees. At a slightly higher level, seven rows of amphitheatre benches are raked at about thirty degrees, and behind them there is a circle of five boxes with five rows of benches. Above that comes a gallery with about eight rows of benches.

The first theatre on the Drury Lane site can hardly have been significantly different. This, broadly speaking, would have been the sort of seating that accommodated that eager audience of 7 May 1663. Unknowingly they were the very first of thousands of Drury Lane audiences, but as their idea of a theatrical night out was so different from ours, it is worth letting the dust settle temporarily on the monopoly controversy and examining in more detail what the Restoration theatre was all about.

CHAPTER TWO

Plaything of the Aristocracy

A theatre under Royal patronage suggests to the unwary that the lowly actors of Tudor and earlier times performing plays in the open air, have become favoured wearers of livery performing indoors to a polite and attentive audience. Nothing could be farther from the truth.

Because we are used to associating the theatre with the gentility of contemporary middle class audiences, it is difficult to grasp what a visit to the original Drury Lane theatre must have been like. To be lifted from a reserved seat in a theatre today, lit only by reflected light from the focus of attention, the stage, and transported bodily to a seething, jostling crowd behind the goal at a football match, would probably be no more traumatic an experience than to take one's place in the Theatre Royal of 1663. The noise and the discomfort would be roughly similar.

No seats were reserved, either one pushed in when the doors opened around noon and sat on a pit bench until the play started at about 3.30 in the afternoon, or one paid a boy or sent a servant to keep a place. If you were less dedicated to seeing a whole play yet concerned to see and be seen in the theatre, one could take advantage of the sampling system. The management allowed one to see one act of a five act play *gratis* and then to pay up and remain for the rest, or alternatively walk out again without paying. Or of course, if you were sufficiently adroit at dodging the doorkeepers from pit to box to gallery and back again, to stay without paying.

If one sat and watched the stage, there was the possibility that Pepys's pretty lady or one of her ilk might expectorate on one. Some of the local prostitutes might be plying their trade in one's direction. Then, perhaps, some of the women selling fruit might be haggling over change, leaning over to deliver messages and drowning the play with their shouts. Even if they subsided temporarily, it was only a matter of time before a drunken party of gallants came in to brawl or review the available women either in the audience or on the stage.

And, if by some unlikely miracle, the acting skill of a Hart or a Mohun managed to still so motley a crew temporarily, one's retina would be dancing with painful images of bright burning candles in the chandeliers suspended above the stage and shining straight into one's eyes. Suffering for one's art was about it.

The more one reads of the plays, and particularly prologues, of the period, the more inescapable evidence there is that the royal theatre was not far removed from a brothel with incidental entertainment. The fops and the beaux brought their licentiousness into the theatre, the depraved women of the court rubbed shoulders with common prostitutes, the actresses leered over the front of the stage with half their minds on the play and the other half on the main chance—an aristocrat prepared to set them up with a wardrobe and a house with or without the happy blessing of matrimony. That some of their numbers arranged their intermittent parturitions to coincide with the summer recess if they were lucky, or waddled around the stage playing virgins with a seven month swelled belly if unlucky, became a standing joke.

The area around the theatre had distinctly seedy connotations. As Gay's *Trivia* puts it:

> Oh may thy virtue guard thee through the roads
> Of Drury's mazy courts and dark abodes;
> The harlot's guileful path who nightly stand,
> Where Catherine Street descends into the Strand.

Most of the denizens of the area found their way into the theatre in some capacity or the other. For one thing, it was an admirable shop window for their more obvious attractions. It was common knowledge at the time that Charles II had made mistresses of actresses in both Killigrew's and D'Avenant's companies. Moll Davis and Nell Gwynne may have hit the Royal jackpot, but there were other prizes well worth catching. Had not Nell herself worked her way up to such dizzy heights with a suspected liaison with Hart the actor, followed as Pepys tells us on 13 July 1667, with a member of the aristocracy?

> . . . my Lord Buckhurst hath got Nell away from the King's House, lies with her, and gives her £100 a year, so as she hath sent her parts to the house and will act no more.

Occasionally, the roles were reversed,

33

... my Lady Castlemayne is mightily in love with Hart of their house, and he is much with her in private, and she goes to him, and do give him many presents.

The raconteur is, as always, Pepys.

D'Avenant's leading ladies were particularly prone to these sorts of deprivations. We have the word of Downes, the seventeenth century prompter, whose *Roscius Anglicanus* is one of the very few accounts of theatrical matters by a genuine contemporary, that 'Mrs Davenport, Mrs Davies, Mrs Jennings & c. The three last by force of Love erept the Stage.' 'Erept' I like, almost as much as his version of Moll Davis's kingly capture.

She performed that ['that' being a song called *My lodging is on the cold ground*] so Charmingly, that not long after, it Rais'd her from her Bed on the Cold Ground, to a Bed Royal.

Not all such suits reached so happy a conclusion. Mrs Marshall who had been prey to the advances of Aubrey de Vere, Earl of Oxford, but held out, was conned into a mock marriage ceremony by the Earl and later kicked out of the house when he tired of her. Her compensation was a £500 allowance which the King ordered the Earl to pay her when he heard of the deception. (That the whole incident sounds like an outline for the plot of a Restoration comedy is not entirely coincidental.)

De Vere and his lack of ethics would have been not untypical of the bands of gallants who habitually frequented the theatre, often without paying. The *Theatre Book of 1663–1700* in the Lord Chamberlain's papers has an entry as early as 7 December 1663 showing that

... divers persons doe rudely presse and with evill Language and Blows force theire wayes into the two theatres ... without paying the prizes established ....

We are considering men like Sir Charles Sedley, Sir Thomas Ogle and Lord Buckhurst, a trio who got drunk at the Cock tavern in Bow Street in 1663 and exhibited themselves in indecent postures on the Balcony and 'gave great offence to passengers by very unmannerly discharges upon them—Sir Charles at last showed himself in his birthday suit, and adapted his conversation to his appearance'. After Sedley was indicted, his one comment was that 'he thought he was the first man that had ever paid for easing himself *a posteriori*'.

And what of men like Buckingham and Rochester 'the two dearest companions of Charles'? 'The latter confessed . . . that for five years successively, he had been in a state of ebriety; and the former, notwithstanding his high rank in life and uncommon vein of wit, became at last so odious for his vices. . . .'

Rochester in *Scanderbeg*, a 1747 guide to playwrights by Thomas Whincop, is outlined like this:

> . . . the eager Tendency and violent Impulses of his natural Temper, unhappily inclining him to the Excesses of Pleasure and Mirth, which, with the wonderful Pleasantness of his inimitable Humour, did so far engage the Affections of the Dissolute, towards him, that, to make him delightfully venturous and frolicksone to the utmost Degrees of riotous Extravagance, they for some Years heightened his Spirits, inflamed with Wine, into one almost uninterrupted Fit of Wantonness and Intemperance.

Sedley, Rochester and Co. and their less talented imitators (like the anonymous gallant of Malcolm's *Anecdotes* who found 'the grand object of his life was making love . . . when a virgin of thirteen was mentioned, he boldy swore miracles had not ceased') made up a curious audience in the playhouse. Tom Brown in his essay on the playhouse in *Amusements Serious and Comical* described them like this:

> There sits a beau like a fool in a frame, that dares not stir his head nor move his body for fear of incommoding his wig, ruffling his cravat, or putting his eyes or mouth out of order his *maitre de dance* set it in; whilst a bully beau comes drunk into the pit, screaming out 'Damn me, Jack, 'tis a confounded play, let's to a whore, and spend our time better'.

The distaff side was no better.

> Here the ladies come to shew their clothes, which are often the only things to be admired in or about 'em; some of them having scabbed or pimpled faces wear a thousand patches to hide them, and those that have none, scandalise their faces by a foolish imitation.

In *The Postboy Robb'd of his Mails*, a satirical book supposedly a series of intercepted letters, 'Young Spark', a gallant, purports to give his recipe for a good night out, and commiserates with his friend who is a married man.

The Night, whilst you in Congugal Fear are confin'd to your Spouse's Arms, I'm carousing it with half a Dozen friends over a Brisk Bottle, which has no Deceit, but gives us fresh Vigor, and elevates our Thoughts above the Brutish Drowsie World; sometimes perhaps, for Variety, we admit a Docil, Super-errogatory Harlot, lewd for our Diversion, not serious Embraces; who for an honest George, and her Dose of Liqour, and a little Victuals to her Empty Stomach, shall give a present View of all the Mysteries of the Kingdom of mighty Lust. . . . From Bed, I retreat to Sylvia's Neat Abode, where I revel in her Arms 'till Play-time, where, if it be a dull One, I pursue some wand'ring Game in the Pit, or Gallery, with whom I frolick, and play, 'till our usual Time of Rendezvous at the Tavern. Sometimes I'm in pursuit of maiden-heads, and try all under Fifteen. . . .

In plays and prologues we get a good many more references to audience composition and behaviour—Saunter in *The Double Gallant*—'[I] go behind the Scenes, make Love in the Green Room, take a Benefit Ticket, ferret the Boxes, straddle into the Pit; Green-Room again, do the same at both Houses, and stay at neither'; or Major Rakish in *Woman's Wit*, with two and a half bottles of liquor inside him 'call'd in at the Play (Impudence my ticket) pick'd up a Parson's Wife, gave her the remains of an old Clap. . . .'

The main problem was that as alcoholic intake increased, tongues and swords rested all too loosely in mouths and scabbards. The phrase 'drunk as a lord' had in those days a contemporary sting, and violence was never far from the surface. In 1664, the unfortunate Clun the actor was fatally stabbed on his way home from the theatre. In 1669, Kynaston, who had unwisely mimicked Sir Charles Sedley, was beaten up by a band of Sedley's bravoes.

In 1670, a similar fate befell Sir John Coventry for a remark passed in the House of Commons. In the course of a debate on a proposed tax on playhouses, Sir John Birkenhead opposed the idea of a tax on the grounds that the King's players were part of the King's pleasure. Coventry wittily, if dangerously, asked 'Whether the King's pleasure lay amongst the men that acted or the women?' Waylaid in Suffolk Street a few days later, Coventry had his nose sliced for his impudence by hired villains. (Hired by Charles himself? Possibly, according to some sources.)

Marvell was luckier with his scurrilous verses penned when the King's latest mistress Louise de Quereuaille arrived in England for the royal

pleasure.

Nell Gwynne displaying some of her most famous attributes. *Enthoven Collection*

And whatever it cost me, I'll have a French whore
As bold as Alice Perrers and as fair as Jane Shore,
And when I am weary of her I'll have more
Which if any bold Commoner dare to oppose
I'll order my bravoes to cut off his nose,
Though, for't I, a branch of Prerogative lose.
I'll wholly abandon all public affairs,
And pass all my time with Buffoons and Players
And saunter to Nelly when I should be at prayers.

Only within the context of the playhouse can one understand how a common prostitute could become the mistress of the King, and that the affair could be obliquely referred to even from the stage. When Nell

37

Gwynne returned to the stage in Dryden's *Conquest of Granada* after a confinement with her elder son by Charles, the Prologue included

> Pity the virgins of each theatre,
> For at both Houses 'twas a sickly year;
> And pity us, your servants, to whose cost
> In one such sickness nine whole months were lost.

If one of the beaux or gallants failed to find what he was looking for among the prostitutes and orange sellers, and tired of parading his finery in front of or on the apron stage—a part of the theatre which became known graphically as Fop Alley—he could pay a fixed charge to enter the dressing or 'tyring' room to consort with the actresses. Wycherley summed up the management's attitude to this invasion in the Prologue to *The Country Wife*:

> We set no guards upon our tyring-room,
> But when with flying colours there you come,
> We patiently, you see, give up to you,
> Our poets, virgins, nay, our matrons too,

Dryden, however, thought the practice had gone too far by 1682:

> We beg you last, our Scene-room to forbear,
> And leave our Goods and Chattels to our care;
> Alas our Women are but washy Toys,
> And wholly taken up in stage employs:
> Poor willing Tits they are; but yet I doubt,
> This double Duty soon will wear 'em out.

Dryden, particularly, was adept at letting the audience know what he thought about them whether or not some of his sarcasm was above the heads of a good many. (He also fell prey to 'a Rose-Alley cudgel ambuscade' one dark night). From two prologues which were used for Dryden's *The Wild Gallant*, the first in 1663 and the second in 1667, we get a strong insight into the effect that an audience such as we have been considering had on the writing of plays. In the second prologue of 1667, Dryden apologizes that his rakish hero now seems so mild—the writer's imagination outdone by real life!

> But since his [i.e. Dryden's] knowledge of the town began,
> He thinks him now a very civil man;

And, much ashamed of what he was before,
Has fairly play'd him at three wenches more.
'Tis some amends his frailties to confess;
Pray pardon him his want of wickedness.

Dryden knew well that the success of his plays depended ultimately on the reaction of the audience, 'the sly she-Jockies of the Box and Pit' as he once called them, that drunken band who wandered in and out:

There are a sort of Pratters in the Pit,
Who either have, or who pretend to Wit:
These noisie Sirs so loud their Parts rehearse,
That oft the Play is silenced by the Farce:

Dryden also knew what they were really interested in:

. . . methinks some Vizard Masque I see,
Cast out her Lure from the mid Gallery:
About her all the flutt'ring Sparks are rang'd;
The Noise continues though the Scene is chang'd:
Now growling, sputt'ring, wauling, such a clutter,
'Tis just like Puss defendant in a Gutter:

and, in a satirical piece *The Fire-Ships* ('fire-ships' being another term for prostitutes) he attacks them again:

The Play-house is their place of Traffick, where
Nightly they sit, to sell their Rotten Ware:
Tho' done in silence and without a Cryer,
He that bids the most, is still the Buyer;
For while he nibbles at her Am'rous Trap,
She gets the Mony, but he gets the Clap.
Intrencht in Vizor Mask they Giggling sit,
And throw designing Looks about the Pit,
Neglecting wholly what the Actors say,
'Tis their least business there to see the Play.

The wearing of 'vizards' or masks by the women in the audience, ostensibly to hide their blushes at any ribaldry spoken on the stage, and in truth, in imitation of the prostitutes whose ravaged complexions well needed concealment, gave the added spice of unknown identity to the formation of on-the-spot liaisons. An orange girl, parading with a basket of fruit, could always be paid to carry a message to a masked and therefore

39

unknown lady a few rows away. If she turned out later to be a friend's wife or mistress, so much the better.

The most famous of all the orange girls, and the one who held the concession for selling fruit at the Theatre Royal, was Orange Moll. According to Pepys on 2 November 1667, she added life-saving to her other services:

> A gentleman of good habit . . . eating of some fruit . . . did drop down as dead, being choked; but with much ado Orange Moll did thrust her finger down his throat, and brought him to life again.

Was she being altruistic, or had he forgotten to pay for the fruit? Either way, Dryden would have been sorry to see Orange Moll or any of her assistants killed in a playhouse brawl:

> . . . I swear we'll pull up all our Benches;
> Not for your sakes, but for our Orange-Wenches:
> For you thrust wide sometimes; and many a Spark,
> That misses one, can hit the other Mark,
> This makes our Boxes full, for men of sense,
> Pay their four Shillings in their own defence:
> That safe behind the Ladies they may stay;
> Peep o'er the Fan, and Judg the bloudy Fray. . . .

The unique relationship between stage and audience could always be exploited for effect by the clever dramatist, and lines that read coldly on the printed page would have a very different effect when delivered by a Nell Gwynne fluttering her eyelashes at the inhabitants of Fop Alley. One wonders if Brecht was being very original with his alienation effects when in 1669, Nell as Valeria in Dryden's *Tyrannick Love*, having delivered her dying speech—

> Stand still but while thy poor Valeria dies,
> And sighs her Soul into her Lover's Eyes—

while sinking on to the green carpet traditionally used in tragedy to protect elaborate gowns and costumes in a dying fall, jumped up when the bearers arrived to remove her 'corpse' from the apron.

> Hold, are you mad? You damn'd confounded Dog,
> I am to rise, and speak the Epilogue. . .

she said and proceeded to deliver it, claiming

I am the Ghost of poor departed Nelly.

Incidentally, the apron stage, which would form about half the full acting area, jutted out well into the auditorium and the curtain was behind the proscenium arch. The old court masque stage with its scenery had been dovetailed to the platform stage of Shakespeare's day, the two divided by the proscenium arch so that the curtain came in the middle. The curtain would be drawn at the start of the play but not closed again until its end. Scene and act changes were performed in view of the audience, with the use of a common device, the 'reveal'. Two painted flats representing one scene would be drawn back like a pair of shutters to 'reveal' another behind it. The actors would then take their places in front of the new scene. At the sides of the stage, cut-outs and flats running along grooves in the floor would increase the effectiveness of the illusion, for the 1660s was an age when perspective was fashionable— gardens were constructed on the principles, Palladio's textbook had been translated into English in 1663, and even Mrs Pepys had been studying the new science in 1669 according to her husband.

The one stage convention that would strike a modern playgoer as a little odd was the use of the proscenium doors. At either side of the stage, as a permanent part of the proscenium, there were two doors through which the actors made their entrances and exits. The use of a door into, say, a woodland glade must have been somewhat disconcerting.

Because the apron stage was so extensive and was used so much, the most accurate way to think of the spectacle is not of actors within a set, but of actors on an open stage with a distant background representing the locale.

Alongside the mechanics of production we must briefly examine the sort of plays that were written during the latter half of the seventeenth century. So many scholars have written of the plays as literature and on the vexed question of the immorality or otherwise of Restoration plays, particularly comedies, that I do not wish to expend space on what has been well covered elsewhere. Nevertheless, I would like to make a few basic points before examining the fortunes of the Theatre Royal for the rest of the century.

Firstly, it still needs reiterating that a play is written for performance. Whatever its literary merit, or its poetic qualities, the first basic demand a true theatre-goer makes of a play is that it shall work in performance before a live audience. Beneath their costumes, and allowing them the idiosyncrasies of the speech of their time, are its characters real flesh and blood? Do they 'live' as assuredly Sophocles' Electra, Shakespeare's Lear, or Jonson's Volpone live?

The difference, to my mind, between the greatness of the best Restoration comedies, and the awfulness of most Restoration tragedy, is precisely this. Wycherley's Horner, Congreve's Millamant or Farquhar's Lady Bountiful, live; Dryden's Berenice, Lee's Roxana or Mithridates assuredly do not. It is the difference between a character displaying the realities of human emotion, for basic emotions like love, jealousy and sexual drive do not change from century to century, and a character conforming to an ideal imposed on him or her by the writer for reasons of morality (or exigencies of plot). Ideals can change from year to year. But while great plays are universal and continue to be performed, bad plays 'date' and disappear. In return for plays like *The Country Wife*, *The Way of the World*, *The Beaux' Stratagem*, and *Love for Love*, one is prepared to allow the period its *Aureng-Zebe*, its *Albion and Albanius* and its *Oronoko*.

It would be too superficial to assume that, because the vices displayed in the theatre and the vices outlined on the stage ran roughly in parallel, Restoration comedy was necessarily a true representation of normal behaviour. I find it difficult to believe that a set of people so concerned to talk about sex, were actually thus engaged as often as they claimed.

Is there not rather an element of wish-fulfilment, a desire to be thought fashionably wicked, and a need to be faintly but deliciously shocked? When Horner in *The Country Wife* adopts the device of spreading a rumour of his impotence as the result of venereal disease to be thought a man who could be given safe access to other men's wives, he is not really representing the behaviour of the gallants in the audience. What Wycherley is doing is giving them an opportunity to indulge their imaginations in wishing they had Horner's wit, ingenuity and particularly opportunity. A case could surely be made that at a much inferior level James Bond has fulfilled the same role in our own age.

With the Restoration, Puritan values naturally fell victim to satire. The Puritans, by their fanaticism had brought decency and purity into disrepute. Piety had become a synonym for hypocrisy. The nature of man had not been changed in the Commonwealth, but it had been forced to wear a different guise. As a character in Shadwell's play *The Virtuoso* succinctly puts it:

I believe there was the same Wenching then: only they dissembled it. They added Hypocrisie to Fornication, and so made two Sins of what we make but one.

The comedies are often attacked by moralists for their ridicule of marriage and their cynical treatment of infidelity and adultery. It can also be said, however, that in one sense they defend the concept of love. The contemporary marriage, let us remember, was an arranged one, and unhappiness and infidelity a frequent consequence. Were the playwrights sometimes not being romantic as much as they were being cynical?

As the century progressed, comedy, except in the hands of the best of writers, did become more cynical and inevitably more gross. Without the compensating wit of a Congreve, who gave up writing for the stage before he turned thirty although he had twenty-eight years to live, less talented writers had to rely on an increase of obscenity in attempts to continue shocking an audience. As always, there is the operation of the law of diminishing returns, for, in any age, what shocks at first soon becomes *passé*, and some fresh excess has to be sought. Nothing succeeds like excess, but strictly short-term.

There were also considerable economic changes outside the world of theatre which had their effect upon the course of the drama. The Restoration land settlements displaced many from positions of power and privilege acquired under Cromwell. They had been replaced by the followers of Charles who had stepped triumphantly into their places. Although it would have been impolitic to voice discontent with the new order, there remained an undercover resentment smouldering beneath the surface.

Because the theatre was so clearly royalist in sympathy, it became a convenient target for the ire of the solid citizen. Furthermore, when William III arrived in 1688, the theatre was robbed of its palace protection, and as soon as new Dutch financial techniques lubricated the wheels of economic development (the Bank of England, for example, was established in 1694), the rise of a whole new mercantile class had considerable effect. Suddenly there were rich merchants, resentful of the fun made of them and their pretensions in a theatre catering for the aristocracy. The Theatre Royal became the focus of attention for the moral reformers and the seventeenth century ends with the most famous, and in many ways, the most effective attack ever made upon the theatre. Because the effects of that attack lie largely in the eighteenth century we will discuss its implications later, but before we leave the seventeenth century in general, we should give some attention to the rhymed tragedy.

To object to tragedy written in rhymed couplets on the grounds that people do not speak in verse, is as absurd as to object to opera on the grounds that people do not bawl arias at one another in real life. Nevertheless, although the tritest of librettos may be rescued by some divine

43

music, it is difficult to find any such compensation in rhymed tragedy. The artificiality of the tragedy was part of its point, but when Thomas Davies, Garrick's biographer, speaks of Dryden's tragedies thus:

> . . . no man will sit down to read them, at this day, without blending laughter and contempt with esteem and admiration . . .

he is voicing as much a twentieth century view as the opinion of his own eighteenth century. Howls of laughter could hardly fail to greet even the most distinguished of our contemporary actresses if she were asked to say as Berenice in Dryden's *Tyrannick Love* that if she should precede her lover in dying she will

> Stop short of Heav'n, and wait you in a Cloud;
> For fear we lose each other in the crowd.

For all their risible aspects and despite the fact that the *genre* was out of fashion by the early 1680s, there are two good reasons for not ignoring rhymed tragedies. Firstly their influence lasted far beyond their vogue, and secondly the fact that they were written and performed alongside the bawdy comedies with considerable popularity, is a useful corrective to the notion that the audience were so obsessed with sex that they never thought of anything else.

This bizarre group of auditors had ideals, particularly lofty ones. They cared about the drama of Spain and of France, they looked for skill, and they looked for what they considered the essential elements of drama. That their ideals are not ours is not to say that they had none. The Lees, the Dennises and the Tates are now condemned for ever to the specialist and the scholar in the quiet contemplation of the study, but they had their day. *Scanderbeg* provides two pithy epitaphs, one for Lee who died insane:

> He had a great genius for Tragedy, but his Sublime Diction was sometimes swelled to Bombast, and that to a ridiculous Degree, which somewhat bordered upon that Madness which afterward possessed the Author . . .

and one for Dennis:

> . . . he laid down Rules for writing good Plays, and shew'd them what were bad, by his own.

The latter could be applied unkindly to the whole of the school.

The obsession with nobility and the sublime also laid its dead hand upon acting styles. We can read reviews of the day where actors like Hart and Betterton are praised to the skies for their portrayals of characters but we can be certain that their performances would be a long way away from anything we would find acceptable. I have mentioned the passions that could be aroused in a member of the audience full of wine and quarrelsome with it, but displays of emotion on the stage itself would have been completely unacceptable.

The tragic actor moved with the fluent mobility of a parking meter. Emotion had to be clothed in formal rhetoric and corseted in an artificial dignity. The left hand was pressed against the heart in case that organ should betray a flutter at a significant moment. The right hand carved elegant patterns in the air to indicate the deepest of feelings, and the lines were intoned rather than delivered.

All was ponderous and slow so that before we marvel too much at a Betterton playing Hamlet in his seventies, it should be remembered that we are thinking not of a youth in Elsinore Castle, but an elderly gentleman concentrating on delivering well cadenced speech in a highly artificial manner, and attired in the formal costume of his own time.

CHAPTER THREE

Closures, Union and Division
1663–1700

THE company started in their new home riding on a boom of popularity and prestige. It would be pleasant to say that so happy a circumstance continued for the rest of the century but in fact, the next forty or so years are as fraught with quarrels, dissensions and financial complications, as a herring with bones.

It was not that they lacked an adequate repertory. They performed pre-Restoration plays like *Othello*, *Henry IV*, *Volpone*, *The Alchemist*, *The White Devil* and many others which a modern playgoer would find familiar. And they could call on the Poet Laureate John Dryden for plays like *The Indian Queen*, *The Indian Emperor*, *Tyrannick Love* and *The Conquest of Granada* as they came from his pen.

They had only D'Avenant's company to fear as rivals thanks to the wide powers of the monopoly. Certainly they had fine actors. *Historia Histrionica*, a dialogue between 'Lovewit' and 'Truman' published in 1699, looked back to the early days of the company with nostalgia.

> [Plays] are all of 'em (some few excepted) as much inferior to those of former Times; as the Actors now in being (generally speaking) are, compared to Hart, Mohun, Burt, Lacy, Clun and Shatterel. . . .

Similarly, a prologue to Fletcher's *Philaster* in a revival of 1695 craves the audience's indulgence because

> For these bold parts we have no Hart, no Nelly,
> Those darlings of the stage. . . .

Downes says that Hart 'might teach any King on Earth how to Comport himself' for he played Alexander 'with such Grandeur and Agreeable Majesty'. Hart was a drawing card, so that 'if he Acted . . . the House was fill'd as at a new Play'. When Hart and Mohun had practically retired in 1679, a Crowne prologue referred to them in flattering terms, as 'the two great Pillars of our Playhouse'. In 1663, the great pillars were continually in support.

By the end of the 1660s, Nell Gwynne's personality was an added attraction—'nature seemed to have qualified her for the stage: her person, tho' below the middle size, was well turned; she had a good natural air, and a sprightliness which promised every thing in Comedy. . .' quotes Genest, who also gives an example of her ready wit when she was assailed in her coach by a mob mistaking her for the French Catholic Duchess of Portsmouth, another of Charles's indulgences. 'Pray, good people, be civil; I am the Protestant whore.'

Mohun, the other leading man of the company, once a major in the Royalist army, was particularly admired for his Iago and for creating roles like Abdelmelech in *The Conquest of Granada* and the title role in Lee's *Mithridates*.

The company also had Kynaston, who despite his beating by Sedley's bravoes, was popular and, as we saw from Pepys, an able actor of male or female roles. On one occasion, however, his late arrival kept the King waiting for the curtain to open and Killigrew had to tell Charles that they were unable to commence because 'the Queen has not yet shaved'.

In competition with Kynaston when he strayed into their particular province, the actresses of the company included Beck Marshall, who had a spectacular quarrel with Nell Gwynne a few years later, and her sister Ann, and Catherine Corey, a specialist in comedy especially in scolding old women roles. Mrs Corey once used a casting as Sempronia in *Catiline's Conspiracy* to mimic a Lady Harvey who was not amused and had the actress imprisoned.

In all probability, they were all ladies stronger in talent than in morals and one wonders how they, and another of their company, Margaret Hughes who was at various times mistress to Sedley and to Prince Rupert, ever managed to find time to learn lines and to act between *affaires* and pregnancies. As Cibber put it later '. . . more than one of them had charms sufficient at their leisure hours to calm and mollify the Cares of Empire'.

Because these extramural activities brought more people into the house than otherwise, they were of no disadvantage. An order from the Lord Chamberlain of 5 June 1665 was much more serious and left the actresses and the rest of the company to fend for themselves for the next twelve months.

Whereas it is thought Dangerous that soo greate a sort of people

47

should be permitted at Yor Theater in this time of Infection of the Plague. These are therefore to require you that you forbarr Actinge any more Playes untill you shall receive further Order from mee.

The further order was a long time coming and, although the cessation of plays gave an opportunity for a widening of the stage, it meant that the house was closed until the end of November 1666. This was serious enough to the health of the company, but a slower and ultimately more serious infection to their well-being was in their own midst—Thomas Killigrew.

His financial affairs moved from the confused to the labyrinthine. To do them full justice in all their tangled glory would fill this or any other book, but thanks to Leslie Hotson's diligent searches in the legal records we have some idea of his mode of operations.

In July 1662, he had granted his son Henry £4 a week which was to come out of the profits on his two shares. Henry, in turn, gave them over to a Thomas Porter for life, presumably in return for ready cash. Porter sold them in his turn to a couple called the Sayers for £600. To do this he had to deed them back to the Killigrews who then assigned them to the Sayers. The Sayers also struck lucky, if financial deals with Killigrew can ever be described as lucky, because even before the 1663 opening of the house, Killigrew made over his nine building shares to Sir John Sayer. After Sayer's death, Killigrew set up a trust in the names of Sayer's widow and a Thomas Elliott, and granted his Patent and all his interests in the Theatre Royal to their keeping for his lifetime in trust for himself. There were various clauses dealing with the shares which might on his death fall to his own widow and to both Henry and Henry's half-brother Charles.

So far, so good. But on 21 June 1673 Thomas was short of money. He borrowed £950 from a Sir Laurence Debusty and made over his shares to him, although they were already held in trust. This must have seemed a stroke of inspiration to Thomas, because he did it again a month later, borrowing £1600 from a Richard Kent and assigning his Patent to an agent of Kent's for 99 years as security. That he did not any longer hold the shares did not deter him.

Killigrew's debt to Debusty was reduced by the incoming profits on the building shares to £500 by 1676. Meanwhile, the interest charges on Kent's loan took that debt up to £1850. Killigrew then made all his interests in the Patent and the Theatre Royal over to Kent for the next 90 years. Kent obligingly paid off Killigrew's debt to Debusty of £500 and was to recoup his money from the theatre profits.

This maze of wheeling-dealing is not untypical. I mention it because it shows that Killigrew had mortgaged all his interests for cash in hand as early as 1673, and that his double-dealing had brought in another eight people with some sort of interest in the theatre's affairs. The ramifications of this and other similar deals are well nigh infinite.

Killigrew was no more conscientious as master of the King's company. From the very start of operations, he delegated power to Hart, Mohun and Lacy. This did not suit some of the other actors who complained bitterly until Killigrew withdrew the Letters of Attorney he had given to the trio. They also complained when Killigrew reassumed power and used it to annex the share of an actor called Bird who died in 1663. This time they appealed to the Lord Chamberlain. A learned trio, Manchester, Lauderdale and Denham, met to consider the matter, and their undated report shows that they could do nothing but accept that the Patent gave Killigrew the right to do just about anything he cared to.

> And wee find by your Maties Letters Patent, that your Matie hath granted to him full and absolute power to make and constitute a Company of Actors or Players, to be under his sole government and authority; and that he shall give them respectively such allowances as he shall think fit; that he hath power to take in, and eject whom he shall think meet. And wee do find that he hath been so far from abusing this power, that he hath made very little use of it hitherto. . . .

There was one compensation to Killigrew as overseer. He told Pepys on 24 January 1669, 'that he is fain to keep a woman on purpose at 20s a week to satisfy eight or ten of the young men of his house'. Probably her weekly salary was much cheaper than a piece-work arrangement.

Such backstage activities may make plays look tame, but for the moment audiences continued to patronize the company. Perhaps the humour was a little broad. *Monsieur Raggou*, a farce by Lacy, exploiting the fact that Nell Gwynne lived near the Strand Maypole, hinted at some very picturesque uses for a miniature maypole, and Dryden's *The Wild Gallant* in which Lord Nonsuch believes himself to be pregnant drew a witticism from the King according to Genest. Knowing that the pregnant Lord had been based on a real incident in the life of his chaplain Dr Pelling, Charles recalled Pelling's large-boned wife and said, 'If any woman could get her husband with child, it must be Mrs Pelling'.

On a more lofty level and decked out with rich costumes and scenery, Dryden treated his audiences to bombastic extravaganzas of noble bosoms torn between love and honour in *The Indian Queen* (1664), *The Indian*

49

Emperor (1665), *Tyrannick Love* (1669) for which a scene painter Isaac Fuller had to go to law to get proper recompense from the company, and *The Conquest of Granada* (1670). After 1671 Dryden was a little more reluctant to lay himself open to ridicule because 1671 saw the first performance of Buckingham's *The Rehearsal*.

The Rehearsal had been planned for 1665, but was postponed because of the plague. It was only a temporary hold-up, and after its première the satire held the stage for the next 150 years. Dryden, who had succeeded to D'Avenant's Poet Laureateship when D'Avenant died in 1668, was the chief target of Buckingham's trenchant wit. John Lacy took the part of Bayes, the hapless and hopeless playwright conducting rehearsals of his latest high-flown and ridiculous tragedy, and faithfully imitated Dryden's mannerisms to drive the shafts home.

Incidentally Lacy's gift for mimicry had got him into trouble in April 1667. Pepys recorded:

> . . . the King was so angry at the liberty taken by Lacy's part to abuse him to his face, that he commanded they should act no more, till Moone went and got leave for them to act again. . . .

A few days' confinement in the porter's lodge did nothing for Lacy's temper, and Pepys gives the sequal:

> [Lacy] . . . met with Ned Howard, the poet of the play, who congratulated his release; upon which Lacy cursed him as that it was the fault of his nonsensical play that was the cause of his ill-usage. Mr Howard did give him some reply; to which Lacy answered him, that he was more of a fool than a poet, upon which Howard did give him a blow on the face with his glove; on which Lacy, having a cane in his hand, did give him a blow over the pate. Many did wonder that Howard did not run him through, he being too mean a fellow to fight with. . . .

Instead, Howard complained to the King and the house was again temporarily silenced. This casts an interesting sidelight on the ambivalence of an actor's position—a sign that familiarity with the gentry was only permitted on sufferance, and that any attempt to cross the class barrier between player and patron was resented.

Most of the wit of *The Rehearsal* would be pointless today because we are so unfamiliar with the targets and unable to recognize the references to plays of the day. However, its accuracy and puns like '. . . putting

Verse into Prose should be call'd Transprosing' had the seventeenth century audience rolling on their benches. If only by the exercise of imagination, we can appreciate the absurdity of a grand stage battle between two men, armed with swords and lutes, fought '*in recitativo*'.

The play was a gratifying success, but it was succeeded in 1672 by a total disaster, the destruction of the new house. A contemporary letter unearthed by Hazleton Spencer tells the sad story.

A fire at the King's playhouse between 7 and 8 pm on Thursday evening last [25 Jan 1672] which half burned down the house and all their scenes and wardrobe; and all the houses from the Rose Tavern in Russell Street on that side of the way to Drury Lane are burned and blown up, with many in Vinegar Yard; 20,000 *l.* damage. The fire began under the stairs where Orange Moll keeps her fruit. Bell the player was blown up.

The Earl of Anglesey, who lived nearby clearly thought there was divine justice at hand in the flames, and finished his own account of the event with the pious note: 'The Lord pardon sin, which brings judgements.'

The event gave rise to a broadsheet which circulated the streets thereafter. It included the lines

> Only the Zealous Hypocrite's o'rejoy'd,
> To see his Scourge thus casually destroy'd;
> He cries, Just Judgement! And wish'd when poor Bell
> Rung out his last, 't had been the Stages kNell. . . .

The interpolation of the capital N in the last line, too pointed to be a compositor's error, cost the printer a term of imprisonment.

Until a new theatre could be built, the company had to eke out a meagre scenery-less and costume-less existence at Lisle's Tennis Court. To add to their gall, D'Avenant's old company had opened barely two months before at the magnificently decorated Dorset Garden theatre. D'Avenant's widow and later his son Charles★ in collaboration with Betterton, had continued the founder's experiments with spectacular operas. They drew large audiences to Sir William's version of *Macbeth*, singing witches and all, and Shadwell's operatic version of *The Tempest*. The travesties done to Shakespeare's texts in the name of scenes and

★ Charles, unlike his father, used the surname Davenant, rather than the older version D'Avenant.

machines hardly bear thinking about but they drew the crowds, and the Duke's company prospered.

A new theatre on the Drury Lane site was not ready until March 1674. It opened with *The Beggar's Bush* and a special prologue by Dryden excusing their inability to match their rivals' decorations:

> A plain Built House after so long a stay,
> Will send you half unsatisfy'd away . . .
> We, broken Banquers, half destroy'd by Fire,
> With our small Stock to humble Roofs retire;
> Pity our Loss, while you their Pomp admire. . . .

Dryden, who had been just as responsible as anyone else for titivating his audience with spectacle, could not resist asserting a lofty, if unjustified, moral superiority. He finished

> 'Twere Folly now a Stately Pile to raise,
> To build a Play-House while You throw down Plays,
> Whilst Scenes, Machines and empty Opera's reign,
> And for the Pencil You the Pen disdain.

However 'plain Built', the house, attributed to Wren who was also the architect of Dorset Garden, lasted until the 1790s despite extensive alterations in the time of Garrick. The company proved more fragile a structure altogether.

The new building cost about £4,000. The capital came partly from arrears due from Charles for performances between 1667 and 1673, although the fees took until 1674 to collect because of Charles's expensive wars. There was also a national church collection but that was for all the victims of the fire, not just the actors. Most of the money came from new articles of agreement. Hart, Mohun and Lacy contributed £200 each and at least five others £160 each. In return they were to get a share of the daily rent until the loans were repaid.

The theory was right, the execution erratic. All the smouldering resentments at Killigrew's shady deals began to come to the surface. Wintershall, Hart, Kynaston and Cartwright tried to retire, and squabbles and dissensions split their ranks. Everyone concerned began to grab what they could, and the health of the company suffered grievously. Most of the original members of the company were old, some were sick, and all began to look first to number one.

Dryden, who had been made a sharer in the company in recognition of his value to the house, broke an agreement he had made to ply them with plays, by supplying a play to the rival Duke's company. Seeing the writing on the wall, he did not wish to see *his* receipts going to other pockets.

In 1675, the Lord Chamberlain's office tried to settle some of the complaints. On 11 January, Kynaston, Mohun, Lacy and others were ordered to attend and explain why it was 'that some of you have violently taken and shared money, against an agreement between you and his [Killigrew's] particular order to the contrary . . . in ye meantime . . . continue Actinge without any disturbance but not to take or share any more money untill I have heard your business'. On the same day, Killigrew had 'agreed and confirmed' to the Lord Chamberlain that he 'expects only his 2 shares and the rest to be divided according to the Articles'.

On 9 December, the company was presenting the Lord Chamberlain with a sort of Code of Conduct for their own 'better regulation'. Its 'shall-nots' with regard to neglecting rehearsals, refusing parts, wearing Theatre Royal costumes outside the theatre, pilfering of feathers, clothes and ribbons, and 'the disorders of the shareing table by an Inundation of People that presse upon them in their businesse' is a sad catalogue of the sort of things which must have been happening.

Despite this worthy document, 1676 was even worse. The actors struck while disputes continued and were ordered to restart on 14 February by Royal Mandate. As the order says, King Charles, hearing of the stoppage, was 'very much displeased thereat'. One supposes he was even more displeased in the spring when Killigrew, perhaps tired of the cares of management, at least by what little of them he chose to take on, called in his son Charles to bring the company to heel. In return, Charles should become the master of the company in his place.

Charles Killigrew adopting the reliable formula of meeting grievance with cash, gave Hart £100 and Kynaston £60 and sat back while the two of them signed themselves, and also persuaded Mohun, Lacy, Burt and Shatterell to sign new agreements. The dubious ethics of Hart and Kynaston in taking bribes pale into insignificance compared with Thomas's next action. Once the new agreements had been signed, he flatly refused to hand over to Charles either his shares or his authority.

Charles had to resort to litigation to get his father to fulfil his part of the bargain and that took until early 1677. In the interim, the Lord Chamberlain had to step in again. On 9 September 1676, he sent an order:

> . . . during the differences between Mr Killigrew and his son. . . [I do] herebye nominate and appoint Mr Michaell Mohun, Mr Charles Hart, Mr Edward Kinnaston and Mr William Cartwright under mee from

tyme to tyme to order and direct all things whatsoever belonging to ye well beinge of your said Company, in distributing of parts, orderinge of playes to be acted and all things thereupon belonging. . . .

Company government by a four-man committee was no improvement, and an entry in the warrant books in February 1677 makes it clear that this was later amended to leave Hart in sole charge.

The same entry records the success of Charles in ousting his father at last.

[Thomas Killigrew] hath resigned and dissolved [?*] all his right power and Authority, with his two voyces as Master of ye Company of His Maties Comedians unto his sonne Mr Charles Killigrew. I do there-fore . . . herebye order that ye said Company do in all things conforme themselves to ye orders and directions of Mr Charles Killigrew as they did unto Mr Thomas Killigrew his ffather. . . .

Charles had won his way to power, but as the profits from his father's shares had to meet the prior claim of Kent, his father's old creditor, he was as reluctant as Thomas had been to fulfil his agreements with his actors. By July 1677, the company was petitioning the Lord Chamber-lain for self-government. Grasping at the slim chance that this would see the end of the turmoil, the Lord Chamberlain was 'pleased to gratifie them in theire proposition of Governing themselves' with the qualifi-cation that they could do so only if Charles's rights to the profits con-tinued to be recognized.

By September, Charles had found another solution to his problems. He won round the younger members of the company, including Cardell Goodman and Philip Griffin, and got them to sign fresh agreements to act in the house and pay the daily rent. The following year, 1678, Griffin, Goodman, Charles and his half-brother Henry were included in the new company as 'master partners'. Henry Killigrew, whose penchant for theatre management stemmed more from the attraction of the actresses than any desire to regulate proceedings, proved more of a hindrance than a help.

Before continuing this chapter of woes, I would like to pay some attention to the new recruits of the company like Griffin and Goodman. We know from Colley Cibber, that these two 'were confined by their moderate Sallaries to the Oeconomy of lying together in the same Bed

* The handwriting of the entry is difficult to read.

and having but one whole Shirt between them'. This fraught sartorial circumstance led to a quarrel between them with drawn swords when both had promised to meet a woman on the same night, and the shirt became essential to the fulfilment of the date.

They had joined a profession which involved at least a three month apprenticeship without salary, and a wait of years to become a proper sworn servant of the King, for there were only sixteen of those allowed at a time. Their daily existence was a round of cadging, borrowing, stealing, and begging for pittances which then went on the usual vices of gambling and drinking. Surviving the rigours of such a life, which, in Goodman's case extended to highway robbery to make ends meet, was only for the resilient.

Goodman was certainly resilient. Notorious for his whoring in his early days, he took the Duchess of Cleveland as his mistress in about 1683. The liaison lasted over ten years which considering her previous record—five illegitimate children by Charles II, and passing affairs with Charles Hart, John Churchill, the future great Duke of Marlborough, and many lesser lights—was something of a bid for the seventeenth century equivalent of the *Guinness Book of Records*. As Rochester unkindly described her:

> Her almost boundless Appetite,
> Cloy'd with the choicest Banquets of Delight,
> She'll still trudge on in tasteless Vice;
> As if she sinn'd for Exercise;
> Disabling stoutest Stallions ev'ry Hour;
> And when they can perform no more,
> She'll rail at them and kick them out of door.

Cardell Goodman (the common epithet 'Scum' Goodman was only applied by Macaulay in the nineteenth century and stems largely from his own Whig view of the Jacobite Goodman) came in for his own share of anonymous verses,

> Goodman the Thief Swears 'tis all Womens Lots
> To dote upon his ugliness and Pox.

In his time he was pardoned his highway robberies, but later condemned by the bloodthirsty Judge Jeffreys for attempting to have two of Lady Castlemaine's children poisoned. He finally absconded to France when out on bail on charges of implication in a Jacobite plot to assassinate William III. Goodman's was a full life.

So was the career of Joe Haines, an earlier recruit to the Theatre Royal as a low comedian. There are almost more anecdotes about Haines than any other man of the time, so I have room only for a few. Even if they are apocryphal, they ought to be true because we know for certain that he was suspended, whipped, jailed and sacked for various escapades.

He once sabotaged a Charles Hart performance in *Catiline's Conspiracy* because Hart had insisted on Haines swelling the numbers of the senators behind himself as he made his big speech. Haines

> . . . gets a Scaramouch dress, a large full Ruff, makes himself Whiskers, from Ear to Ear, puts on his head, a long Merry Andrews Cap, a short Pipe in his mouth, a little three Leg'd stool in his hand, and in this manner, follows Mr Hart on the Stage, sets himself down behind him, and begins to smoke his Pipe, to Laugh, and Point at him. Which Comical Figure, put all the House in an Uproar, some Laughing, some Clapping, and some Hollowing . . .

says his 1701 biography. Hart, his big speech spoiled, was not pleased, any more than he was when Haines 'appointed' a parson to attend the theatre, and call the players to prayers. Solemnly, he instructed the noble divine that 'there is one Thing that I must particularly desire to your care

Joe Haines, the low comedian, speaks a prologue from the back of a donkey.
Enthoven Collection

viz, on the 3rd Door of your left hand, lives one Mr Hart. This Gentleman, whether he be delirious or frantick, or whether he be possest with some Damn'd Notions of Atheism, if you mention Prayers, he'll laugh at you, perhaps Swear, Curse and Abuse you . . . [but] leave him not, till you have oblig'd him to come along with you to Prayers. . . .'

Haines's facility for getting into scrapes was matched by his ingenuity in getting himself out again. When the cleric's infuriated son heard that his father had been used by Haines in a practical joke, he challenged Haines to a duel. Haines agreed to give the man a chance to resuscitate the family honour, but craved an opportunity to retire to an adjoining room to pray before the swords were drawn. Leaving the door open, he knelt and prayed loudly enough to be overheard. Craving the Lord's indulgence for the seventeen people he had already slain in combat, he then earnestly asked to be forgiven for the slaying he was about to commit. The parson's son took the hint and fled!

Charles Killigrew could have done with some of Haines's *chitzbah** in the next few years. Not all his troubles came from within the company. The years from 1678 to 1681 were also the period of the political uncertainties of the Popish plot.

Stirred up by the ridiculous business of Oates and his discovery of a 'plot' by the Catholics against the English Church and State, and fanned by rumours and scurrilous broadsheets, fear of popery became universal. Parliament was stampeded into anti-Catholic legislation, and authority generally reacted nervously to any hint of sedition creeping into plays.

Lee, Tate and Crowne all had plays banned for their possible parallels with contemporary politics, and Dryden and Lee's *The Duke of Guise*, as loyal a work as could be wished, was delayed for months by the Lord Chamberlain suspicious that there were 'great persons' depicted in it.

The Duke of Guise satirized citizens, Whigs, Nonconformists and the Duke of Monmouth from a Tory point of view. The effect of the censorship was that the Tory dramatists had freedom of speech from the stage but the Whigs had their plays banned. The Tories like Dryden, lashed their opponents in Prologues and Epilogues, although one would imagine the couplet in Dryden's Epilogue to *The Loyal Brother*

> Let Husband or Gallant be what they will,
> One part of Woman is true Tory still . . .

was the sort of compliment his own party could have done without.

---

* The Yiddish term once described as the quality shown by a man who murdered his father and mother then pleaded clemency on the grounds of being an orphan.

The only recourse left to the Whigs was to attend the theatre and register their audible resentment. And while Tories and Whigs cheered and counter-cheered, and the theatre became a political battleground, the apolitical stayed away in droves. At times in 1681, the company had to dismiss the audience and return their money because there were too few receipts to justify a performance.

Symptomatic of a final crumbling of the company, are the charges and counter charges which were made later that Charles Killigrew, Henry Killigrew and some of the actors had been guilty of pilfering from the company's stock. The sad and inevitable end came in April 1682 when the theatre was forced to close its doors. From a position of helpless mendicants they had virtually to beg the Duke's company to take them over. For the next twelve years London was to have not two but one company of players.

Thomas Betterton, the leading actor of the Restoration stage, was nearly fifty but his unique abilities made him the natural leader of the new united company. High flown rhetoric fitted his low pitched voice, and his tread was stately and dignified. Anthony Aston gives what sounds a truthful picture in that he

> . . . (although a superlative good actor) labour'd under ill Figure, being clumsily made, having a great Head, a short thick Neck, stoop'd in the Shoulders, and had fat short arms which he rarely lifted higher than his Stomach—His Left Hand frequently lodg'd in his Breast, between his Coat and Waist-coat, while with his Right, he prepar'd his Speech . . . his Aspect was serious, venerable and majestic; in his latter Time a little paralytic—His Voice was low and grumbling; yet he could Tune it by an artful Climax, which enforc'd universal attention, even from the Fops and Orange-Girls.

I think we would also agree with Aston that in *Hamlet* 'his Repartees seem'd rather as Apopthegms from a sage Philosopher, than the sporting Flashes of a Young Hamlet', but undoubtedly the man was considered by his contemporaries to be a giant.

He was of sufficient stature to draw fire from carpers like Tom Brown—

> . . . if you go to desire a piece of courtesy of him, you must attend longer than at a secretary's of state. His gravity will not permit him to give you audience till the stateliness of his countenance is rightly adjusted, and all his high-swelling words are got in readiness . . .

Thomas Betterton, the foremost actor of the Restoration stage; colleague and sometimes rival of the King's company at Drury Lane.

Enthoven Collection

and the anonymous sneers of the unknown author of *Satyr on the Players*—

> For who can hold to see the Foppish Town,
> Admire so sad a wretch as Betterton?
> Is't for his Legs, his Shoulders, or his Face;
> His formal Stiffness, or his awkward Grace?
> A Shop for him had been the fittest Place.

This unknown gentleman also doubted that Betterton's long-lived marriage to actress Mary Sanderson necessarily implied fidelity:

> . . . Methinks I see him mounted, hear him Roar,
> And foaming Cry, Odsblood, you little Whore,
> Zounds, how I f——k! I f——k like any Moor.

Not only modern stars had to contend with scurrilous attacks on their private lives.

59

In addition to Betterton, the Duke's company had William Smith for heroic roles; Sandford—'Meagre-fac'd, Spindle-shank'd, Splay-footed, with a Sour Countenance . . . the best Villain in the World'; Nokes—whose homosexuality drew epithets like 'You Smockfac'd Lads, Secure your Gentle Bums. For full of Lust and Fury See he comes. . . '; Leigh; Underhill—whose 'Nose was flattish and short, and his Upper Lip very long and thick' and whose monkey-like appearance was matched by his actions, 'leaping often up with both Legs at a Time, when he conceived any Thing waggish, and afterwards hugging himself at the Thought'. Mrs Barry also drew Tom Brown's fire. He suggested that she would lie with anyone for a night and not speak to them in the morning unless they could raise another £5 for the privilege. The object of Otway's devotion and known as the Restoration's greatest actress, she once appeared as Roxana to Mrs Boutell's Statira in *The Rival Queens*. Mrs Boutell won an argument about the ownership of a veil, only for Roxana to give Statira a nasty flesh wound with a dagger in the last act. 'As it was well known these ladies were not vestals; it was reported jealousy gave force to the blow.'

From the old King's company came Kynaston, Goodman, Griffin, Haines and Powell, whose drunkenness was notorious. Powell 'often toasted, to intoxication, his mistress, with bumpers of Nantz-brandy; he came sometimes so warm, with that noble spirit, to the theatre, that he courted the ladies so furiously on the stage, that, in the opinion of Sir John Vanbrugh, they were almost in danger of being conquered on the spot'.

The gout-ridden Hart, Mohun, Cartwright, Burt and Shatterell retired around this period. Mohun, by a plea to his old admirer the King, managed to secure a pension. Hart and Kynaston made their own private arrangements. Shabby the arrangements were, but by contemporary standards not outrageous. As Percy Fitzgerald's *Life of Betterton* makes quite clear, Hart and Kynaston accelerated the demise of the King's company by taking money from the Duke's company *not* to act, and agreed secretly to promote a union between the companies. Kynaston also agreed to try to get free to join the Duke's company himself if the merger was not forthcoming.

The union concluded between Charles Killigrew and Charles Davenant agreed that they would run the new company under their own joint direction. Killigrew agreed to dissolve the Drury Lane company and unite his father's Patent with that of Davenant. The opening of the new company was actually under the authority of the Davenant Patent and the Killigrew Patent became dormant.

Killigrew's right to make such an agreement rested on slender ground. He was under fire in the courts from Richard Kent to whom his father had assigned the rights in the theatre. The judgement in December 1682 upheld Kent's claims to the property. When Thomas Killigrew died in March 1683, he left his estate to Charles's half-brother Henry, and Henry showed his brotherly love by suing Kent for the return of his father's Patent, disclosing that Kent had let Charles take over the interests for '£500 and a greater sum to be thereafter paid'. Kent was obviously something of an optimist in agreeing to a sum 'thereafter' as his holdings had brought him less than a third of what he should have earned in the last seven years. Henry also tried to lure some of the actors away in the hope that he could get another patent himself.

Charles Killigrew had his father's talent for bluff. He reached the agreement for union with Charles Davenant; yet he had only a disputed claim on the Patent, a tiny holding in actors' shares, only a quarter of the thirty-five building shares, and a lease from the Earl of Bedford which had only a few years to run. From this limited power base, he somehow persuaded a majority of the building shareholders to accept the new company as tenants at a lower rent than before, pleading that the expenses of continuing to run Dorset Gardens for occasional performances in addition to Drury Lane would otherwise prove too high.

Under the new régime, the theatre moved into a new era of prosperity. The combined talents drew good audiences and there was but one market for plays available to contemporary writers. The Duke's company had drawn on the extraordinary woman playwright Aphra Behn, and her Tory play *The Lucky Chance* was performed by the united company at Drury Lane in 1686.

Notorious for her ability to match any male writer in obscenity, she had a chequered career. She was once an English spy in Holland and conducted some notorious affairs including one with John Hoyle 'an Atheist, a Sodomite professed, a corruptor of youth and a Blasphemer of Christ'. Her work has high comic moments although hardly ripe for a modern revival. At least our age would be unlikely to dismiss her work as did one Victorian lady as the products of a mind 'tainted to the very core'. She died in 1689.

Dryden continued to write for the new company, the young Congreve gave them his first two plays, *The Old Bachelor* and *The Double Dealer*, Otway supplied *Venice Preserved* and there were many distinguished revivals.

Behind the scenes all was still not well. Charles Davenant became plagued with fraternal troubles similar to Killigrew's. He himself was

61

short of cash and in August 1687, his brother Alexander offered him
£2,400 for the family Patent and for his interests in the theatre. Charles
agreed, without realizing that the money was not Alexander's own but
came from a deal Alexander made with Sir Thomas Skipwith. Skipwith,
a Lincolnshire baronet who is described in the Skipwith family history
as a man 'of unenviable notoriety, even in those days, for his *bonnes
fortunes*', gave £2,000 towards the purchase and agreed to lease his five-
sixths of the whole back to Alexander for seven years in return for free
tickets and £6 a week.

Two years later, Alexander was even more in need of ready money and
he leased his remaining sixth to Christopher Rich for £300, in return
agreeing to pay Rich £1 4s a week. Alexander had the escape route that
at the end of the seven years he could pay Skipwith £2,000 and Rich
£300 and reclaim his rights to the theatre and the Patent. As Skipwith
and Rich undoubtedly knew, he was unlikely ever to be able so to do.
They allowed his weekly payments to lapse by more than twelve months
and patiently waited.

Alexander, joined by another brother Thomas, ran the company from
1688, moved Ralph Davenant in as treasurer, and although the company
was taking something like £10,000 a year, used his status to get bogus
credit and to swindle actors, creditors and others by such charming
devices as selling property three times over. For five years he sowed the
wind, and in 1693 when he was about to reap the whirlwind, he escaped
arrest by fleeing to the Canary Islands.

By December, Skipwith and Rich had asserted their rights, showed
Alexander to have been in arrears and claimed the theatre. Of the two
Rich was by far the most powerful and his soon became a one-man rule.
History has given him something of a bad press. Cibber's 'as sly a tyrant
as ever was at the head of a theatre; for he gave the actors more liberty,
and fewer days pay, than any of his predecessors' is invariably quoted, and
A Comparison Between Two Stages, published anonymously in 1702, has
him as 'an old snarling Lawyer Master and Sovereign; a waspish, ignorant
pettifogger in Law and Poetry; one who understands Poetry no more
than Algebra; he wou'd sooner have the Grace of God than do every
body Justice. . . .'

Rich was no different to many another of his age. He cheated, he
double-dealt, his interest in theatre was minimal; his interest in lining
his own pockets was legendary—he was just better at it than most. He
could not however keep the company together. Mainly because Rich
refused to conform to agreements the actors had reached with the management during the brief reigns of Charles Killigrew, Charles Davenant and

Alexander Davenant, and instead drove harsher bargains with them himself, the most prominent members of the company petitioned the Lord Chamberlain in December 1694 for a redress of their grievances.

A long document giving details of the reductions in salary, the pocketing of 'after-money' (the money taken at the door from those only wishing to see the latter part of the proceedings) and the making of 'not King's Servants . . . but the Claimers Slaves', was appended. The petition came from Betterton, Underhill, Kynaston, Mrs Barry and nine others. This drew an even longer reply in equally tedious detail from Rich. This correspondence in the Public Record Office viewed dispassionately shows that there were faults on either side—Rich was not the only sinner.

Just after the correspondence had been delivered to the Lord Chamberlain's office, there was a suspension of theatrical activities owing to the illness of Queen Mary. Betterton used the period to do some unofficial canvassing of the Lord Chamberlain, and in March 1695 gained a private audience of King William. By dint of his considerable prestige and persuasive powers, he managed to obtain a special licence to act elsewhere —the first breach in the monopoly foreseen in the two original Patents. In the names of himself, Mrs Barry, Mrs Bracegirdle, Mrs Verbruggen, Mrs Leigh, Bowman, Williams, Underhill, Doggett, Bowen and Bright, the licence granted them power 'to Act and Represent all manners of Comedys, Tragedys, Plays, Interludes, Operas and all other Theatricall and musicall entertainments'. The rebellious group opened up at Lisle's Tennis Court in Lincoln's Inn Fields in competition to Rich and the remainder of the company at Drury Lane.

The rivalry between the two companies became an all-out theatrical war. Betterton started brilliantly with the first presentation of Congreve's classic *Love for Love* but the main weapons in the battles for audiences were somewhat less distinguished. As actors now had an alternative market to ply their services there were also some unseemly disputes about poaching and bribery between the two companies until the Lord Chamberlain forbade anyone to leave either company. Both had 'seduced Actors'.

Desperate for audiences, both houses tried to seduce spectators as well 'with absurd and foreign Diversions'. The stage became 'prostituted to Vagabonds, to Caperers, Eunuchs, Fiddlers, Tumblers and Gypsies'. Drury Lane put on Signior Clementé 'the famous Eunuch, Servant to the Elector of Bavaria'. He was a hit for 'he got more by being an Eunuch than if he had the best Back in Christendom; the Ladies paid more for his Caponship than they wou'd ha' done for his virility'. At least Vanbrugh's *The Relapse* and *The Provoked Wife* are rather more lasting

63

contributions from the Drury Lane reportory of the 1690s than Signior Clementé.

Disorder in the theatre itself kept many potential patrons away. In 1699 *The Country Gentleman's Vade Mecum* talked of

> . . . what's worse still . . . comes in a drunken Lord, with a Party of Low Country Warriours; or what's more common, a Country Squire, that has lately taken up the Noble Profession of Scowring and Revelling; and to shew their Parts and their Courage, raise a Quarrel, and put the whole House into a Hurly-Burly; then you'll see fine Work indeed; the Whores tumbling over the seats, and the poor Squires and Beaus tumbling after 'em in a horrible fright, and disorder; the whole Pit's in Arms in a Minute, and every Man's sword drawn. . . .

The enemies of the theatre registered all these things and over the last decade of the seventeenth century moved increasingly on to the attack. Because the effects of their moral attitudes shaped the eighteenth century in a particular way, before we continue to trace further the fortunes of Christopher Rich and his rivals, it is worth looking first at the background of the next hundred years.

PART II

*The
Eighteenth
Century*

CHAPTER FOUR

Size and Sentiment

THE death of Charles II in 1685 had profound effects upon the royal theatre. Where the company had been guaranteed an enlightened and sympathetic ear for their troubles and tribulations, and a tolerance for anything that smacked of the risqué in their plays, the advent of William III in the Glorious Revolution of 1688 meant they, like everyone else, had to toe a moral line. William's Queen Mary was genuinely pious, and her successor Queen Anne even more a champion of decorum. Instead of a court monopoly, Drury Lane became merely a fashionable rendezvous.

The change was important because court protection was replaced by the house becoming the target for social reformers. The immorality of plays, the frequent outbreak of disorders in the house, political demonstrations, pickpockets and prostitutes combined to give the stage an aura redolent with brimstone and sulphur. For half a century, the Devil had had all the best lines.

Just as the Restoration of Charles II had seen a reaction against Puritan values, so the coarseness of the intervening years provoked a change in moral tone. There was a resurgence of Puritanism which lasted until the coming of Wesley. Between 1698 and 1800, there were more than fifty diatribes published attacking the playhouses on moral grounds.

Now, there was no one to say as Charles had, when approached by the Lord Mayor and his Puritan supporters to get Lady D'Avenant's nursery company at the Barbican closed in 1671, 'that the Playhouses should be pulled down when the Meeting Houses were!' The moral code of the aristocrats was gradually being replaced by that of the upper middle class in an increasingly mercantile society. The ridicule in which representatives of the class had been held on the stage gave an added venom to the attacks.

The Lord Chamberlain sent orders, relating to the licensing of plays

and the striking out of obscenities, in 1696, 1697, and 1699. The Master
of the Revels, none other than our old friend Charles Killigrew, threw
himself into the moral crusade with all the fervour of a recent convert.
The *Daily Courant* of 24 January 1704 reports Queen Anne's decree
making her attitude quite clear:

> Whereas we have herebye given orders to the Master of Our Revels,
> and also to both the companies of Comedians acting in Drury Lane
> and Lincoln's Inn Fields to take special care that nothing be acted in
> either of the Theatres contrary to religion or good manners upon pain
> of our high displeasure and of being silenced from further acting and
> being further desirous to reform all the indecency and abuses of the
> stage which have occasioned great disorders. . . .

This change in official attitudes reflected the changes in public opinion,
or, more accurately, represented the increasing importance of people
outside the coterie of the Court who held different opinions. The solid
citizens who made up the Grand Jury of Middlesex in 1703, for example,
were demanding a voice:

> We, the Grand Jury of the County of Middlesex do present, that the
> Plays which are frequently acted in the play-houses in Drury-Lane and
> Lincoln's-Inn-Fields in this County are full of prophane, irreverent,
> lewd, indecent and immoral expressions, and tend to the great dis-
> pleasure of Almighty God and to the corruption of the auditory, both
> in their principles and their practices. We also present, that the common
> acting of plays in the said play-houses very much tend to the debauching
> and ruining the youth resorting thereto, and to the breach of the peace,
> and are the occasions of many riots, routs and disorderly assemblies,
> whereby many murders and other misdemeanours have been frequently
> done, and . . . further that the common acting of plays at the said play-
> houses is a public nuisance.

We cannot afford to scoff too readily. Our own times have seen just as
many attacks upon the arts which continue to draw the fire of moral
reformers. In the *Western Mail* of 15 September 1971, a report on a debate
of the Flintshire County Council included the following:

> Alderman Tom Fish said deteriorating moral standards and depravity
> were sponsored by the arts, literature and the theatre.

Almost any provincial paper today could produce similar examples. What made the late seventeenth and early eighteenth century attacks particularly important is that they found a focus in two men who gave articulate voice to the inarticulate feelings of many, and that they had a lasting and damaging effect upon the drama of a whole century.

Like Flintshire's Alderman Fish, unable to see that drama is a mirror of its own times and not a root cause, the first of the two men was a non-juror and pamphleteer called Jeremy Collier. In 1698 he published a *Short View of the Immorality and Profaneness of the English Stage*. The view, neither short nor accurate, betrays an unwholesome lack of a sense of proportion and a fair amount of ignorance of the history and techniques of theatre. The amazing thing was that because he struck so sympathetic a chord in the hearts of his readers, the champions of drama went down before him like a pack of cards.

Collier's thunder was joined by the persuasive tones of Sir Richard Steele. Steele was all for the reform of drama and saw the stage in terms of a pulpit whereby morality could be transferred from the printed page into people's minds. To him a play had to point a moral lesson; villainy and immorality had to receive their come-uppance and virtue its just reward. That life is not like that, and that Restoration tragedy had already shown the futility of writing plays to conform to ideals, did not concern him. His journalism and his political connections enabled him to get power at Drury Lane, and, unlike Collier, the opportunity to put his ideas into practice.

While he preached for plays as 'Representations as tended to the Instruction and Ornament of Life', he could meanwhile have pleasure in poking fun at the sort of after-pieces, 'mimical Dances and fulsome Buffooneries', that both theatres were putting on. He was joined in this by Addison whose review of the labours of Mr Higgins a contortionist, is a minor classic.

> ... to my unspeakable amazement there came up a monster with a face between his feet; and as I was looking on, he raised himself on one leg in such a perpendicular posture that the other grew in a direct line above his head. It afterwards twisted itself into the motions and wreathings of several different animals, and after great variety of shapes and transformations, went off the stage in the figure of a human creature ... the admiration, the applause, the satisfaction of the audience ... is not to be expressed.

Similar fare was common. Contemporary advertisements promised a

Mr Evans 'vaulter of the managed horse, where he lies with his body extended on one hand, in which posture he drinks several glasses of wine with the other, [then] . . . throws himself a somerset over the horse's head to the admiration of all'; and a Mr Clinch whose speciality was an 'imitation of an organ with three voices, the double curtel, and the bells, the huntsman with his horn and pack of dogs; all which he performs with his mouth on the open stage, being what no man besides himself could ever yet attain to'.

It would be unrealistic to expect an audience happy to applaud the efforts of Messrs Higgins, Evans and Clinch, to discriminate against the sentimental twaddle that passed for the average eighteenth century play. Based broadly on the themes and characters of Restoration plays, the bite and the vigour has been sweetened with a saccharine layer of sentiment. Sops for the squeamish brought in their wake countless numbers of reformed sparks, and innocent heroines protecting their virtue and putting evil to shame by their colossal naïvety and ignorance.

There was also a Rousseau-like admiration for the innocence of the country which contrasted nicely with the corruption of the town. Rakes reformed, dimple-cheeked damsels simpered their way to triumph and irascible old gentlemen found hearts of gold beneath their gruff exteriors in time for the fifth act curtain.

Perhaps the first of the sentimental comedies, *Love's Last Shift* by Colley Cibber, made its appearance in 1695 and had a great success. It was the father of some monstrous progeny; and by the operation of a theatrical version of Gresham's Law, bad plays drove out the good. Can we wonder that the wit of Congreve's brilliant *Way of the World* (1700) was so ill received that he gave up the stage in disgust with another twenty-years to live? To add to the irony, '. . . the Play was hissed by barbarous Fools in the Acting, and an impertinent Trifle was brought on after it, which was acted with vast Applause'.

Significantly, Shakespeare who had been re-written in the seventeenth century because he was not sufficiently 'modern' or to excuse displays of scenes and machines, was travestied in the eighteenth century unmercifully. He was performed only in versions we would find totally unacceptable. *King Lear* at the hands of Tate has Cordelia happily marrying Edgar, Cibber's *Richard III* remains famous for one line 'Off with his head—so much for Buckingham!' and Garrick had both Juliet declaiming 'Bless me, how cold it is!' on her awakening in the tomb, and Macbeth delivering a dying speech. (D'Avenant's version of the Thane's last breath was 'Farewell, vain world, and what's most vain in it, ambition'.)

The only crumb of comfort one can glean is that the phenomenal growth of pantomime during the century probably preserved the bard from some of the operatic-spectaculars that would have been otherwise done in his name.

The pantomime was not what we would recognize as such. Rather it was an entertainment composed half of scenic surprises and magical transformations, and half of tumbling and comic antics. The harlequin figure, which Grimaldi turned into the clown at the end of the century, was a prominent feature. The success of the *genre* is unquestionable.

A review of the years from 1747 to 1776 when Garrick ruled Drury Lane will show that three pantomimes by Henry Woodward—*Queen Mab, The Genii* and *Fortunatus*—and one by Garrick—*Harlequin's Invasion* —received more performances than any other work. For the 259 performances of *Queen Mab, Romeo and Juliet* (and that more Garrick than Shakespeare) got 142.

Garrick changed the Drury Lane building itself considerably. The first gallery was enlarged in 1747. The boxes at the Russell Street side were given a new entrance in 1750, and special provision for ladies' carriages was made two years later. Lacy, Garrick's partner, supervised an increase of seating capacity in 1762 and after an interim repainting for the 1771-2 season, the summer recess of 1777 was used for the construction of a brand new auditorium designed by Robert Adam. Extensively decorated in the Adam style, much of its elegance was regrettably forsaken when Messrs Greenwood and Capon refurnished it in 1783.

Were Garrick's changes for the better? When he took over in 1741, the theatre held 1,000 people and the annual receipts were £18,276. When he retired in 1775, the house had been remodelled to hold 2,362 people and took £33,615. The importance of this is that one would no more think of staging intimate or *avant garde* entertainments in a theatre of such size, than one would of getting a string quartet to play in Wembley Stadium. By its very size therefore, the Theatre Royal was committed to the safe, the spectacular and the large scale entertainment which would draw popular taste. In one sense, a pattern, which has remained constant to our own time, had been formed.

The succession of official orders, and the gentility of the entertainment, was not necessarily paralleled by improvements in audience behaviour. Garrick particularly was a notable reformer of many of the malpractices we have noted in previous years, but although the century opened to rowdyism and riots and closed in comparative calm, it is easy to overstate the improvements. Full scale riots were always a possibility—1743 saw a two day riot, 1755 a six day riot, 1763 a two day riot, 1770 a three day riot, 1776 a four day riot—quite apart from the normal day to day hazards of the theatre, prostitutes and pickpockets. As late as 1791, a German visitor recorded:

> The uproar before the play begins is indescribable . . . frequently spectators are wounded and their clothing is soiled. . . . At Drury Lane I wished to look around at the gallery in order to examine its structure, but a heap of orange peels, striking me with considerable force in the face, robbed me of all curiosity. The best plan is to keep your face turned towards the stage and thus quietly submit to the hail of oranges on your back. On one occasion my hat was so saturated (I really do not know with what watery ingredients) that I was compelled to have it cleaned next day. . . .

A subsidiary reason for Garrick's structural changes and increase in seating accommodation, was to abolish spectators from the stage itself. The practice took a deal of killing and the *Actor* of 1755 shows how irritating the intrusion could be.

> The keeping up of the illusion of carrying on an appearance of reality is the great merit of theatrical representation, but that is impossible under this disadvantage. Let the decorations of the house, the dress and deportment and recitation of the players be ever as proper, this destroys all. The head of some cropped beau among a set of full-bottomed conspirators destroys all the look of reality.

The century saw the focus of the stage action pushed gradually back from the apron to within the proscenium arch and nearer to the scenery. Practical doors and open flats are evident at the back of the stage in the Garrick period, occasionally lateral flats were turned to oblique positions, and although box sets were unheard of until the 1830s, ground rows and raking pieces increasingly made their appearance.

These improvements were only possible because of improvements in lighting. Until 1765, the stage was lit by six chandeliers over the stage, each with a dozen wax candles. These chandeliers could be raised or dropped to affect the amount of light on the stage but that was obviously limited and unsatisfactory. Garrick imported an Alsace painter called Philippe de Loutherbourg who had made a particular study of stage illusions. By changing the main source of light to battens behind the proscenium arch, and exploiting the possibilities of coloured lights and coloured transparent silk screens turning on pivots in the flies and the wings, de Loutherbourg conjured sunsets, moonlight, cloud and fire effects at Drury Lane, particularly in the pantomimes.

The *Public Advertiser* was astonished by the possibilities of concealed lighting:

> ... the Drury Lane Managers have absolutely created an artificial Day; or, to vary my Expression and Sentiment, they seem to have brought down the Milky Way to the Bottom of the Stage; or, to vary once more, they have given us a perfect Meridian of Wax.

Before we get too carried away with these advances towards naturalism on the stage, let us not forget that Garrick was still playing Lear beardless and dressed in a velvet robe with ermine trimmings, a white wig, lace hose and high heeled shoes with silver buckles.

Dialogue in most plays carried just the same sort of conviction. The immortal exchange in Dr Brown's *Barbarossa* for example:

> *Othman*   ... Besides he wears
> A mark indelible, a beauteous scar,
> Made on his forehead by a furious pard,
> Which, rushing on his mother, Selim slew,
>
> *Achmet*   A scar!
> *Othman*   Ay, on his forehead.
> *Achmet*   (lifting his turban) What, like this?
> *Othman*   Whom do I see?
> Am I awake? My Prince!
> My honour'd, honour'd king!

With this background in mind, let us return to the doings of Christopher Rich and Co.

CHAPTER FIVE

Triumvirate and Trade Union

1700–34

THE Betterton company did not reap all the benefits that the break-away might have brought. In the battle which broke out between the new company and the old at Drury Lane, Rich more than held his own. The weapons used in the battle were sometimes clever and well chosen; on other occasions, petty and silly. Betterton announced *Hamlet* for a Tuesday. The Theatre Royal announced *Hamlet* for the Monday. Betterton then changed his *Hamlet* to Monday. This provoked Powell, who was in effect Rich's acting manager, to revive *The Old Bachelor* instead, planning to 'mimick Betterton throughout the whole Part'. As a result of the change, Cibber had to learn the part of Fondlewife at a few hours' notice, and added to a growing reputation in so doing.

Colley Cibber plays a major role in the history of Drury Lane. Leaving behind him an entertaining autobiography, he spent some forty years at the theatre as actor, manager and author. 'His thin, sharp features, aquiline nose, bright small eyes, together with his solemn strutting air, giving him the appearance of some grotesque bird, at once venerable and vindictive looking', wrote one contemporary witness, and we hear that later, 'he plumped out like a partridge'.

An inveterate gambler, with a continuing eye for the pleasures of the flesh despite two wives and a succession of children, Cibber grew in stature from spear-carrier to Poet Laureate and the G.O.M. of the first half of the eighteenth century. Tactless, rude to those of a lesser stature and snobbishly obsequious to those of a higher, he wrote plays like *The Careless Husband*, among twenty-five original works and many adaptations. *The Careless Husband* became a model of gentility, politeness and sentiment.

His acting in comedy inspired Vanbrugh to write the role of Lord Foppington in *The Relapse* for him, the play itself a sequel to Cibber's own *Love's Last Shift*, and he scored a brilliant success. His playing in tragedy was less sure. In his own adaptation of *Richard III*, a version which kept Shakespeare's off the stage until well into the nineteenth century, *The Laureat* tells us:

> He screamed through four acts without dignity or decency . . . when he was killed . . . one might plainly perceive that the good people were not better pleased that so execrable a tyrant was destroyed than that so execrable an actor was silent.

When he stayed out of the coffee houses, taverns and gambling halls, Cibber moved somewhat nearer to Rich who found him a potential ally. Rich had a deal of talent at his disposal but he had few allies, particularly on the basis of his capacity to drive hard bargains with his actors— 'he would laugh with them over a bottle, and bite them in their bargains'. Rich, normally 'a close, subtle man', consulted Cibber about the growing rivalry between Powell and Wilks.

In addition to his drinking habits, Powell had the added disadvantage of a natural arrogance and intractability. Steele in the *Tatler* talks of 'Mr George Powell, who formerly played Alexander the Great in all places, though he is lately grown so reserved as to act it only on the stage'.

Robert Wilks was an Irishman who originally had been engaged by Rich on Betterton's recommendation. He was paid 15s a week at the start, but, a typical Rich ploy, deducted 10s a month for dancing lessons. Wilks brought to England with him a fellow actor George Farquhar and a life-long friend. Farquhar's career as an actor was short-lived because he was unlucky enough to wound a fellow actor in a duel scene and turned to playwriting instead. As the wound indirectly brought us *Love in a Bottle*, *The Constant Couple*, *The Recruiting Officer* and *The Beaux' Stratagem*, our sympathy for the unknown recipient has to be somewhat tempered.

The acting honours went not to Farquhar but to Wilks. His dedication to the preparation of a part, such as Sir Harry Wildair in *The Constant Couple*, became legendary and gained him 'an Immortal Reputation'. Wilks, according to Cibber, 'in a great measure wore out the Organs of Life in his incessant Labour to gratify the Publick'. He fathered ten children, adopted four, and was as lively on stage. In the *Comparison Between Two Stages*, we learn

> His Feet never stand still; he is like the Pendulum of a Clock, perpetually shuffling from one side to t'other . . . [he has] affected levity in his heels.

and John Downes mentions his occasional 'Unnatural Rants'.

Wilks's successes did not please Powell whose 'pretended contempt . . . began to sour into an open Jealousy'. There was talk of a duel but instead Powell 'grew so out of Humour that he cock'd his Hat, and in his Passion walk'd off to the Service of the Company in Lincoln's Inn Fields'. Wilks succeeded to the head of the company, partly due to Cibber's advice to Rich who preferred Powell both as an actor ('when he was, what he seldom was, sober'), and as a manager—Powell had once kept the actors quiet for six weeks without pay! Powell did not last too long at Lincoln's Inn Fields either and returned two seasons later when he had to humble himself under Wilks. It was the lesser of two evils for all was not well with the Betterton company.

Rich judged plays by receipts. His adroit mixture of novelty diversions and good plays in harness drew audiences. Betterton and his company found that 'Experience in a Year or Two shew'd them that they had never been worse govern'd than when they govern'd themselves . . . many of them began to make their particular Interest more their Point than that of the general'.

They also lost Thomas Doggett to Rich. In Downes's words, Doggett was 'very Aspectabund, wearing a Farce in his Face; his Thoughts deliberately framing his Utterance Congruous to his Looks: he is the only Comick Original now Extant'. Although, or perhaps because, Doggett was so proficient at comedy, he had a contempt for tragedy. He 'could not with Patience look upon the costly Trains and Plumes of Tragedy, in which knowing himself to be useless, he thought were all a vain Extravagance'.

Rich devised a scheme whereby footmen, who had been sent to keep places for their betters, were admitted free to the upper gallery at Drury Lane. The noise, orange pelting and uproar which frequently resulted, Rich thought a small price to pay in return for the free publicity below stairs in the houses of people of quality. The scheme, in income at least, paid off. Most of his ideas did.

One less commercial idea, which became something of a hobby with him, was a 'genius in nook-building'. He took Cibber on a conducted tour of 'fifty little back-doors, dark closets, and narrow passages' which he had constructed at the theatre. It could be that when Rich carried out these brick-laying operations, some unknown assassin took advantage of the fact to conceal a murder. All that we know is that late in the nineteenth century, a wall was taken down revealing a tiny room containing a corpse in the remnants of an early eighteenth century costume with a dagger sticking between its ribs. This is the only instance which I can find which may give some credence to the theatre's famous ghost.

Thomas Doggett—comedian, theatre manager and staunch Whig. *Enthoven Collection*

In common with most people, I can believe in a ghost when it manifests itself in my presence. Until that event takes place, I must remain on the side of the doubters. Nevertheless, it must be recorded that many observers, throughout both nineteenth and twentieth centuries, have reported seeing an amorphous grey gentleman in wig, cloak, three-cornered hat and riding boots who, for his own reasons, occasionally appears, doing little more than appearing at one side of the Upper Circle, walking across and disappearing at the other side. That is all I can say,

77

although if the gentleman cares to get in touch with me, I can promise him his first-hand testimony will be incorporated in any future editions of this book. Answers, on a postcard, will be given careful consideration . . . .

If any of the figures of the period were genuinely to manifest themselves today, I would like to see Mrs Oldfield. She was discovered by Farquhar, serving in the Mitre Tavern in St James's Market, and was introduced by Vanbrugh to Christopher Rich. She took some time to establish herself but her creation of the role Lady Betty Modish in Cibber's *The Careless Husband* in December 1704 brought her into the front rank. The author himself said 'all that Nature had given her of the Actress seem'd to have risen to its full Perfection'. When she went on to play in *The Provok'd Husband* to similar acclaim, the management was constrained to award her an extra 50 guineas for her efforts. This, I need hardly add, was after Rich's time.

Her rise to fame was too much competition for the former leading lady Mrs Bracegirdle, who duly retired. Famous for her chastity in a licentious age, although her relations with Congreve were, to say the least, regarded with suspicion, 'she was of a lovely Height, with dark-brown Hair and Eye-brows, black sparkling Eyes, and a fresh blushy Complexion'. The description comes from Anthony Aston, who adds that 'Genteel Comedy was her chief Essay', and that she particularly shone in 'Men's Cloaths, in which she far surmounted all the Actresses of that and this Age . . . .' Her virginity, real or pretended, was once the subject of a collection of 1,000 guineas made by some noble lords especially to commend it. For once, virtue brought a cash reward.

In 1705, Betterton's company moved to a new house built for them by Sir John Vanbrugh, playwright and architect of Blenheim, in the Haymarket. Unfortunately, the attraction of the new house was more visual than acoustic. Cibber tells us that 'scarce one Word in ten could be distinctly heard in it . . . generally what they said sounded like the Gabbling of so many people in the lofty Isles in a Cathedral'. The venture was so unsuccessful that Vanbrugh was seeking a union with the Drury Lane company after the first three months, petitioning the Lord Chamberlain for his assistance in bringing about the merger.

Rich saw no reason why he should bail out his erstwhile rivals. He said that his existing shareholders would 'tear him to pieces with lawsuits' if he took in further sharers, just as, at last, he was beginning to reap reasonable profits. Vanbrugh then turned to Owen Swiney, a friend of both Cibber and Rich, and an Irish actor and manager. After Swiney had had consultation with Rich, he leased the house, company and scenery from Vanbrugh at £5 a day.

What was said between Swiney and Rich will never be conclusively known, but in all probability Rich agreed to let Swiney take any Drury Lane actors he wanted except Cibber. (Rich knew he could keep some sort of repertory going with dancers and musicians and one 'tolerable Actor'.) In return, Swiney promised to split the Haymarket and Drury Lane profits with Rich. If this surmise of the agreement between them is accurate it means that Rich was letting Swiney take all the risks of putting on legitimate drama, while he knew he could keep Drury Lane open

Colley Cibber, actor, manager, playwright and the author of an entertaining autobiography. *Enthoven Collection*

himself with sundry entertainments, and he would still get 50% of any profits the actors earned in the new house. Swiney was given no written agreement that Rich would keep his side of the bargain. Heads Rich wins, tails Swiney loses.

Full of optimism, Swiney took Wilks, Mrs Oldfield and others off to the Haymarket and wrote to Cibber who was on holiday in Gloucestershire asking him to join the company. Cibber was reluctant to leave Rich despite the weakness of the company around him. When Swiney

79

and Rich quarrelled about the non-fulfilment of Rich's side of the bargain, Cibber eventually joined the Haymarket company in November 1706. Rich consoled himself for the absence of Cibber by negotiating for an attraction bigger in every sense—an elephant. It was only when it emerged that a wall essential to the stability of the structure of Drury Lane would have to be knocked down to make way for the pachydermous performer, that Rich gave up the idea.

Meanwhile, his old partner Skipwith was quietly withdrawing from the scene. Skipwith met a Colonel Henry Brett, one of Cibber's old friends and one responsible for introducing Cibber into higher social circles than the actor would have been otherwise able to patronize. Skipwith was very taken with Brett's 'uncommon share of sociality' and their first meeting 'ended in an agreement to finish our bargain that night over a bottle'—the bottle 'the sire of many a jolly dozen'. Skipwith, in an alcoholic haze, signed over to Brett his entire share in Drury Lane 'in consideration of friendship, love and affection . . . [and] the sum of ten shillings to him in hand paid by the said Henry Brett'. Believing his holding to be worthless, Skipwith had given away a valuable *entrée* to the Theatre Royal for ten shillings! He tried to recover it later.

Brett came to London and consulted Cibber who suggested 'That he should produce his Deed to the other Menaging Patentee of Drury Lane, and demand immediate Entrance to a joint Possession of all Effects and Powers to which that Deed had given him an equal Title'. Brett did just this and became a joint manager. One doubts that Rich was too pleased.

Brett also had influence at Court and, wanting to get the actors back to Drury Lane, he was probably behind a decree from the Lord Chamberlain on 31 December 1707 which insisted that from 10 January onwards, only the Haymarket would be allowed to do operas and music, and only Drury Lane would be allowed to perform legitimate drama. It was in effect another union, and by 13 January 1708 the actors had returned to Drury Lane.

Three months later, Brett delegated his power to Wilks, Cibber and Estcourt. Estcourt, a minor comic actor, Downes tells us had the power 'always to laetificate his audience, especially the quality'. Laetificated or not, whatever that happy state might be, his fans had to do without him when Estcourt gave up the theatre and opened a tavern which 'enlarged his acquaintance, and . . . shortened his days', so he need not concern us.

Rich again reduced salaries and began to operate a system whereby he demanded a third of the profits from any benefit performances. Actors complained to the Lord Chamberlain, and Cibber, Wilks and Doggett reached a secret agreement with Owen Swiney that they would return to the Haymarket in the autumn and share with him in the company profits which resulted.

Rich was also under fire from the Lord Chamberlain who sent an order on 30 April 1709, requiring Rich to pay actors full benefits, deducting only £40 for house expenses. Like most of the orders from the same source, Rich ignored it. This was a tactical error because it was followed on 6 June 1709 by a Silence Order forbidding any more performances at Drury Lane.

The delivery of the Silence Order bringing Rich's long reign to an end was almost pure melodrama. Cibber on one of his frequent backstairs canvasses, had already seen the Silence Order at the Lord Chamberlain's Office, and arrived at the theatre to tell the other actors the glad news. A rehearsal was in progress. Modestly, his account is in the third person. He is 'the actor' and

. . . when being call'd to his part, and something hastily questioned by the patentee [Rich] for his neglect of business; this actor, I say, with an erected look, and a theatrical spirit, at once threw off the mask, and roundly told him—'Sir, I have now no more business here, than you have; in half an hour, you will neither have actors to command, nor authority to employ them'—The patentee, who though he could not readily comprehend his mysterious manner of speaking, had just a glimpse of terror enough from the words to soften his reproof into a cold formal declaration, 'That if he would not do his work, he should not be paid'. But now, to complete the catastrophe of these theatrical commotions, enters the messenger, with the order of silence in his hand, whom the same actor officiously introduc'd, telling the patentee that the gentleman wanted to speak with him, from the Lord Chamberlain.

When the messenger had delivered the order, the actor throwing his head over his shoulder, towards the patentee, in the manner of Shakespear's Harry the Eighth to Cardinal Wolsey, cry'd—'Read o'er that! and now—to breakfast with what appetite you may'.

As usual Cibber got the quotation slightly wrong, but as a moment of pure theatre it must have been uniquely satisfying.

Rich made surprisingly little of a comeback, and apart from some accounts supplied by his treasurer Zachary Baggs to cast doubt on the truth of the actors' complaints, he did not protest as volubly as one would expect. He did, however, sit tight at the silent theatre. An advertisement appeared in the newspapers to rub salt in the wound:

> That a Magnificent Palace with great Variety of Gardens, Statues and Waterworks, may be brought cheap in Drury-Lane ... several Castles to be disposed of, very delightfully situated, as also Groves, Woods, Forests, Fountains and Country-Seats, with very pleasant Prospects on all Sides of them, being the Moveables of Ch——r R——ch Esq, who is breaking up House-keeping. ...

Rich was also faced with a powerful enemy who had bought his way into a small share of the Patent. This was William Collier, a Tory member of Parliament who was prepared to use his influence at Court to further his cause and in the meantime to form temporary alliances with any of the interested parties. The alliances tended to last only as long as Collier benefited from them. Alliances and cross-alliances formed which would be too tedious to follow in all their details.

Swiney was full of confidence that with the silencing of Rich, he would be sitting pretty. Hopeful that he would eventually have the Haymarket for opera and the Lane for plays, he promised high salaries, reconstructed the Haymarket to improve the acoustics, and launched the 1709–10 season. In fact, the season lost £206, but in June 1710 Swiney went off to Ireland leaving his acting partners Wilks, Cibber and Doggett to give benefit plays for themselves.

Collier launched into action on 22 November 1709. Deciding that even against a master lawyer like Rich, possession might prove nine tenths of the law, he organized an invasion of the building. He claimed later that he had no control over the proceedings, but as a body of soldiers and a plentiful supply of liquor appeared by some happy co-incidence at an opportune moment, we can assume that he did. The *Tatler* of 24–26 November 1709 gives a humorous account of the way Collier's supporters moved in only to be pre-empted by Rich ('Divito') who had moved out all the valuables the night before:

> On the 22nd Instant, a Night of publick Rejoicing, the Enemies of Divito made a Largess to the People of Faggots, Tubs and other combustible Matter, which was erected into a Bonfire before the Palace. Plentiful Cans were at the same time distributed among the Dependences of that Principality; and the artful Rival of Divito observing them prepared for Enterprize, presented the lawful Owner of the neighbouring Edifice, and showed his Deputation under him. War immediately ensued upon the peaceful Empire of Wit and the

Muses: the Goths and Vandals sacking Rome did not threaten a more barbarous Devastation of Arts and Sciences. But when they had forced their Entrance, the experienced Divito had detached all his Subjects, and evacuated all his Stores. The neighbouring Inhabitants report, That the Refuse of Divito's followers marched off the Night before disguised in Magnificence; Door-Keepers came out clad like Cardinals, and Scene-Drawers like Heathen Gods. Divito himself was wrapped up in one of his black Clouds, and left to the Enemy nothing but an empty Stage, full of Trap-doors, known only to himself and his Adherents.

Next day, the Drury Lane company opened up again. Audiences were very small and Collier turned the running of the house over to a group of seven actors. Apart from the right of conquest, his authority for running the house was as slim as that of Rich. He had no lease (he did not obtain one until a year later), no contracts and he soon had a rebellion on his hands. When the company scored a notable success in February with Shadwell's *Fair Quaker of Deal* and finances looked up, he deposed the seven actor-managers and put his own man Aaron Hill in charge instead. That worthy gentleman who was attacked by an angry armed mob of actors, fled to find the Lord Chamberlain, could not do so and returned to find himself locked out of the theatre. Rich may well have been behind this episode, for he walked past the theatre to be cheered by the rebellious band and greeted by Leigh with 'God bless you, master! See we are at work for you!'

Swiney had his own troubles at the Haymarket. He returned from Ireland to find that Cibber, Wilks and Doggett had drawn £350 from the funds and divided it between themselves. Although he opened a new season on 4 October, he had to close after three days, because he could not pay his singers.

Complicated negotiations started to resolve all the conflicts. As a temporary result two companies were set up at the Haymarket, and a licence was issued to Swiney, Wilks, Cibber and Doggett on 6 November 1710, to give them authority to act. Collier took charge of the opera and the two companies shared the house between them. Three weeks later, Collier obtained a lease at Drury Lane, and the acting side, under Swiney and the three actors, moved there instead but agreed not to play on the same nights as the opera, and to contribute to the rent of the Haymarket.

Once they were installed at Drury Lane, Wilks, Cibber and Doggett took a different view of the justice of the proceedings. As they saw it, they were burdened with Swiney who was to get a share of any profits

83

they earned, without contributing anything to their success, and they were expected to subsidize the opera by leaving them the best nights of the week. Arbitrarily they reduced payments to Swiney. He went to the Lord Chamberlain and to the law courts but this 'troublesome person', as Doggett called him, eventually settled out of court for a fixed £600 per annum.

This £600 Swiney then used as a bargaining weapon in a new deal with Collier. Collier gave up the management of the opera in Swiney's favour, and in return took the £600 and moved to Drury Lane. On 17 April 1712 two more licences were issued—one to Collier, Cibber, Wilks and Doggett for Drury Lane, and one to Swiney for the opera. It did Swiney little good, for after the presentation of two Handel operas, he had to flee to escape his creditors. Collier, content to draw £600 per annum for very little, sat back and allowed Wilks, Cibber and Doggett to run Drury Lane.

This famous triumvirate then began to run the theatre in a democratic but business-like fashion. No payments were allowed without the agreement of all three, but for once creditors' demands were met and the company made a profit. They made £4,000 in 1712–13, £3,600 in 1713–14 and took £1,700 in the first twelve weeks of the 1714–15 season. This is not to say that all was sweetness and light in the relations between them.

The hot-tempered Wilks was a typical Thespian for whom artistic standards were paramount, providing that is, that he was involved himself. Once he adopted a role, he was prepared to spare no expense on costumes and productions. Doggett, whose antipathy to the trappings of tragedy had brought him to Drury Lane from Betterton, was of a more conservative ilk and inclined to take an accountant's view of unnecessary expenditure. Where Wilks saw a glittering robe, Doggett saw the price tag. Cibber, who one cannot help thinking was more than a little afraid of Wilks, steered an uneasy path of compromise between them. 'I was rather inclin'd to Doggett's way of thinking, yet I was always under the disagreeable restraint of not letting Wilks see it.'

The three of them were in accord so far as giving the public what it wanted, whether it was a genteel comedy by Cibber, a travestied Shakespeare or a noble tragedy. Therefore with the change of power from Tories to Whigs, they took advantage of the political climate in 1713 to stage Addison's *Cato*, a play full of liberal sentiments. *Cato* reads somewhat like an opera libretto today, but its rhetoric struck answering chords in contemporary hearts.

The Tories of the day were too clever to go along and boo at the opening performance. Instead they stole their opponents' clothes by cheering every speech in favour of liberty as if that were a specifically Tory virtue. The actor Barton Booth was presented with fifty guineas collected from the boxes in recognition of Cato's 'honest opposition to a perpetual dictator; and his dying so bravely in the cause of liberty'. Doggett, a staunch Whig who was not to be outdone in zeal by his political opponents, insisted that the trio presented Booth with another fifty guineas to cancel out the first.

Booth was after bigger spoils. He was educated at Westminster School, came from a good family and thought himself as fit as the trio to manage a theatre. Playing up his political connections to the hilt, he succeeded in getting an order from the Lord Chamberlain insisting that he be made a partner at Drury Lane, and that the triumvirate were to negotiate a satisfactory price for his admission. Despite their opposition to the idea, and their placing an absurdly high valuation on a share (£1,300) the Lord Chamberlain over-ruled them and insisted that Booth be admitted immediately for £600.

This was more than Doggett's Whig convictions would allow him to stomach. His devotion to party had led him to set up a race for Thames Watermen for the Doggett Coat and Badge, a competition which continues even today, and a Tory partner at an arbitrary price was too much. He departed the theatre and the partnership in high dudgeon and over the next few years there was another flurry of law suits. Doggett sued the partners, the partners sued Doggett, Collier sued for a share of the £600 Booth had contributed, and also for his annual payment which had been stopped by Cibber.

Cibber was not just trying it on in suspending payment to Collier. Drury Lane had competition from a new quarter. Its old master, Christopher Rich, died in 1714 leaving his theatrical interests to his sons John and Christopher Moyser Rich. He had been preparing a new theatre at Lincoln's Inn Fields, and although he died before the house was ready, his son John opened it up in December 1714 in competition to Drury Lane. Operating under the authority of the Davenant Patent, John was a formidable competitor. Supporting plays with musical entertainments and particularly pantomime for which he became famous as both promoter and performer, he bit deeply into the Drury Lane audiences and profits.

Cibber, Wilks and Booth were forced to follow suit and tried to woo audiences back with all the spectacle that scenes and machines could offer. Like Cibber, like Wilks, Booth was also a realist. Once when he was asked in a tavern after one of his appearances in tragedy, why the tragedy had been followed by a debased pantomime, he 'frankly answered,

That he thought a thin Audience was a much greater Indignity to the Stage than any they mentioned . . . He begged them to consider there were many more Spectators than Men of Taste and Judgement; and if, by the Artifice of a Pantomime, they could induce a greater Number to partake . . . of a good Play than could be drawn without it, he could not see any great Harm in it'. He was expressing a truth first seen by Rich, and which could serve as a motto for the house for the rest of its history. The philosophy recurs like a leitmotiv throughout the succeeding centuries.

The death of Queen Anne and the succession of George I, changed the political climate and indirectly favoured Cibber and Co. They had an unwelcome Tory partner in William Collier. The new King was likely to be rewarding men who had been loyal to the Whigs and the Protestant succession in the last years of Anne. The most prominent of these was Sir Richard Steele, the self-appointed keeper of the theatre's moral conscience. The trio replaced Collier with Steele, and a new licence was issued incorporating Steele's name in the place of Collier's.

Once Steele was in, the trio explained that they could not pay him a fixed sum in the face of the Rich competition, but promised him an equal share of the profits instead. Steele agreed and for good measure promised to use his influence to obtain a new Patent. As a Patent, unlike a licence, gave them the power to defy the Lord Chamberlain if necessary they readily agreed. Steele duly obtained a Patent on 19 January 1715.

The Patent and the Governorship of Drury Lane were given to Steele, the champion of virtuous drama, specifically because it was thought that he would be the one man to reform what the Patent called, in almost Jeremy Collier phraseology, 'indecent and immodest expressions . . . prophane allusions to Holy Scripture . . . [and] abusive and scurrilous representations of the clergy'. Like any government elected on a high sounding prospectus of promises, Steele did nothing to bring promise to fulfilment. Sure of a share in the profits, and a theatre for his own plays, he plunged back into his political career, and let the trio continue with masques, operettas and vaudeville turns in opposition to Rich. Cibber meanwhile used the Patent to defy the Lord Chamberlain, and refused to submit either plays or fees to that worthy gentleman.

Neither Steele nor Cibber escaped scot free. Cibber was suspended by a new Lord Chamberlain, Lord Newcastle, when he refused New-castle's request to cast a specific actor in *The Spanish Friar*. Steele had his Patent revoked when his energetic campaigning against the Peerage Bill which young Newcastle (who was only 22 when he took up the office in 1717) had championed, helped to defeat the bill. Steele was also removed from the Governorship of the theatre but reinstated in 1721, when his fellow opposer to the South Sea Bill, Walpole, became First Lord of the Treasury and Chancellor of the Exchequer.

However, apart from one financial success given to Drury Lane with his *The Conscious Lovers* in 1723, Steele played no major role in the affairs of the theatre in the 1720s, and he died in 1729 leaving the trio to buy out his interests from his daughter.

Although fortunes varied as audiences fluctuated between Drury Lane and Lincoln's Inn Fields, the trio soldiered on until the early 1730s. In 1723 their pantomime *Harlequin Doctor Faustus* proved no match for Rich's *The Necromancer*, and in 1728 the phenomenal success of John Gay's *The Beggar's Opera*, which was wittily and accurately said to have made Gay rich and Rich gay, were body blows to Drury Lane. But they survived.

It was just as well, because the most famous of all their rivals started in 1732. Riding on the wave of success of *The Beggar's Opera*, Rich raised a subscription for the building of a new playhouse. Small but beautifully decorated, this was the playhouse in Bow Street, Covent Garden, and became what we know today as the Royal Opera House. The battle a Drury Lane theatre had to fight to survive was moving quietly into the heavyweight division.

A minor irritant was the opening of unlicensed theatres beyond the boundaries of the Cities of London and Westminster. The best known of these was the Goodman's Fields Theatre running under Henry Giffard in Ayliffe Street. This became important during its brief life, as we shall see, but closed in 1742.

The triumvirate began to come to an end when all three actors came to the end of their careers. Booth stopped acting in 1727 but before he retired, he, Cibber and Wilks managed to get a new Patent for twenty-one years from July 1732. That their intention was to sell it when they got it, became clear very soon. Ten days after the Patent was issued, Booth sold half of his share to a John Highmore for £2,500. This was the first move in a new power struggle which rivalled earlier ones in its ferocity.

In September 1732, Wilks fell ill and asked Colley Cibber to look after his interests. Cibber agreed but when Wilks died, his widow had other ideas and appointed John Ellys a painter to act for her instead of Cibber. Cibber was bitter at the slight, and in October got out of the management by renting his share of the Patent to his son Theophilus for the rest of the season, becoming a salaried actor in the company himself.

Two personalities merit attention—Theophilus Cibber and John Highmore. Highmore was a wealthy amateur gentleman with pretensions, and the wherewithal to indulge them. Benjamin Victor tells us that Highmore had

> . . . offered himself (by way of Frolic for one Night) to play the Part of Lothario, prompted to that Extravagance by a Wager at White's, of one hundred Pounds . . . the Managers readily accepted the Proposal. . . .

A full house duly saw Highmore play Lothario and win his bet, the novelty of the occasion being sufficient to draw a crowd. That would have been just about acceptable, but Highmore became convinced that he, the amateur, was at least the equivalent of the professionals, if not God's gift to the boards. He went on to play other roles including Hotspur, 'till he was in Danger of obtaining a Cure from some Part of his Audience, who thought themselves injured, instead of being entertained'.

One can imagine what Theophilus Cibber thought of Highmore's attempt at Hotspur. He himself had joined the Drury Lane company at the age of 16, but his early determination to be an actor was in the face of parental opposition. Probably Colley did not want his son to spend his youth as he had himself, now that he was a respected figure in London society. Theophilus repeated the paternal pattern, and his undoubted talent had to be weighed against his general indiscipline. He played good minor roles like Abel Drugger and Pistol, but he was known as Pistol outside the theatre as well as in. He worked his way up through the company and, allowing for his father's unpopularity, that was probably the hard way. By the 1727–8 season he was assistant manager to Wilks.

As he saw it, he was the professional man of the theatre, able and willing to take over when the triumvirate retired. The triumvirate had proved that actors could adequately manage their own affairs—he was the obvious successor. The sudden influx of amateurs like Ellys and Highmore was anathema.

He made the best of it at first. Renting his father's share temporarily, he began to organize the repertory for the 1732–3 season. Undoubtedly, the actors were on his side, particularly when he secured them an immediate rise in salary. He conducted rehearsals of a pantomime *The Harlot's Progress* but fell ill. When he returned to the house, he found his production had been abandoned by Highmore and Ellys who planned another pantomime instead—one by Ellys himself who had suddenly forsaken the brush for the pen. Naturally, he was furious at this confirmation of his prejudices against meddling amateurs and he protested volubly. For the moment, the amateurs gave in.

What they did however was to work surreptitiously to oust Theophilus by removing his authority. Highmore, knowing that money was the most eloquent of all persuaders, secretly offered Colley Cibber 3,000 guineas to sell him the share of the Patent that he had rented to his son for the season. Without a word to Theophilus, Colley agreed. Highmore then took pleasure in telling Cibber Jnr that he would have to leave when the season ended on 1 June.

'Pistol', despite his father's dubious deal, was not finished so easily. He emerged as the natural leader of the actors who already had a legitimate grievance that Rich at Lincoln's Inn Fields, and Wilks at Drury Lane, had fixed salaries between them and secretly agreed not to employ anyone from either company who was dissatisfied with his lot. They saw that if Highmore and Rich formed a similar employers' cartel, Highmore could reduce salaries without fear of losing his actors. With Theophilus at their head, they formed a rudimentary trade union.

Their first action as a union was not particularly militant, but it was pretty inspired. In May 1733, they persuaded a majority of the building shareholders to lease the theatre to them on a sub-lease for fifteen years. With one fell swoop, Highmore was left holding most of the Patent but not theatre. He was then told by the union that he could accept 200 guineas a year to keep out of the way while they ran the theatre, or alternatively he would need to find himself a new theatre and a new company of actors if his Patent was to be more than a useless scrap of paper.

At this turn-up for his book, Highmore turned decidedly nasty. On 26 May he hired a band of armed ruffians to possess the theatre and exclude the actors. Theophilus sued for a writ of ejectment but meanwhile led the union of actors off to the Little Theatre in the Haymarket which had opened in December 1720. Here they drew good audiences and quietly waited for Highmore's fight to collapse.

Together with Rich, Highmore tried a new tack. They sued Giffard of Goodman's Fields (who, by the way, had bought the remaining half of Booth's share of the Patent when Booth died, but was clearly not prepared to fight on Highmore's side against Cibber Jnr) and Mills of the Haymarket theatre, on charges of vagrancy. The J.P. who heard the case laughed it out of court. The next time, they were more successful. On the same day that Theophilus's ejectment suit was heard against them, they disrupted that evening's performance of *Henry IV* by the union actors, by getting Harper, the Falstaff, committed to Bridewell Prison on vagrancy charges.

That evening, Cibber read the part of Falstaff and explained to the audience why Harper was missing. Next evening an angry audience went to Drury Lane and disrupted the performance there. Highmore and Rich's victory proved even more hollow when Harper came up for trial. The Lord Chief Justice both released him and strongly censured Highmore and Rich. Their cause collapsed completely and Theophilus had won.

I have given this account of the events of 1733, gleaned from the pages of the contemporary papers like the *Grub Street Journal* and the *Daily Post*, and the public statements that both sides made in print, in some detail, because it casts a different light on Cibber Jnr than the one commonly accepted.

Throughout the whole affair, he behaved ethically and within the bounds of the law, which is more than one can say for his opponents. Now *The Oxford Companion to the Theatre*, for example, mentions the 'worthless son of Colley Cibber' and says he 'soon forfeited all claims to respect by his insolence and complacency'. These sorts of emotive dismissals are made because he was involved in subsequent years in a scandalous triangle with his second wife Susanna Maria Cibber (she was the sister of Dr Arne the composer but not, as the *Penguin Dictionary of the Theatre* suggests, *Colley*'s second wife.) The rights or wrongs of that affair need not concern us. In the Drury Lane struggle of 1733, he is the only person one can feel sympathy for.

With the demise of Highmore's aspirations, that unhappy gentleman cut his losses by selling his half of the Patent for £2,250 to Charles Fleetwood, a landed gentleman worth £6,000 a year. Fleetwood was in a mood for shopping that day because he also bought Wilks's old share for another £1,500. Five-sixths of the Patent to the good (Goodman still held the remaining sixth) and £3,750 out of pocket, he was the next to negotiate with the actors.

CHAPTER SIX

The Coming of Roscius
1734–76

A meeting between Fleetwood and the actors, one side holding a lease on the theatre and the other a Patent to perform, brought the actors back to Drury Lane where they opened on 8 March 1734. Charles Fleetwood met some stiff demands from Cibber and Co. but he got them back, and he got the theatre open. He was to remain in charge for the next eleven years.

The decline in the quality of playwriting continued, reaching some sort of nadir in 1762 with Whitehead's *The School for Lovers*, a play, according to W. J. Lawrence, 'in which the characters were all remarkable for elegance of sentiment, purity of expression, and propriety of manners, but in which there was not the slightest scintillation of wit or leaven of humour'. What, however, makes the eighteenth century so fascinating is that the decline in writing was paralleled by a remarkable flowering of acting talent. With a few honourable exceptions, one can search in vain for a good play, but players force themselves upon our attention. Considering the transience of the art, that so many of their names should live today is a phenomenon.

Theophilus Cibber soon quarrelled with Fleetwood and departed. He returned later for a few seasons only. His successor as stage manager was the Irishman Charles Macklin. Even for the eighteenth century, Macklin was an overpowering personality. Most records give him as being born about 1700, but on one occasion he admitted to 1690. He lived until 1797 and, although unable to finish the performance, played Shylock in May 1789! In the 1730s and 40s he was brimming with energy and physical vigour, alternating his acting with fives, boxing, running and love-making.

When someone spoke to him at Spranger Barry's funeral, he turned to say, 'Sir, I am at my rehearsal, do not disturb me'. And he said of Garrick's well-known parsimony, 'Yes, Sir, in *talk* he was a very generous man, a humane man and all that; and by God Sir, I believe he was no hypocrite in his immediate feelings; but, Sir, he would tell you all this very plausibly at his house in Southampton Street, till turning the corner, the very first ghost of a farthing he met with, would melt all his fine resolutions into air, into thin air, and he was then a mere Manager'.

Regrettably, Macklin's tongue was not his only resource in times of conflict. He once strode from the stage and felled an over-conscientious prompter who, as he explained to the audience on his return, had 'interrupted my Grand Pause'. In May 1735, he quarrelled in the Drury Lane Green Room with a fellow actor Hallam about the ownership of a wig from stock. There was an angry exchange, and Macklin thrust a stick into Hallam's eye which killed him. Although he retained his freedom, he was brought to trial and found guilty of manslaughter.

Fleetwood also engaged an actor called James Quin. Quin, a stickler for preserving the manners and costumes of the Betterton era, had an even sharper tongue than Macklin. His view of Macklin's grim visage was 'If God Almighty writes a legible hand, that fellow is a villain'. Garrick, who was notably small of stature, drew several of Quin's shafts of wit. When he was asked what he thought of Garrick's Othello, he evoked one of Hogarth's paintings with a negro page boy—'Othello, Madam, no such thing! There was a little black boy, like Pompey attending with a tea-kettle, fretting and fuming about the stage; but I saw no Othello'. When Quin and Garrick were caught in the rain, and only one sedan chair was available, Quin suggested that they share it—'I will go in the chair and you can go in the lantern'.

He once put down Peg Woffington beautifully. Playing Sir Harry Wildair, one of her most famous trousers roles, she came off the stage to rounds of applause and said, 'Mr Quin, I have played this part so often, that half the town believe me to be a man'. As her numerous affairs were well known, Quin rejoined, 'Madam, the other half *knows* you to be a woman'.

Apart from this, and an exchange on the weather—'Mr Quin, do you ever remember such a summer?' 'Yes, last winter!'—it is worth recalling some of his wit on stage. Playing the role of Cato, a messenger's Welsh accent for the line 'Caesar sends health to *Keeto*' provoked the audible reply from Quin, 'Would he had sent a better messenger!' Announcing an indisposition, he once told the audience: 'I am obliged by the manager to inform you that the dance intended for tonight will be omitted because Madam Rollan has broken her ankle—I would it had been her neck!'

Between two such personalities as Macklin and Quin, there had to be

Charles Macklin as Shylock—one of the greatest triumphs of the eighteenth century stage. *Enthoven Collection*

an explosion. It came when they were cast together in *The Plain Dealer*. During a Quin speech, Macklin inserted some comic business and the Green Room saw a furious row between them. It culminated in Quin throwing an apple into Macklin's face followed by a fist. Macklin's face swelled until he was unable to finish the performance. Only Fleetwood prevented a subsequent duel, and the two survived, to achieve a drunken reconciliation some years later.

In 1741, Macklin was responsible for one of the great triumphs of eighteenth-century acting. *The Merchant of Venice,* in Granville's adaptation of 1701, was well known to contemporary audiences. It rested on low comedy of the Doggett school from Shylock, which was neither a star role nor even an opportunity to steal the play in performance. Macklin persuaded Fleetwood to revive *The Merchant of Venice* and to give it in its original form. One doubts that the text was a pure Shakespeare version but it was nearer than Granville's.

Fleetwood, who had revived *As You Like It* and *Twelfth Night* (with Macklin as Malvolio) earlier in the season without much success, was

93

naturally reluctant to give another Shakespearean comedy. Macklin was persistent and eventually he conceded. Quin consented to play Antonio, but considered Shylock beneath his dignity and preached the gospel of disaster to Macklin. Undeterred, Macklin studied Jews in the coffee houses and read up the subject, but concealed his real intentions throughout the rehearsals.

On the opening night, 14 February, he went out, played Shylock straight with all the venom and malevolence he could muster, wrung cheer after cheer from an astonished audience, and simultaneously wrote himself permanently into theatre history. The *Dramatic Censor* records his 'forcible and terrifying ferocity'.

Fleetwood embraced him fervently. Macklin's own memory of the occasion is touching—'By God, Sir, though I was not worth fifty pounds in the world at that time, let me tell you, I was Charles the Great that night'. Pope is supposed to have marked Macklin's achievement with the tribute

This is the Jew
That Shakespeare drew.

Sorry as I am to dispel popular myths, the story was started by Kirkman fifty years after the event and has been repeated many times since, but there is no evidence to show that Pope, who was ill at the time, either saw Macklin or commented on his performance.

Later in the year there was another acting sensation in London, but first let us look more closely at Charles Fleetwood. He was indolent, dissipated and an inveterate gambler. His gambling career started when he was a rich dupe and the costly tuition he received in the school turned him into as dishonest a sharp as any of his tutors. The theatre's accounts became inextricably confused with his own, and his wild extravagances were supported by Drury Lane finances. Bailiffs called regularly and carried off pieces of scenery in lieu of repayments of loans. 'Though conscious of his incapacity to repay any sums he borrowed he still borrowed on; his best friends were no exceptions to his art.' His eventual bankruptcy was inevitable; the wonder is that he survived so long. The probable reason is that he could, when necessary, be ruthless.

Under him, the status of the Theatre Royal declined and he was constantly at variance with his actors, usually on non-payment of salaries. However, when the Goodman's Fields Theatre presented him with competition, he joined with Rich and got it closed permanently in 1742. When a new pantomime with Madam Chateauneuf was staged,

Fleetwood knew well that the lady was ill but he continued to advertise a grand dance finale which had, in her absence, to be abandoned. He got away with it for two nights but the third night, the audience

> . . . ushered out the Ladies, and then went to work on the House. The first Motion, and made by a most noble Marquis, was to fire it! but that being carried in the Negative, they began with the Orchestra, broke the Harpsicord and Base-Viols, broke all the Looking-Glasses, pulled up the Benches in the Pit, broke down the Boxes, even the King's Arms in front . . . fell victim to their Rage!

So Benjamin Victor tells us. Next day, the Marquis donated £100 towards paying for the damage, so perhaps he had a more satisfying evening than if Madam Chateauneuf had appeared.

Just nine months after Macklin's Shylock, London was taken by storm with another acting sensation. At the theatre in Goodman's Fields, a 'young gentleman' supposedly made his first appearance on the stage as Richard III. The claim was inaccurate, because the 'young gentleman' had already played under the name of Lyddal in Ipswich where Giffard had given a summer season. That did not matter. As the word spread, a traffic jam of coaches from Whitechapel all the way back to the Temple Bar gave testimony to the appeal of the new star. David Garrick had arrived.

His interpretation of Gloucester 'threw the critics into some hesitation concerning the novelty as well as the propriety of his manner' but as soon as they attuned to his exciting innovations, he was greeted with 'loud and reiterated applause'. As Davies, his first biographer put it, Garrick

> shone forth like a theatrical Newton, he threw new light on elocution and action, he banished ranting bombast and grimace; restored nature, ease, simplicity and genuine humour.

Traditionalists like Quin were less sure. 'If the young fellow is right, we have all been wrong' he said as if that settled the matter conclusively. When it emerged that Garrick's innovations drew crowds, Quin assumed the fashion would soon pass. 'Garrick is the new religion: Whitefield* was followed for a time; but they'll all come to church again,' said

---

* The great evangelical preacher who had drawn huge crowds to open air meetings in 1738.

Quin. When Garrick heard of this remark, he published his own reply. It included the lines

> Pope Quin who damn's all churches but his own . . .
> . . . When doctrines meet with gen'ral approbation,
> It is not heresy, but reformation.

It is a good answer, although it does reveal Garrick's sensitivity to criticism, a trait that remained with him throughout his life.

Garrick's success at Goodman's Fields was the main reason for Rich and Fleetwood's getting the theatre closed down. This was easy because Walpole, who had been angered by Henry Fielding's satirical attacks on him staged at the Haymarket, had pushed through the 1737 Licensing Act to get unlicensed theatres closed down, and incidentally to confirm the monopoly of Drury Lane and Covent Garden.

Fleetwood followed up by signing Garrick for a season at Drury Lane for 600 gns. As a sop to the dispossessed manager, Giffard and his wife were engaged too. Garrick then justified the salary by playing thirteen separate roles including Hamlet in his first season.

He had come to London from Lichfield with his friend Dr Johnson and entered the wine trade. Forsaking so respectable a trade for the stage, he felt he had to explain to his brother, was not necessarily a drop in social status. One letter of 1741 went

> . . . As for ye Stage, I know in ye General, it deserves Yr Censure, but if you will consider how hansomely how reputably Some have liv'd as Booth Mills Wilks Cibber & c & admitted into, & admir'd by ye Best Companies. . . . As to Company ye Best in Town are desirous of Mine, & I have rec'd more Civilities & favours from Such Since my playing than I ever did in all my Life before. . . .

Truth to tell, Garrick was a bit of a snob and like many snobs, his over-consciousness of social status led him to be often jealous of rivals, and small-minded when he thought his own position threatened. The tendency sometimes led him to prevarication for Murphy says '. . . his temper was naturally wavering and irresolute' and he would often 'flutter and hesitate, and feel a conflict of various sensations working at his heart'.

Davies confirms this reading of his character.

> He had justly acquired a very great reputation, and he feared lest the base, unfounded aspersions of men, who had no character of their own

David Garrick, the Roscius of the eighteenth century, who made Drury
Lane the most famous theatre in Europe. *Enthoven Collection*

to lose, should make more impression on the world than it was possible they could . . . [he] was weak enough to be alarmed at every shadow of a rival.

Amusingly enough, if one apocryphal story is true, Garrick's own acting skill once went against him in his determination to be respectable. His brother was supposedly told by a local grocer who had seen Garrick play Abel Drugger in *The Alchemist*, 'Though he is your brother, I must say, he is one of the shabbiest, meanest, most pitiful hounds I ever saw'.

After his first season, he went to Dublin for the summer with Peg Woffington. They had a well-publicized affair until her infidelities brought it to an end. At one stage they lived together but there were frictions between them, particularly over house-keeping. Peg's hospitality was liberal, David's particularly frugal.* When Dr Johnson came to take tea with them, Garrick complained bitterly that she used too much of so expensive a commodity—'Tea, madam, 'tis as red as blood'.

Their relationship apparently reached the brink of matrimony but broke up in 1745. Garrick celebrated the occasion with some remarkably ungentlemanly verses in an *Epistle to Mrs Woffington* ('Flatter or pay, the nymph is yours'). She merely pointed out that her most expensive present to him, shoes with diamond buckles, were never returned.

Garrick returned for the next Drury Lane season as part of a strong company—Macklin, Quin, Garrick, Mrs Clive and Mrs Pritchard—under a failing manager, Fleetwood. At the end of the summer of 1742, Garrick took over Theophilus Cibber's old role of trade union organizer and negotiator.

Faced with so strong and slippery an opponent as Fleetwood, the players' only hope of success was solidarity. Nine of the company with Garrick and Macklin at their head drew up and signed a document declaring that no one would re-sign for the coming season unless all their demands were met. There was an alternative if Fleetwood refused to listen, to do what Betterton and others had done—appeal to the Lord Chamberlain for a separate licence to act. Macklin was all for a direct approach to Fleetwood, but Garrick's suggestion, that the Lord Chamberlain be approached first, prevailed.

Garrick went to see the Duke of Grafton, the Lord Chamberlain.

---

* Stories of Garrick's care with money are common. It was said that Fielding gave Garrick's servant a miniscule tip. When Garrick remonstrated, Fielding said that to give a small amount was the only way he could be sure the man would be allowed to retain it for himself.

Grafton asked Garrick what salary he was receiving. When Garrick told him, he cuttingly, if irrelevantly, pointed out to Garrick that Grafton's own son was risking his life in the army for a fraction of the sum, so Garrick could re-sign with Fleetwood and be duly grateful.

This meant that Garrick had to negotiate with Fleetwood. Fleetwood meanwhile prepared to open the theatre without the nine. Like any strike, successful or unsuccessful, events had reached an impasse and it became a battle of wills. As we have seen, Garrick's will was weaker than most people's and he took up an offer from Fleetwood of 700 gns for the season. The other players Fleetwood was also prepared to take back, some at three-quarters and a half of what they had been getting, but Macklin he would not have at any price. This was because Fleetwood had been instrumental in keeping Macklin out of prison after the Hallam killing, and saw Macklin's action in joining the group as gross ingratitude. An unholy public row, with both men publishing their case, broke out between Garrick and Macklin. Garrick tried to put the best possible gloss

Zoffany's painting of a rare Garrick excursion into drag. *Enthoven Collection*

on his action by offering to pay Macklin £6 a week himself until such time as Fleetwood would readmit him. Macklin threw some of Garrick's militant words of a few months before back at him—that he (Garrick) would be the last person to sign with Fleetwood, for example—and reminded Garrick that they had solemnly agreed to stand or fall together, if necessary going off to act in Dublin together.

Macklin supporters invaded Drury Lane when Garrick next appeared as Bayes in *The Rehearsal*. His appearance was greeted with shouts of 'Off! Off! Off!' and a shower of peas was thrown on to the stage. Fleetwood had been expecting tumult and had laid his own plans. When the clamour began, large gentlemen armed with sticks and bludgeons, who had been recruited among Fleetwood's friends in the Jack Broughton prize-fighting fraternity, stood up and dealt with the offenders. In fairness, we cannot blame either Macklin or Garrick for the excesses of their supporters, but it must have been an ugly scene.

The quelling of Macklinites was Fleetwood's last victory. An attempt to raise prices in 1744 was greeted with another round of riots, and shortly afterwards, Fleetwood sold all his interests in the Patent and the sub-lease to a partnership of City bankers called Green and Amber. Green and Amber put up £6,750* but as the property was already mortgaged for £5,000, Fleetwood had to be content with a guaranteed annuity of £500 per annum for the remaining years of the Patent. The bankers had no desire to run the theatre themselves, but they put up the capital, in return for two-thirds of the profits, to allow Lacy, John Rich's assistant at Covent Garden, to run it for them.

James Lacy, a Norwich business man, had forsaken accounts books to act, which he did with little success, but under Rich he had built a reputation for being an able manager with the rare quality of integrity. Lacy made overtures to Garrick to share in the management, but Garrick was more cautious. Knowing that rebellion had broken out in Scotland, Garrick took up an offer from Thomas Sheridan to act in Dublin.

News of the eventual failure of the rebellion and the defeat of the Young Pretender at Culloden, reached George II in his box at Drury Lane. An announcement was made to the audience and patriotic fervour reached new heights with the singing of a recently composed royalist song attacking the Young Pretender. We know it better as 'God save the King' though the then topical fourth verse about Marshal Wade has long since disappeared.

The Jacobite rising had a side-effect, a run on banks. Many banks

* Davies says £3,200.

closed as a result and among those who went bankrupt, were Lacy's financers. It was a red light for Green and Amber but Lacy somehow managed to carry on.

When Garrick returned from Ireland, he went not to Drury Lane but to Covent Garden under Rich. Both theatres were marshalling strong forces. Rich had Garrick, Quin, Susanna Cibber, Mrs Pritchard and Henry Woodward; Lacy had Macklin, Yates, Mrs Clive, Peg Woffington and his import from Ireland, Spranger Barry. Garrick and Quin alternated as Richard III and Othello and played together if a play offered two strong roles. This was not to Quin's advantage. One of his favourite long pauses as Horatio in *The Fair Penitent*, which followed a line from Lothario (played by Garrick) 'I'll meet thee there', was interrupted by a voice from the gallery saying 'Why don't you tell the gentleman whether you'll meet him or not?'

Lacy, worried about the drift of audiences to Covent Garden, re-doubled his efforts to get Garrick as a sharer. Because he had assiduously cultivated the Duke of Grafton, the Lord Chamberlain, he was able to promise that a new Patent would be available when the present one ran out. Eventually, Garrick agreed and they arranged to share responsibility for the accumulated debts hanging around the house from Fleetwood's and Green and Amber's bankruptcies.

In many ways, it was an ideal partnership. Garrick dealt with authors, acting, casting and rehearsals. Lacy dealt with the care of properties, the wardrobe and finances. They got a Patent in June 1747 for twenty-one years, and also obtained a lease that placed all the power into their own hands. The stability of the arrangement moved the theatre into a new era of prosperity and good management enabled them eventually to pay off all the accumulated debts; they remained together until Lacy died in 1774. They had their differences. Garrick once called Lacy 'a mean mistaken creature', and on another occasion, 'a maggot-breeding pericranium', and Lacy probably replied in kind for he was known to be 'rough and sometimes boisterous in his language', but in the context of thirty successful years, it was an excellent relationship.

Garrick was less lucky in his first season with the actresses he had to deal with. He was not always treated with the respect his new managerial status should have warranted. When he entered the Green Room in a resplendent silver costume, Kitty Clive said, 'My God! Make way for the Royal Lamplighter!'

Mrs Clive, who had played Portia in Macklin's famous *Merchant* performance and used the opportunity to forget Portia and mimick the mannerisms of well-known barristers, was a handful. Plain of features

A Van Loo portrait of Peg Woffington, Garrick's one-time mistress, and a brilliant exponent of breeches roles. *Enthoven Collection*

but animated, she had succeeded by force of personality and had a sharp tongue. She remained with Garrick at Drury Lane throughout his long reign but the relationship was based on a sneaking regard for each other's talents, usually well concealed, and on what has been called euphemistically a 'creative tension'.

She was not his only problem. There was also the embarrassing presence of his ex-mistress Peg Woffington. Beautiful, charming, talented, particularly in dashing breeches roles or as woman of spirit, she was sufficiently hot-tempered to come to blows with Kitty Clive in the Green Room and chase George Anne Bellamy with a dagger. And there was Susanna Cibber, Theophilus's ex-wife, excellent in tragic roles, and from the tone of some of her letters, enamoured of Garrick. He probably welcomed the affection, but resented the way she tried to use it to poach others' favourite roles. To complete his unlikely aviary, there was Mrs Pritchard who resisted any attempts to relieve her of the young lady roles no longer suitable to her expanding girth.

Problems with intractable actresses plagued him throughout his career. His eventual retirement was said to have been precipitated by Mesdames Abington, Pope and Younge. He found the first named 'false, treacherous . . . (and) the worst of bad women'. Always prone to fall ill in sympathy if the box-office takings did not look too healthy, she was too popular with the public to be dispensable. Dr Johnson, trapped in an abominable seat with a restricted view for an Abington benefit performance was later asked, 'Why sir, did you go to Mrs Abington's benefit? Did you see?' 'No, sir.' 'Why then did you go?' (It is amazing to me how many straight men Johnson managed to find. They never learned, and this one was crushed like the rest.) 'Because, sir, she is a favourite of the public; and when the public cares the thousandth part for you that it does for her, I will go to your benefit, too!'

Despite Garrick's wariness of rivals, most of the prominent male actors of his day appeared at Drury Lane at some time or another. Spranger Barry—'Silver Tongued' Barry—was over six feet tall, 'elegantly shaped, and his natural bearing . . . full of grace and dignity. His features were regular, his eyes bright and blue, his hair fair gold.' He appeared at the Lane in 1747–50 and 1767–74. Henry Woodward, who rivalled Garrick in comedy and John Rich in pantomime, stayed from 1748 to 1758. Tom King, the creator later of Sheridan's Sir Peter Teazle, Puff and Sir Anthony Absolute, was there from 1748 to 1750 and from 1759 onwards as Garrick's assistant. Dick Yates, a disciple of Doggett was with Garrick twenty-two years. However, when Thomas Sheridan scored against Garrick in *King John* both as the King to Garrick's Bastard and the Bastard to Garrick's King, 'his [Garrick's] uneasiness . . . began every day to be more and more visible'.

I have already given some indication on pages 70–1 of the most popular works in the repertory during Garrick's time. Pantomimes, farces, ballad operas and musical entertainments were the staple fare, with the occasional appearance of such acts as Seignor Capitello Jumpedo, who it was promised 'after a Hornpipe, will, in a manner entirely new, Jump down his own Throat'. I doubt it was a feat which could be done more than once.

How then does Garrick measure up to his reputation as the great champion of Shakespeare? When Lacy hired a rope-dancer in 1752, Garrick was horrified at this 'defilement and abomination into the house of William Shakespeare', but the only honest answer to the question is that with friends like Garrick, the Swan of Avon hardly needed enemies. If Shakespeare was done, he was done in doctored versions that reverently observed eighteenth-century tastes and travestied the original texts. When Garrick put on *Hamlet* for example, there was no Osric, no gravediggers, a Gertrude who goes mad, the duel between Laertes and Hamlet was followed by one with the King, and when Laertes' dying speech started to get applause regularly, Garrick transferred the words to Hamlet.

In a prologue to *Florizel and Perdita*, which you would be forgiven for not knowing is a Garrick adaptation of only three of the five acts of *The Winter's Tale*, Garrick talks defiantly of his reverence for Shakespeare:

> Lest, then, this precious liquour run to waste,
> 'Tis now confin'd and bottled for your taste.
> 'Tis my chief wish, my joy, my only plan,
> To lose no drop of that immortal man.

A less biased observer would be bound to admit that Garrick had duly spilled him by the bucketful. When it came to the rain-affected Stratford Jubilee of 1769 held at Stratford under Garrick's direction, the celebrations planned for three days featured the firing of cannons, an oratorio, a public breakfast, fireworks, a horse race, a pageant, a ball and not one word of Shakespeare from start to finish.

Garrick's main contributions to theatrical history, were his own playing, which, if not as natural as all the contemporary accounts might suggest, was a significant advance on anything that had gone before; his improvement of rehearsals and preparations whereby unpunctuality and slipshod line-learning became less common; his technical innovations based on observations made on his tours abroad; his patronizing of de Loutherbourg and his abolition of malpractices like spectators on the stage. Hardly, however, can he be called the defender of the Shakespearean faith—the title he would most probably have cherished.* Instead, we can remember him as his contemporaries did, the man who made his theatre the most famous in Europe, and for whom was revived the name of Roscius, the Ancient Roman actor praised by Cicero.

---

* In the Stratford Memorial Gallery, a painting by George Walker, *The Apotheosis of Garrick*, shows Garrick being lifted from his tomb by angels as Shakespeare descends from the clouds to greet him. If the apotheosis took place, one imagines William S. had a few well-chosen words to say to him.

The mediocrity of most of the repertory under him can be explained by the continuing competition of Covent Garden and the need to do more and more farces and pantomimes to rival a house where audiences were said to be 'fiddled out of their senses'. It demonstrated the fundamental truth that was captured by Samuel Johnson in three lines of the Prologue he wrote for the opening night in 1747 of the Garrick and Lacy partnership:

> The stage but echoes back the public voice,
> The drama's laws, the drama's patrons give,
> For we that live to please, must please to live. . . .

Johnson showed he had not entirely grasped the point himself by his play *Irene*, which despite an excellent cast—Garrick, Barry, Mrs Pritchard and Mrs Cibber—failed after nine performances in 1749.

The unlucky lady *Irene* was also symptomatic of the chronic shortage of good plays—Garrick must have doctored some fifty or sixty scripts to fit them for the stage, usually to the authors' dissatisfaction. Taunts like 'Jackanapes' and 'Theatrical Dictator' were generally his only thanks.

(Some of the gibes rubbed off on Garrick's brother George who was rumoured to be paid hush-money, because no one knew what he did except follow David around saying 'Hush' when the great man was either to act or to pronounce. George was famous for entering the theatre daily and asking, 'Did David want me?' He died three months after Garrick himself. 'How extraordinary!' said one man. 'Not at all,' said Charles Bannister, 'David wanted him.')

The menace of Covent Garden brought matters to a farcical level in 1750 when both houses played *Romeo and Juliet* and battled it out for twelve days running—Barry and Susanna Cibber *v.* Garrick and George Anne Bellamy. One town wit encapsulated the public's attitude in verse:

> Well, what's tonight, says angry Ned
> As up from bed he rises.
> Romeo again! And shakes his head
> A Pox on both your houses.

The anger of the public could be a dangerous thing to rouse, as Garrick found to his cost in 1755. Jean Noverre, one of the greatest figures in ballet history, had staged in Paris in 1754, *Les Fêtes Chinoises*, a musical entertainment decked out in Chinese gauzes and taffetas. Billed as *The Chinese Festival*, Garrick persuaded Noverre to come to Drury Lane with his dancers and give a repeat. Just at this time Britain was teetering on the edge of war against France, and although Garrick announced that Monsieur Noverre was a Swiss Protestant and that there would be few French dancers in the company, the distinction was too subtle for many.

Despite the presence of the King who chuckled happily, the opening night was roundly booed from all the cheaper parts of the house. The following night, swords were drawn in the auditorium but the ferocity of the gentry to any interrupters prevented serious disorder. The next night, not a word nor a note was heard for noise, and on the Saturday, the situation exploded into total war. Seats were torn up, mirrors and chandeliers were smashed, the stage was stormed and the rioters only driven back with cudgels by Garrick-imported bravoes.

At this point, discretion might have proved the better part of valour, but Garrick was determined to recoup the money he had sunk into the *chinoiserie*. Monday night, an unadvertised performance was given, and Garrick announced a repeat for the Tuesday. It was a showdown. The theatre was packed hours before the curtain rise. A chanting audience demanded *Roast Beef of Old England*, and *The Chinese Festival* never really

The Robert Adam auditorium of 1775. *Westminster Local Collection*

started. A few tinkling bars of music provoked a hail of peas and nails, the gallery patrons invaded the pit, fighting broke out everywhere, and when the house was eventually cleared, the windows of Garrick's house were smashed by the mob. The festival was over.

Similar scenes took place in 1763 when a man called Fitzpatrick organized a protest against full prices for revived plays. Garrick tried to address the house to explain that nightly expenses of the house had nearly tripled since the beginning of the century, but he was howled down. The following evening a performance of *Elvira* by Mallet (which was supposed to have been staged by Garrick in return for a favourable mention in Mallet's latest biography—of the great Marlborough!) brought a repetition, with an actor called Moody drawing the wrath of the mob for stopping a member of the gentry setting fire to the house.

The audience bayed for Moody to bend his knee and crave their pardon. Moody, who was made of sterner stuff than Garrick, shouted 'I will not, by God!' and strode off. Garrick, typically weakening, promised the audience that they would have their wish on prices and that Moody would not appear again. He salved his conscience by promising Moody that he would continue to pay his salary. Perhaps Goldsmith had a point when he wrote of Garrick:

> He cast off his friends like a huntsman his pack
> For he knew, when he pleas'd, he could whistle them back,
> Of praise a mere glutton, he swallowed what came,
> And the puff of a dunce he mistook it for fame;
> 'Till his relish grown callous, almost to disease;
> Who pepper'd the highest was surest to please.

Let us rather remember him at a moment of dignity, taking a final farewell of his public on 10 June 1776. Having played Don Felix in a comedy called *The Wonder*, he spoke a final epilogue. 'This is to me a very awful moment . . .'—then 'he bowed respectfully to all parts of the house, and in a slow pace, and much hesitation, withdrew for ever. . . .' For once, the audience had no stomach for an after-piece and the evening closed there.

CHAPTER SEVEN

Port and Anchovy Sandwiches
1776–1800

JUST before Garrick's sad farewell in 1776, Covent Garden had scored heavily over its rival with three works from the pen of a new Anglo-Irish dramatist. In 1775, he gave them a polished comedy *The Rivals*, a farce called *St Patrick's Day; or The Scheming Lieutenant*, and a comic opera *The Duenna*. So successful was *The Duenna*, the ageing Garrick was said to be so worried that the 'old lady' would be the death of 'the old man'. The outstandingly talented writer, who was only 24 at the time, was, of course, Richard Brinsley Sheridan.

With the possible exception of Garrick himself, Drury Lane has never had a more distinguished manager than the man W. A. Darlington so accurately described as 'this casual young genius'. For once the word 'genius' is not too extravagant a term. Not only was he to write the most frequently performed play in the English language outside Shakespeare, who had a few years' start on him, but his political career dazzled even in an age of political giants. He entered the world of Burke, Fox and Pitt, and proved himself their equal. That his career in the affairs of the state was ultimately less successful than theirs, should not conceal the fact that to them and to the public he was a highly important figure. His speeches at the impeachment of Warren Hastings, and his oratory in the controversy surrounding the Prince Regent's morganatic marriage to Mrs Fitzherbert, were masterpieces.

Byron, who wrote a *Monody* on the death of Sheridan, suggested that he wrote 'the best comedy, the best drama, the best farce, the best address and delivered the best oration ever conceived or heard in this country'. This is putting it a bit strongly but it gives some idea of the stature of the man.

Alongside the massive intellect, wit and ability that brought these achievements within Sheridan's grasp, one would expect to find evidence of order, organization, logic and industry. Not a bit of it. In him, genius,

Richard Brinsley Sheridan, the 'casual young genius', before alcohol had taken its toll. *Enthoven Collection*

indolence and waywardness were equally distributed. Never during his life had he sufficient funds to sustain all the activities he thought important, but he survived by the simple expedient of using his immense personal charm and humour to make up the deficit.

His entry into the Drury Lane management was typical. In conjunction with a Dr James Ford, and his father-in-law Thomas Linley, who was a composer and also joint manager of oratorios at Drury Lane, Sheridan bought Garrick's share in the Patent and the leases for £35,000. He and Linley were certainly both on heavy mortgages to raise the money. Sheridan also bought the Lacy share in 1778 for another £31,500 although that share was subject to mortgages plus two annuities totalling £1,000 per annum. He himself mortgaged or sold some of his interest in the meantime, but still paid £18,000 for Ford's share in 1788. (That a physician like Dr Ford should be involved, Kitty Clive found highly amusing—'I thought I should have died laughing when I saw a man mid-wife among them . . . I suppose they have taken him in to prevent miscarriages'.)

Sheridan had something like £1,000 of his own yet had somehow spent about £80,000, a feat beyond most men. Still, as Michael Kelly, the Irish tenor who joined Drury Lane and who was the creator of Basilio and Curzio in Mozart's *Figaro*, once said, 'tomorrow was always his favourite pay-day'.

Sheridan was not dishonest in any moral sense. He worked on the supposition that if money could be bought at 5% and used to earn 10% it would allow him to do all he desired. Whereas a capitalist *manqué* would triumph with such a formula, he was basically too uninterested in money* to bother with the attendant accountancy. Joseph Richardson suggested: 'Could some enchanter's wand touch him into the possession of fortune, he would instantly convert him into a being of the nicest honour and most unimpeachable moral excellence.' It is seldom noted that the Lord Chamberlain *twice* reported that Sheridan, despite the massive debts around him, could be cleared of all charges of mismanagement.

His elusiveness was not reserved for creditors. The affairs of the theatre were delegated by default. When Tom King gave up as manager, he wrote to the *European Magazine* in October 1788:

Should anyone ask me, what was my post at Drury-Lane—and add the further question, If I was not Manager, who was? —I should be forced to answer . . . to the first, I don't know; and to the last, I can't tell. I can only once more positively assert, I was not Manager; for I had not the power . . . nor indeed had I the wish to approve or reject any dramatic work, the liberty of engaging, encouraging or discharging any one performer, nor sufficient authority to command the cleaning of a coat, or adding, by the way of decoration, a yard of copper lace; both which . . . were often much wanted. . . .

He added that a certain 'gentleman' promised to visit him, 'for which call I waited with great temper till past three in the following morning'. He was lucky, some people waited for Sheridan for days.

---

* His first wife could have earned him large fees for her singing, but after their marriage, which had been preceded by an elopement and two duels, he refused to let her give concerts, probably because he thought it unbecoming for a future statesman's wife to perform publicly.

Sheridan's other distinguished manager was the great John Philip Kemble. Before Kemble finally gave up and joined Covent Garden, the stately, pompous and talented John Philip suffered a multitude of indignities under Sheridan (he was once arrested for one of Sheridan's debts) as he desperately tried to pin Sheridan down to paying attention to some matter of theatrical business or other. Sheridan's standard tactic, for they were both considerably addicted to the bottle, was to get drunk with Kemble and watch resentments disappear temporarily in an alcoholic haze of *bonhomie*. Occasionally even this could not appease the affronted Kemble and there was one richly comic scene good enough to have come from the pen of Sheridan himself; when Kemble emitted a

. . . humming sound like that of a bee, and groaned in the spirit inwardly . . . at last, like a pillar of state, slowly rose up Kemble, and in these words addressed the astonished proprietor 'I am an EAGLE, whose wings have been bound down by frosts and snows; but now I shake my pinions, and cleave into the general air, unto which I am born'. He then deliberately resumed his seat, and looked as if he had relieved himself from insupportable thraldom.

Even at such moments, I doubt that George Cooke was strictly accurate in describing Kemble as having 'the face of an itinerant Israelite and the voice of an emasculated French horn'.

Sheridan's manner of composition was little different from his general unreliability. In February 1777, he wrote *A Trip to Scarborough*, a relatively feeble adaptation of Vanbrugh's *The Relapse* to accord with the sensitivity of his times. This was written without too much trouble, but its successor *The School for Scandal*, and Sheridan's masterpiece, was subject to continual delay in the writing. At last complete, Sheridan penned 'Finished,Thank God. RBS' on the title page and handed it to Hopkins the prompter, who added with feeling, 'Amen'. Two years later, he went through the same process with *The Critic*, a lively satire based on Buckingham's *The Rehearsal*.

The cast and the rest of the theatre's staff got it page by page and began to despair that the play would ever be completed. They got it finished by the adroit device of luring Sheridan into the Green Room where pen and paper, two bottles of port and a plate of anchovy sandwiches awaited him, locking the door and allowing him out only when it was finished. Sheridan was amused, but duly complied.

It was almost the end of his career as an author. This was only 1779, but politics became his major preoccupation from his entry to Parliament

Gillray's caricature of the later Sheridan with a brandy nose as the adaptor of Kotzebue's *Pizarro*. 'Pizarro' contemplates the returns from his new Peruvian mine and says: 'Honor? Reputation? a mere Bubble!—will the praise of posterity charm my bones in the grave?—psha! my present purpose is all!—O Gold! Gold! for thee I would sell my native Spain as freely as I would plunder Peru.' *Enthoven Collection*

in 1780 until his death in 1816. He did write *Pizarro*, an adaptation of a play by Kotzebue which was so popular that it was translated back into the original German, and that brought the same attendant delays in 1799. However dreadful a play, *Pizarro* came at a time when England was alarmed by the French Revolution and the rise of Napoleon. Kotzebue, against liberty of thought and the freedom of the press, fitted the current mood. The public was lucky to get it at all.

Michael Kelly tells us that

. . . at the time the house was overflowing on the first night's performance, all that was written of the play was actually rehearsing and . . . incredible as it may appear, until the end of the fourth act, neither Mrs Siddons nor Charles Kemble, nor Barrymore had all their speeches for the fifth. . . .

The delays were so long that the after-piece started after midnight to seventeen people in the whole dress circle and twenty-two in the pit. It made £15,000 in the season. In every sense, Sheridan had done it again.

That Sheridan did not continue to write plays is obviously a tragedy. A man who could so casually produce so fine a play as *The School for Scandal*, had he chosen to remain in the theatre, might have achieved almost any heights. After him, literature and drama were to drift apart for nearly a hundred years.

The School for Scandal itself could only be an eighteenth-century play, but how its characters live! Full of scintillating wit:

Lady Teazle. For my part, I should think you would like to have your wife thought a woman of taste.
Sir Peter. Aye—there again—taste. Zounds! madam, you had no taste when you married me!

and in Joseph Surface, the play has the ultimate condemnation of contemporary 'sentiment'. The play is brilliantly constructed, and the famous screen scene alone shows how inherently *dramatic* a writer Sheridan was. The revelation of Lady Teazle at the falling of the screen brought such a roar at the first performance, a passing journalist fled believing that the building was falling in.

Sheridan's long tenure at Drury Lane was not only marked by his own talents. Two of the great ladies of the stage graced the house with their presence in the period. Dorothy Jordan, who had thirteen illegitimate children to interrupt her career, ten of them by George III's son, the Duke of Clarence and later William IV, brought memories of Peg Woffington in her brilliant assumption of tomboy or high-spirited comic roles. Charles Lamb thought her 'a privileged being sent to teach mankind what he most wants—joyousness' and Leigh Hunt talks of her 'happy and happy-making expression of countenance'. Her rivalry with Mrs Siddons over salaries and position became notorious, and was a contributing factor to the Siddons's eventual departure to Covent Garden.

Sarah Siddons remains the greatest tragic actress of the English stage. Hazlitt's testimony—'Power was seated on her brow; passion emanated from her breast as from a shrine. She was tragedy personified'—must have been accurate. The perfect contrast to Dorothy Jordan—her private life was exemplary—she was sufficiently prudish to refuse to wear breeches as Rosalind, appearing instead in an unbecoming androgynous monstrosity. (The miscasting brought the remark from Colman that she played Rosalind as 'a frisking Gog'!) She was a model of all the tragic virtues. 'Make love to Mrs Siddons?' asked Sheridan, 'I would as soon have thought of making love to the Archbishop of Canterbury.'

It was an era of tragedy. Instead of the effects that had been achieved earlier in the century by sudden almost violent transitions from elegance to explosions of passion, pathos began to take over. A typical Siddons performance would be aimed at a more even tragic solemnity, evoking floods of tears from the audience. Public expression of grief had become fashionable; weeping and swooning common. Burke, Fox, Pitt, Liverpool, all sobbed openly at moments of high drama, and Mrs Siddons herself is supposed to have swooned at Burke's invective against Warren Hastings. Her playing, and her strikingly dignified presence, was perfectly in tune with the prevailing emotional climate.

Her first appearance under Sheridan was in October 1782 as Isabella in *The Fatal Marriage*, a typical blend of overflowing grief and betrayed innocence. It took London by storm as it had the provinces, and represented a personal triumph for it was not her Drury Lane debut. That had been under Garrick in 1775 as a 'young lady' playing Portia. It was not a success. The *Gazeteer* thought,

> . . . from the specimen she gave, there is not room to expect anything except mediocrity. Her figure and face, tho' agreeable have nothing striking; her voice (that great requisite of all public speakers) is far

(Opposite) A contemporary playbill for the eighteenth century's greatest comedy—credits for everyone but the author. *Enthoven Collection*

PERFORMED but ONCE.

At the Theatre Royal in Drury-Lane,
This present Friday, the 9th of May, 1777,
Will be presented a NEW COMEDY, call'd THE

School for Scandal.

The PRINCIPAL CHARACTERS by
Mr. KING,
Mr. YATES,
Mr. DODD,
Mr. PALMER,
Mr. PARSONS,
Mr. BADDELEY, Mr. AICKIN,
Mr. PACKER, Mr. FARREN,
Mr. LAMASH, Mr. GAUDRY,
Mr. R. PALMER, Mr. NORRIS, Mr. CHAPLIN,
And Mr. SMITH.
Miss POPE,
Miss P. HOPKINS
Miss SHERRY,
And Mrs. ABINGTON.
The Prologue to be spoken by Mr. KING,
And the Epilogue by Mrs. ABINGTON.
With NEW SCENES and DRESSES.
To which will be added a Musical Drama, call'd

The DESERTER

Henry by Mr. DAVIES,
Russet by Mr. BANNISTER, Simkin by Mr. CARPENTER,
Skirmish by Mr. PARSONS, Flint by Mr. WRIGHT,
Soldiers by Mr. Legg, Mr. Kear, Mr. Griffith, Mr. Chaplin, Mr. Follet,
Jenny by Mrs. DAVIES,
Margaret by Mrs. LOVE,
Louisa by Miss COLLETT,

The Doors will be opened at Half after Five, to begin exactly at Half after Six o'Clock.

from being favourable to her progress as an actress. It is feared she possesses a monotony not to be got rid of, there is also a vulgarity in her tones, ill-calculated to sustain that line in a theatre she has at first been held forth in. . . .

Later, she blamed Garrick for her lack of success in this and other appearances and thought she had been used by him to score off the other ladies in the company. She may well have been right.

Now five years later, and five years maturer, apart from the occasional sulk in her tent about terms, she paralysed Drury Lane audiences with Isabella, Jane Shore, Belvidera in *Venice Preserved*, and, although Sheridan was very dubious of the propriety of departing from the Pritchard tradition by putting down the candles to wash her hands, Lady Macbeth. If any inventor had been able to come up with Kleenex at the time, he would have made a fortune.

Other notable talents of the time, even if dwarfed by Siddons, Jordan and Kemble, were John Henderson, and Mrs Robinson who began a Royal Command Performance of *The Winter's Tale* as Perdita, and finished the evening as the mistress of the Prince of Wales.

Not all the entertainment offered was on the same lofty level as la Siddons by any means. Sheridan was just as aware of the importance of pantomime, after-pieces and novelties as the next man. Although he had written a comic opera, the musical side had been handled by his father-in-law. Sheridan himself had 'not the smallest idea of turning a tune' and his singing was 'a sort of rumbling noise with his voice resembling a deep, gruff bow-wow-wow'. He did however realize the popularity of opera and duly supplied it, provoking heavy sarcasm from Horace Walpole:

. . . the ladies, forgetting their delicacy and weakness clapped with such vehemence that seventeen broke their arms, sixty-nine sprained their wrists, and three cried bravo! bravissimo! so rashly that they have not been able to utter so much as no since. . . .

William Hazlitt spoke primly of 'intellectual prostitution'.

Their hostility troubled Sheridan not at all. When the house was packed to see the antics of Carlo the dog in *The Caravan* by Frederick Reynolds (the dog rescues a child) Sheridan rushed back-stage. 'Where is my preserver?' he said. 'I am here,' said Reynolds. 'No,' said Sheridan, 'I mean the dog.'

Perhaps the most notorious of all such occasions of tapping contemporary fads and fancies was the *Vortigern* scandal of 1796. A nineteen year old youth called William Ireland began to discover in some un-named house, legal and personal documents of Shakespearean interest. This caused some stir, and Ireland's father, who was a dealer in rare books and prints, pronounced them genuine. Contemporary scholars became more and more excited, until at last there emerged from the same source, an unknown Shakespearean play *Vortigern and Rowena*. The enthusiasm was no less than if a hitherto unknown Shakespeare play were to be found tomorrow. Sheridan and Kemble moved in and it was announced that *Vortigern* would be played at Drury Lane with Kemble and Mrs Siddons.

Meanwhile, doubts began to creep in. The divine Sarah withdrew from the cast. The scholar Malone pronounced the play to be a fraud, but with Kemble and Mrs Jordan in the cast, the play was given to a packed house on 2 April. Whether Sheridan and Kemble were fooled by the claims, or whether they were cynically exploiting the controversy will never be conclusively known. (The evening took £725 2s 6d.) As the performance proceeded, it became painfully obvious to the increasingly restive audience that *Vortigern* was not from the great William. In the fifth act, when Kemble, whose convictions had been visibly disturbed by the reception, reached the immortal line 'And when this solemn mockery is over . . .' and stopped, to Sheridan's annoyance; howls of

Henry Holland's grandiose if short-lived building of 1794. *Westminster Local Collection*

The interior of Henry Holland's building. *Westminster Local Collection*

mirth and censure brought the proceedings to an untimely but welcome end. It was just as well: the youth Ireland, who had written it himself in a cleverly assumed Tudor hand, had already written a *Henry II*, and was half way through *William the Conqueror*. One of those might have seen Sheridan's new theatre pulled down around his ears.

Sheridan, anxious to support his political expenditure from his theatrical interests, had commissioned Henry Holland to pull down the existing theatre and to build an even larger one on the site, so the old building had been demolished in 1791–2.

The rebuilding was not without problems. The capital was raised by selling 300 subscribers shares at £500 each. In return, each subscriber got free admission and 2s 6d per acting night (an annual commitment for Sheridan of £7,500!). Sheridan acquired a new ground lease from the Duke of Bedford for a larger site, but there were protracted difficulties with regard to a Patent, which brought building to a halt. The Garrick and Lacy Patent ran out in 1795, and Sheridan needed authority to run a theatre for far longer than that before his subscribers were prepared to put up the money. Therefore he had to buy the Killigrew Patent, partly in the possession of Harris at Covent Garden, but dormant since the silencing of Rich.

Harris's right to sell it was contested by a man called White. The matter was the subject of protracted negotiation with Sheridan's friend Fox as an intermediary. White was offered £5,000 for his 14/60ths of the document but the deal fell through. In 1793 Harris got £11,667 for his 46/60ths. It took until 1813 to get the remaining 14/60ths from succeeding owners when it cost another £9,561 19s 8d. It was never sub-divided again and it still remains in the hands of the Theatre Royal Drury Lane Ltd, today appearing among the company's assets at a nominal £100. That it was necessary to talk of 1/60ths of one piece of paper is eloquent testimony to the tangled web the original financing led to, and why the document has had to occupy so much space in this book.

Two views of Sarah Siddons, the tragedy queen, as Lady Macbeth and Isabella. *Enthoven Collection*

There were other more minor suspensions in the rebuilding, including a carpenters' strike in September 1793. Typically, Sheridan himself settled it—with a free barrel of ale! At last, on 12 March 1794 the new theatre holding 3,611 people was opened to a concert of sacred music performed in a stage setting of a Gothic cathedral.

The opening night of the play season on 21 April featured Sarah Siddons as Lady Macbeth and a special commemorative prologue spoken by Miss Farren. The prologue, written by George Colman the Younger included the lines

> The very ravages of fire we scout
> For we have wherewithal to put it out
> In ample reservoirs our firm reliance
> When streams set conflagration at defiance.

To the admiration of the audience, an iron safety curtain was lowered, it was struck with a hammer to show that it was indeed metal and was raised again to reveal water cascading into a large tank in which a man was rowing a small boat. The Fire God, however, had the last word fourteen years later when the building burnt down.

A more lasting innovation of 1794 stems indirectly from the death that year of Robert Baddeley, the creator of Moses in *The School for Scandal*. In his will he left an invested £100 with the instructions that the interest was to be used for the provision of a cake every Twelfth Night to be consumed by His or Her Majesty's Comedians. This bid by Baddeley for lasting fame was so successful, he is commemorated at the theatre still by the cutting of a cake on every January the 6th.

PART III

*The
Nineteenth
Century*

CHAPTER EIGHT

Size and Sensation

SHERIDAN'S short-lived theatre of 1794 with its seating for 3,611 people and its 1812 successor, which held 3,060, were both built on huge lines and on one giant assumption—that the Patent which had been the subject of so many deals, litigation and confusion would continue to hold sway and that apart from Covent Garden there would be no competitor in the field of legitimate drama. The assumption was wrong. In 1843, the increasing agitation against so artificial a monopoly was given the final seal of approval by Parliament. The Theatres Act of that year in one fell swoop destroyed their privileged position and left them to fend for themselves against all comers. Covent Garden became a house almost exclusively devoted to opera from about 1847 onwards. Drury Lane had to find other solutions.

It would not be accurate to suggest that all was well before the 1843 Act and that the legislation alone brought trouble. The Act was rather a recognition of events that had already taken place. Between 1800 and the 1850s, London's population tripled. In 1807, there were ten London theatres, in 1870 there were thirty. Of the original ten, only Drury Lane and Covent Garden offered drama; of the thirty, at least half. The 1870s was the start of a new era of prosperity to managers as the increasing urbanization of London brought more and more people from the middle and working classes into theatre audiences, but the drama had some traumas to survive first.

In broad outline, the nineteenth century represents first a decline when the upper classes were lost to the theatre, driven away by events like the nightly riots at Covent Garden for 'old prices' which continued for over sixty nights in 1809, and other disorders—as late as 1844 the *Theatrical Journal* spoke of the theatres as 'great public brothels'. Drury Lane had its own riot in 1848. The house was described by Dickens as 'a bear-garden, resounding with foul language, oaths, cat-calls, shrieks, yells, blasphemy, obscenity: a truly diabolical clamour'. As the expensive seats emptied, it became more and more necessary to resort to spectacles of equestrianism, aquatics and performing menageries to keep the pit and the gallery full.

The divergence between literature and drama continued. Writers found a new public for novels which brought a wider audience and higher profits for their labours than if they had written plays. Any poets who attempted a play seemed doomed to producing endless monologues in turgid blank verse. When the Romantic movement flourished, popular taste was drawn not to its lyric or more lasting virtues, but to the mock-Gothic horrors of Romanticism at its most lurid and Teutonic.

A few people, notably Macready, Madame Vestris and later Charles Kean, fought against the trend by trying to make theatre respectable, and by wooing back the aristocracy. It was an uphill struggle and it almost bankrupted Macready. Only after 1843, did upper class interest return.

Men like Samuel Phelps, who produced all but four of Shakespeare's plays between 1843 and 1862, were able to tap the reviving interest. From the patronage of Victoria and Albert, from the new legality of the small theatres, from the respectability of Macready, from the realism introduced into drama by Thomas Robertson and his followers, a new climate of opinion was created. By the end of the century Jones, Pinero and Shaw, together with the growing influence of Ibsen, had restored theatre to its rightful place in our culture and laid the foundation stones of modern drama as we know it today.

There were technical developments which made this possible—the gas lighting which reached the Olympic theatre in 1815 and Drury Lane in 1817 was replaced in the 1880s by the spread of electricity. Even with the improvement of gas over oil lamps and candles, subtlety of expression or economy of gesture would have been useless. Only the grandiose and the artificial was possible. As J. C. Trewin described it so beautifully, the early nineteenth century was when

> Drama was written largely in exclamation marks and in the stage directions of the mock-Gothick shocker. It plunged into blazing gulphs. It was lit by Germanic marsh-lights. It rattled its skeletons. It was emptily spectacular. It strutted and bellowed, volleyed and thundered, and in the Patent theatres it had to shout if the audience were to hear it at all. Meaning could flicker away in the racket. English poetry and fiction were in high summer; but the stage could only shake a thunder sheet.

To think of Chekhov by gas-light, to realize how profound a change electricity brought! Alongside it, came reserved stalls with every auditor in his own seat, an audience in darkness concentrating on the picture before them in a small theatre, the brightly lit stage the constant focus of their attention. At last, this was what the theatre had to offer those who had been seduced away previously by the opera and the printed word.

It was what the theatre in general had to offer. It was not what Drury Lane could supply. Its present capacity is 2,226, on the basis of the last reconstruction of the auditorium in 1922, which may be 800 down on its nineteenth century capacity, but is still vast by any standards. There was no possible way in which a theatre of this size could be in the vanguard, or even among the camp followers, of the development of naturalistic domestic drama.

As early as March 1813, the *Theatrical Inquisitor* pointed out that Garrick's style of playing would have carried no further than the orchestra, but it is extraordinary how few people grasped the fact. From the middle of the 1820s until the Act of 1843, neither Patent theatre succeeded in paying its way. Successive managers went bankrupt in trying desperately to fill it, and for two decades after the Act, if Drury Lane was open at all, it was open for circuses, music and four legged performers. Instead of the sympathy which in many ways it deserved, it was attacked bitterly on all sides for failing to measure up to its history.

Joseph Knight, in 1875, was only repeating what had been said a hundred times before when he spoke of

... the ignorant pleasure-seekers who, flocking to Drury Lane, have turned what should be a national theatre into something not widely different from a circus. ...

F. B. Chatterton, who opened his management bravely with serious plays and turned by 1868 to offerings like *The Great City*, mostly as an excuse to get a real hansom cab and horse on to the stage, left an immortal phrase 'that Shakespeare spells ruin and Byron bankruptcy'. It brought him such notoriety that he felt impelled to publish a self-justification in 1875, demonstrating conclusively that the sensational plays he put on made money, and the more worthy offerings were financial disasters. To a man in his position as manager of Drury Lane in his particular time, he was right—Shakespeare did indeed spell ruin and Byron bankruptcy. Contemporary taste was undoubtedly appalling but that was hardly Chatterton's fault. We know from Joseph Knight that in the 1870s:

It is hopeless to fight a battle of fidelity to the text of Shakespeare. Colley Cibber's Richard III has driven the original play out of the field.

One production of *Henry V* drew the acid comments of the *Athenaeum* in January 1875:

> It is, to speak plainly, as glaring an instance of literary cobbling as has ever been attempted. However, the less said about literature in connection with this revival the better. The play, such as it is, had obviously been chosen and arranged merely with an eye to spectacular effect. One 'set piece' succeeds another with a rapidity which our fathers would have declared impossible. The stage is always crowded with supernumeraries, arrayed in every conceivable variety of brilliant attire, military and other; the air is filled with shouting and confused with noise, all the paraphernalia of warfare being employed to give additional sound and fury to the spectacle. All this may be magnificent, but it is not Shakespeare.

Audiences who could tolerate this, received sensation and melodrama with relish. Offerings like Dion Boucicault's *Formosa* featuring the Oxford and Cambridge Boat Race may have 'desecrated the National Theatre', but they brought in an audience. Chatterton was following Johnson's dictum and pleasing to live.

With the demise of men of literature and culture in the theatre, the hack writer moved in, particularly in the field of melodrama. The extremes of sensation and pathos that make up so much of Victorian fiction meant that novel after novel was adapted for the stage—how often Scott's novels were plundered would be impossible to count. The crime headlines disclosing the grimmer realities of a gaslit London were another rich source of dramatic material. Henry Arthur Jones, talking disapprovingly of 'the Theatre and the Mob', in 1895 put it thus:

> On the whole, a melodrama has succeeded much in proportion as the general impression left by it is the same as the general impression left by the front page of the *Illustrated Police News*.

The irony is that melodrama, to a major extent, grew from the existence of Drury Lane's monopoly rights. The smaller theatres, forbidden by the 1737 Licensing Act to perform legitimate drama, catered for a working class audience with melodrama. A play performed to a musical accompaniment—the word itself comes from the Greek *melos* (music) and the French *drame* (drama)—was an adroit way of avoiding the law. As the century progressed, the small theatres took more and more liberties. Music became less and less a feature of the performance, merely a token nod to legality.

Having spawned the illegitimate child outside, the Lane eventually welcomed it to the family home with open arms, taught it some manners, played down its working class origins by transferring its settings to the stately homes of England, and brought vast scenic resources to increase its quota of thrills. In return, the bastard saved its parent's life, and the theatre survived. For the last two decades of the century, Drury Lane drama meant melodrama.

Augustus Harris, manager of the Lane from 1879 to his death in 1896, had to face his share of criticism for forsaking literary merit for a blend of spectacle and sensation. An unidentified newspaper cutting of 1880 in the Enthoven Collection snobbishly proclaimed:

Regarding the responsibility of management from a purely practical point of view, and looking to the possibility of pecuniary profit from the support of the multitude rather than the probability of patronage from those whose tastes incline to plays of a poetical kind, Mr Augustus Harris has commenced his season at an earlier period than usual with a direct appeal to that section of the playgoing community whose avocations enforce their stay in town while fashionable society seeks autumnal recreation elsewhere.

As I hope has become clear from our examination of the previous centuries, neither Harris nor Chatterton were turning their backs on the history of the Lane. In fact, they were considerably nearer to following tradition than their critics realized. Beneath the romantic patina with which time has coated the achievements of Betterton, of Cibber, of Garrick, of Sheridan, lies the reality. The reality is that each of those gentlemen catered for the taste of their time. Often it was a debased taste, but if the vulgar was financially successful, it was the vulgar they presented. Betterton thrived on scenes and machines, Garrick on pantomimes and farces, Sheridan on performing dogs. Any one of them taking over a vast theatre in 1879 would have had no hesitation in packing the crowds in with melodrama, or, let it be added, in 1972 with musicals.

CHAPTER NINE

Kean

1800–19

A T Drury Lane, the century almost opened with a bang. King George III settled into his box to enjoy a performance of *She Would and She Wouldn't* on 15 May 1800, and was greeted with loyal applause and a gun-shot from a would-be assassin. A bullet embedded itself in a pillar at the side of the box, but before another shot could be fired, an ex-soldier called Hadfield was seized by fellow members of the audience. The failure of the assassination was commemorated by the striking of a special medal, although Sheridan got in before the mint with a hurriedly scribbled extra verse to the National Anthem which was duly sung by the assembled company:

> From every latent foe
> From every assassin's blow,
> God save the King!
> O'er him thy arm extend,
> O Lord our God defend
> Our Father, Prince, and Friend,
> God save the King!

Sheridan's attempts to persuade Kemble to share with him in management failed, partly because Kemble's lawyers were unable definitely to establish Sheridan's full rights to the property. Considering the confusion, mortgages and loans that surrounded them, this was hardly surprising. Instead, Kemble spent his money (some £22,000, which shows Sheridan often *did* pay up) on buying one-sixth of the Covent Garden Patent. His distinguished sister also transferred her services to the other house.

In 1806 there was a quarrel over salary with Joe Grimaldi and he also took a short walk up Bow Street to remain at Covent Garden from 1806 until his retirement in 1823. The illegitimate son of a syphilitic Italian ballet master and a chorus girl over forty years his junior, Joe Grimaldi became synonymous with the term clown. The Joeys of today's circus demonstrate the lasting power of the legend. He was an accomplished acrobat, a nimble dancer and made comic songs his own.

Drury Lane paid a belated tribute to him by staging his farewell benefit in June 1828. Then, he was too infirm to do other than sit in a chair which was carried on to the stage for him to pronounce, after one song, that he had jumped his last jump, filched his last custard, and eaten his last sausage. It must have been a poignant moment for both audience and performer.

Without Kemble, Siddons or Grimaldi, Sheridan should have been in trouble. That he was not, was due to an extraordinary theatrical phenomenon which sent the London theatre public temporarily near to a mass outbreak of insanity. Instead of a wolf at the door, Sheridan found crowds literally fighting to get to their seats to see, believe it or not, a thirteen-year-old child called Master Betty playing major Shakespearean roles. As an early exercise in advance puffing and publicity, it could prove a model to a modern pop promoter, for Bettymania rivalled the Beatlemania of 160 years later in its frightening emotional and commercial appeal. In his fascinating book, *The Strange Life of Master Betty*, Giles Playfair has told the full story of how the talented child was exploited by his father

Fun and games with Joe Grimaldi, the most famous clown in history.
Enthoven Collection

The strange phenomenon of Master Betty—a watercolour by Sir Martin Archer Shee. *Enthoven Collection*

and an unscrupulous manager. The implications of that lie outside the scope of this history. All that concerns us here is that in 1804, both Patent theatres were prepared to pay inflated fees for the privilege of presenting the tiny prodigy going through his paces. The inherent absurdity of a thirteen-year-old Hamlet or Macbeth was ignored, and the child was hailed as 'Garrick reborn' and 'The Infant Roscius'. He played twenty-six nights at Drury Lane and took relatively more money at the box office than Sarah Siddons.

When he fell ill under the strain of nightly performances, Southampton Row was blocked by carriages of the quality carrying people to read the daily medical bulletin on the railings outside the house. It was as if a favourite monarch was about to pass away. Even the best reference books

An 1804 view of a Drury Lane audience. *Westminster Local Collection*

tend to repeat the myth that Pitt adjourned the House of Commons to allow members to see a Master Betty performance, but that the prodigy was lionized by society and that Pitt, Fox, the Prince of Wales and Lady Caroline Lamb were all his fervent admirers, is certain. Possibly Giles Playfair is correct in reading something sexual into the universal ardour. His playing of Young Norval was said to leave not a dry eye in the house; perhaps it left not a dry seat either.

Sheridan was no more beguiled by the new actor than he had been by Carlo the Dog. When it was suggested that Drury Lane cancelled out the Covent Garden Master Betty performances by putting up another child (the period brought an inevitable rash of child stars) he refused, saying: 'No, one bubble at a time is enough; if you have two, they will knock against each other and burst.' The bubble lasted long enough to make the house a deal of money; that was enough.

After the Betty episode, Sheridan handed matters more and more to his son Tom. Tom was something of a wit in his own right. When Sheridan claimed that he was descended from the O'Sheridans but had dropped the 'O' out of modesty, Tom replied, 'Who has a greater right to the O than we have? We owe everybody!'

DRURY LANE THEATRE,
taken from Westminster Bridge during the Conflagration on the Night of 24th February, 1809.

The Ruins of the Theatre from Bridges Street, after the Fire.

London Published August 7th 1811 by Robert Wilkinson, N.° 58 Cornhill.

The 1809 fire bringing the end of the Henry Holland building and of Sheridan's career. *Westminster Local Collection*

Sheridan wanted the house merely as a source of income to support his political career, so the catastrophe that came in 1809 was, to him, a total disaster. On 24 February of that year, he was in the House of Commons waiting to speak in a debate on the Spanish War, when the news was brought that the Theatre Royal was on fire. Members sympathetically offered to adjourn the debate, but Sheridan, probably befuddled with drink, refused to allow his private affairs to take precedence over matters of state. He was as noble when he reached the Piazza Coffee House later. Watching the fire put an end to his income and his career, he stood with a bottle in his hand and said, 'Cannot a man take a glass of wine by his own fireside?'

Very little was rescued from the fire, and the building which had cost £150,000 was insured for a paltry £35,000. Accumulated debts alone came to £436,971. Probably a large proportion of the debts was due to unscrupulous creditors who wrote up their amounts knowing Sheridan's casual approach to such matters. It was still a formidable obstacle.

Sheridan co-opted Samuel Whitbread, who had casually mentioned that he would like to be on the rebuilding committee. Once Whitbread, a brewer and fellow M.P., was officially in, he took over. He saw himself as the saviour of the national theatre, and threw himself into two industrious years of raising rebuilding capital, persuading creditors not to oppose rebuilding but to accept annuities in the new theatre instead. He formed a distinguished committee which included Lords Holland and Byron, two representatives of the Royal Family, two from the House of Commons and one from the City of London. Personally, he got 134 friends to take shares at £100 each, and he was instrumental in defeating a group of City business men who petitioned Parliament for the issue of a *third* patent. Without his energy and fervour, the story of Drury Lane would probably have had to stop here.

Whitbread, in the handling of the finances, saw it as imperative to do everything by the book. The casual accountancy of a Sheridan was unthinkable. He withheld £12,000 from Sheridan to cover claims against the old theatre. Indirectly, this cost Sheridan his Stafford seat at the 1812 election, and although Whitbread secured his release from a debtors' prison, Sheridan bitterly blamed Whitbread thereafter.

On 10 October 1812 the large new theatre opened, designed by Benjamin Wyatt (not as the *The Oxford Companion to the Theatre* has it, Henry Holland, who was responsible for the 1794 structure), and a full house of 3,060 people saw *Hamlet* and a musical farce *The Devil to Pay*. It was preceded by a special address by Lord Byron, delivered by R. W. Elliston who also played Hamlet.

On view in today's theatre, the bust of Samuel Whitbread, M.P., who raised the rebuilding funds after the 1809 fire. *Peter Abbey*

The address provoked a minor drama of its own. On 10 September, Byron wrote to Lady Melbourne,

> Today I have had a letter from Lord Holland, wishing me to write for the opening theatre, but as all Grub Street seems engaged in the contest, I have no ambition to enter the lists, and have thrown my few ideas into the fire. . . .

In their infinite wisdom, the committee had organized an open competition for a new address to be spoken at the ground opening. All that Grub Street actually produced was a pile of mediocre versifications ranging from the functional to the ridiculous. As a result, Whitbread persuaded Byron to write an address instead, firmly censoring some of the poet's remarks on contemporary taste. The unsuccessful competitors swore favouritism had been at work. The controversy eventually died with the publication of a volume of *Rejected Addresses*, a set of parodies on leading poets in the form of prologues, but it was fun while it lasted.

The committee had appointed Samuel Arnold of the Lyceum theatre as manager, but as a body they were better supplied with peerages than with theatrical experience—they were amateurs in a ruthlessly professional world. For two years they struggled to fill their vast theatre. As Coleridge said, 'our theatres are fit for nothing—they are too large for acting and too small for a bull-fight'. By one of those strange quirks of history, as the arena stood empty, they stumbled accidentally on the one man who could fill it. His name was Edmund Kean.

To understand the complex personality of Kean, it is as well to shut out the memory of Alan Badel's recent performances as the wise-cracking charmer of the Sartre and Dumas play *Kean*. The romantic and sentimental conception of Dumas, even with Sartre's existentialist jokes, bears little relation to the grim reality of the original. This is not said in the spirit of criticism, for *Kean* is written as a comedy. The career of the real Edmund Kean was nothing short of high tragedy.

He almost failed to appear at Drury Lane at all. Found by Arnold in the obscurity of a Dorchester theatre, he had already been engaged by R. W. Elliston, who doubled his own acting at the Lane and elsewhere, with the managership of some of the minor theatres. Elliston did not really want Kean, whom he had agreed to take on as an obscure knock-about harlequin. On the other hand, when Kean wrote to him, saying that he would have to break off the engagement in view of 'a very liberal offer from the proprietors of Drury Lane Theatre', and he also saw Drury Lane puff the arrival of a new actor as comparable to Garrick for 'voice, passion energy and expression', Elliston seized the opportunity to indulge his favourite great impresario role. He told Kean that he would be held to the terms of his agreement. Meanwhile Arnold, furious with Kean for having contracted to appear at the Lane when Elliston had a prior claim, was particularly unsympathetic. He refused to pay Kean any money until he was free of Elliston.

For three interminable weeks, the tragedian was stranded without money in an unfriendly city, his wife and child half-starved, and with the searing memory of his eldest six-year-old son having died the previous month for the want of the medical attention a full salary might have brought. To spend Christmas 1813, when the Thames was frozen solid, in these circumstances, with eight long years of starvation and obscurity as an unknown strolling player behind him, would have embittered more saintly a man than the twenty-six-year-old Kean.

As arbitrarily as he had entered into the agreement, Elliston then grandly waived his claim. Kean's first appearance as Shylock in *The Merchant of Venice* was billed for Drury Lane on 26 January 1814. Through drizzle, snow and slush, Kean, shabbily dressed with wig and costume in a pitiful parcel under his arm, trudged to the Drury Lane theatre. At last he was to be given a chance to show what he could do.

The most amateur of psychologists can hazard a reasonable guess at what his feelings were on that walk. To survive at all, his emotions had had to be forced deep down into himself, as he presented a hard outer casing to the world. Without such a shell, he would have been a broken man. All the pent-up emotions and frustrations were held in check until he was out on the stage before an audience barely filling a third of the vast auditorium. Then, as Shylock, the flood gates opened and all the pent-up passion spilled out into the auditorium, electrifying spectators with its hypnotic power. Even to the most prosaic of auditors, it must have been obvious that something truly terrible was taking place. Com-

Edmund Kean as Sir Giles Overreach in Massinger's *New Way to Pay Old Debts*, a performance that put some into convulsions. *Enthoven Collection*

parable only to Macklin's Shylock, or Siddons's Isabella in impact, it was one of the greatest débuts in theatrical history.

However cathartic an experience for those lucky few privileged to be in the theatre that night, it was not cathartic enough for Kean. The evil that the world had done him in his luckless life could not be expunged so easily. He continued to vent his awesome passion in role after role including Richard III, Othello and Sir Giles Overreach in Massinger's *A New Way to Pay Old Debts*, a performance which put some members of his audience into convulsions. He was an almost perfect representative

An 1813 engraving of the sort of audience that flocked to Kean's performances. *Westminster Local Collection*

INTERIOR VIEW OF DRURY LANE THEATRE.

of the Romantic and this was the Romantic age. However, he not only acted the wild hero, he lived it.

Because his new found fame and fortune were still inadequate to wipe out the tragedies of the preceding years, Kean was untrusting and truculent. He paraded with a tame lion, threw himself into the Bacchanalian revels of the notorious Wolves Club, and chose his company in low taverns. Any attempt by the quality to lionize him in their drawing rooms, met with an angry refusal to be a society pet, and he is believed to have conducted *affaires* with upper class ladies as if each conquest was a blow in the class war.

He also nurtured so much resentment at a public so fickle that it could condemn him to starvation one day, and herald him as a god the next, that he sometimes failed to appear at all after some drunken exploit or other, or failed to learn his part properly. He parted with money with the wild extravagance only possible to those who have been so long without it that it has to be spent immediately before fortune can frown and take it away again.

Before his unique genius crumbled under the twin assaults of alcohol and illness, his performances provoked so many ecstatic notices from intelligent, sophisticated men, that we would be justified in taking at least some of them at face value. Coleridge said that, 'To see him act, is like reading Shakespeare by flashes of lightning'.

Hazlitt said,

Mr Kean's acting is like an anarchy of the passions, in which each upstart humour, or frenzy of the moment is struggling to get violent possession of some bit or corner of his fiery soul and pigmy body—to jostle out and lord it over the rest of the rabble of short-lived and furious purposes . . .

and on another occasion,

He fought like one drunk with wounds: and the attitude in which he stands with his hands stretched out, after his sword is taken from him, had a preternatural and terrific grandeur, as if his will could not be disarmed, and the very phantoms of his despair had a withering power.

Leigh Hunt, who incidentally was one of the few to remain balanced amid the hysteria surrounding Master Betty, wrote,

138   Kean we can never see without being moved; and moved too in fifty

ways—by his sarcasm, his sweetness, his pathos, his exceeding grace, his gallant levity, his measureless dignity: for his little person absolutely becomes tall. . . .

Whatever his faults as an actor or as a man, can we doubt that Kean was something special? For all the ranting and bombast that disfigured the theatre of his time, and for all the contemporary penchant for seeing plays in terms of histrionic boxing matches; he scored heavily over all his rivals. John Philip Kemble attempted Overreach, failed and he retired to the safer ground of Coriolanus for his 1817 farewell. Junius Brutus Booth, the head of the Anglo-American acting family of Booths which produced Abraham Lincoln's assassin, was unwise enough to play Iago to Kean's Othello and was ruthlessly upstaged and out-gunned.

The eventual decline of Kean was as spectacular as his successes. Firstly, the committee, £80,000 in debt themselves, resigned in 1819.* Kean hoped to become the lessee. Instead, his old enemy Elliston took over. Forced to play a season under Elliston by the terms of his contract, he then went off to America. There he had initial triumphs but nearly provoked a riot in Boston by refusing to play to a small house. He returned to England where Elliston astutely organized a hero's welcome. The crowds came to see him, but his non-appearances became more frequent.

In 1825, he was involved in an unsavoury law case when an Alderman Cox sued Kean for the criminal conversion of his wife. Kean's letters to Mrs Cox were read in court and ridiculed, and he was ordered to pay £800 damages. He was bitterly attacked in *The Times*, particularly when he defiantly played Richard III less than a week later. *The Times* leader was virulent and unpleasant:

> He is not merely an adulterer, he is an adulterer anxious to show himself before the public with all the disgrace of the verdict of guilty around his neck, because that very disgrace is calculated to excite the sympathies of the profligate and to fill the theatre with all that numerous class of morbidly curious idlers who flock to a play or an execution to see how a man looks when he hanged, or deserves to be hanged. . . . His immediate appearance is as great an outrage to decency, as if he were to walk naked through the streets at mid-day.

---

* Byron described the sub-committee running affairs thus: ' . . . we were but few, and never agreed. There was Peter Moore, who contradicted Kinnaird; and Kinnaird who contradicted everybody.'

After that, the performance itself had to be unruly. Enemies and friends shouted each other down, culminating in an ugly brawl when Kean reached the all too appropriate lines:

> I do suspect I have done some offence
> That seems disgracious in the City's eye. . . .

Kean somehow survived all this but on his next visit to America, Boston revenged itself on him by pelting him off the stage. On his return to Drury Lane in 1827, he ruined a new play *Ben Nazir* by his inability to learn the lines. His drinking and his behaviour became wilder. In 1830, he essayed *Henry V* for the first and only time, and again the words were beyond the grasp of his once razor-sharp mind. His uncanny powers were beginning to evaporate but in 1832 he played Othello against the Iago of Macready, a confrontation both men had avoided for years. G. H. Lewes recorded later a moving account of what happened:

> I remember, the last time I saw him play Othello, how puny he appeared beside Macready, until in the third act, when roused by Iago's taunts and insinuations, he moved towards him with a gouty hobble, seized him by the throat, and, in a well-known explosion, 'Villain! be sure you prove etc.' seemed to swell into a stature which made Macready appear small. On that very evening, when gout had made it difficult for him to display his accustomed grace, when a drunken hoarseness had ruined the once matchless voice, such was the irresistible pathos—manly not tearful—which vibrated in his tones and expressed itself in look and gestures, that old men leaned their heads upon their arms and fairly sobbed. It was, one must confess, a patchy performance considered as a whole . . . but it was irradiated with such flashes that I would again risk broken ribs for the chance of a good place in the pit to see anything like it.

Despite such flashes, the end was near. On 25 March 1833, he played Othello to his son Charles's Iago at Covent Garden, collapsed into his son's arms in the third act, preceding the seizure with 'O God, I am dying—speak to them for me'. He was carried from the stage, and, despite a partial recovery, he died in May at Richmond .The fiercest of flames had finally been extinguished.

To do justice to Edmund Kean, I have moved ahead of the story of the theatre which saw most of his acting life. Let us return to the 1819 accession to power of Robert William Elliston.

CHAPTER TEN

Musical Chairs for Managers

1819–79

THE advent of Elliston brings us to a sixty-year period when Drury Lane management was as hazardous an occupation as tightrope-walking. At times it looked like an apprenticeship preparatory to the bankruptcy court. As a result of the general decline in theatre, managers came and went; some stayed a decade, some stayed a week, very few even paid their way. Elliston had to pay £10,000 a year rent for the building; by the 1830s the rent the proprietors could ask had plummeted to £5,000, by the 1850s to £3,500. Only in the 1880s was the house restored to the position it had achieved under Lacy and Garrick of a valuable business proposition.

Elliston, the man John Hamilton Reynolds proclaimed as 'Oh! Great Lessee! Great Manager! Great Man! Oh, Lord High Elliston!' did all he could to live up to the billing. An anthology of contradictions rolled into one; at times his feet were more firmly on the ground than those of the Statue of Liberty, at other times he took off to some cloudy world of the imagination which could be reached only by himself.

He had fingers in more pies than Simple Simon. He took over innumerable small theatres, opened a subscription library, and in his early days, broke his rounds of gambling, drinking and fornication only to give a series of lectures on morality during Lent. He was ruthless enough to get his actors running from the Olympic theatre to the Surrey and back again to save on the wage bill, yet when it came to staging a special 200-strong coronation procession in *Richard III* to commemorate the coronation of George IV, Elliston got so carried away with the role he advanced on an astonished pit in his full regalia and intoned 'Bless you, my people!'

Addressing the audience was an Elliston speciality. In Birmingham, he had once had the cheek to puff the appearance of the Great Bohemian, a Teutonic strong-man who had supposedly felled an ox with one blow

Actor, manager and eccentric, Robert William Elliston—'O Great Lessee!'
Enthoven Collection

of his fist and would now, for the delectation of the audience, handle a rock weighing a ton like a tennis ball. With a house packed to the rafters with curious Midlanders, the programme reached the point for the appearance of the Great Bohemian. With the curtain still down, Elliston strode on to the stage.

He told the audience that the great man would not be appearing after all, but before they had a chance to start a riot, he pulled a sheaf of paper from his pocket and flourished it as conclusive proof of his agreement with the 'faithless foreigner'. Any member of the audience . . . providing they could read German (!) was welcome to see the documentary evidence of his good faith. 'Deceived me—that I could have pardoned; but he has

142

deceived my friends—he has deceived *you*!' Elliston buried his face in his hands at the thought. Then came the master-stroke: 'But my friends, as a special treat, at least I am able to show you *the rock*!' Up went the curtain to show an otherwise empty stage with a vast boulder in the middle. Duly impressed, the audience cheered the spectacle, and went away heavy-hearted that their beloved manager had been so cruelly deceived.

He once addressed a Drury Lane audience, angry at the non-appearance of Joe Munden, on one knee, his hand clasped to his breast. 'Gentlemen, press not too hardly on a fallen man.'

One of the most priceless of his more abstracted moments came during a rehearsal. Immaculately dressed, the great Robert William stepped on to the stage with a faraway look in his eye and said with no apparent relevance, 'Violino obligato'. The stage manager asked his pardon. 'Violino obligato.' The stage manager called the conductor who was told firmly, 'Violino obligato'. At this point a printer appeared who asked for the title of the after-piece for next week's bill. 'Violino obligato.' To the astonishment of the company, Elliston then scribbled a hurried note and left it behind as he moved to the stage door. The note was opened. It read 'On no circumstances allow me to forget Violino obligato in the morning'. Meanwhile, outside the theatre, Elliston climbed into a coach. 'Where to, sir?' said the driver. 'Violino obligato,' said Elliston.

In his managership of the Lane, Elliston dealt with Kean's tantrums, hostile audiences, an angry Alderman Cox looking for Kean with a pistol, the ill-tempered Macready, Mesdames Vestris and Catalani and press criticism of his Falstaff, all with the same superb aplomb. The last named, possibly under the influence of alcohol or more probably illness, was captured by *John Bull* in a phrase—'Elliston fell *off* in the fourth act, and fell *down* in the fifth'.

In 1826, Elliston, in arrears for the rent for £5,500 went bankrupt, but considering that he spent £22,000 of his own money on redecorating the interior of the theatre in 1822, he was harshly treated by the proprietors. Mixing legitimate drama with pantomimes and melodramatic after-pieces like *Cataract of the Ganges* with £5,000 worth of waterfall, he also made vain attempts to persuade Sarah Siddons to come out of retirement and to get Sir Walter Scott to write him a play. If ever a man deserved to succeed, it was Elliston. As Lamb said: 'Wherever Elliston walked, sat, or stood still, there was the theatre.'

His successor was Stephen Price, an American manager who took the theatre at a rent of £10,000. He did not actually pay it, but that was the agreed sum. He not only ran the Lane for four seasons, but he organized the export of many a London actor to the Baltimore–Boston–Philadelphia circuit until he became known by the unofficial title of Star Giver General to the United States. The upright Macready did not care for the Price methods of theatrical management; he described him as 'a reckless speculator . . . boastful and overbearing . . . in short, he was not a gentleman'.

After Kean's disgrace in *Ben Nazir*, the tragedian stalked off to Covent Garden. Much to Kean's disgust, Price engaged his son, Charles Kean, and put up son against father. Charles appeared first at Drury Lane in October 1827, and although he had little of his father's passion, by the 1850s he had risen to the top of the profession, pioneering lavish and historically accurate stagings of Shakespeare and others at the Princess's theatre.

Price finally fell by the wayside, but his unique achievement was to get the proprietors to pay him to leave, although he owed them for the rent. He was followed by an Alexander Lee, who was financed by the Member of Parliament for Bedford, Captain Polhill. Polhill's mistress in the company used her influence with the backer to compete for parts with Lee's wife, who acted under the name of Mrs Waylett. The two ladies quarrelled so incessantly, Polhill took the easy way out and ensured his own domestic harmony by dispensing with the services of Lee. As a replacement, he promoted Elliston's stage manager Alfred Bunn.

Even by Drury Lane standards, there were few more extraordinary men than Bunn. The model for Thackeray's Pendennis:

> . . . a portly gentleman with a hooked nose and a profusion of curling brown hair and whiskers: his coat was covered with the richest frogs, braiding and velvet. He had under-waistcoats, many splendid rings, jewelled pins, and neckchains. When he took out his white pocket-handkerchief with the hand that was cased in white kids, a delightful odour of bergamot and musk was shaken through the house.

His elegant appearance belied a vulgar turn of phrase when the occasion demanded. His advice for the correct method for dealing with one actress was, 'Kick her arse and send her back again'. In his career so far, he had seen Drury Lane present both Shakespeare, and a spectacle with boa-constrictors and an elephant (how old Rich would have loved that!), and he had counted the respective receipts. Against novelty, Shakespeare was a loser. Bunn duly took the hint.

According to the *Theatrical Times*, Bunn was 'the presiding genius of dramatic humbug, the great incarnation of managerial quackery', but

The Brydges Street façade in an 1828 engraving. *Westminster Local Collection*

remarks like that were like drops of water off a mallard's back. He went on his own sweet way. He became the Lessee of Drury Lane and Covent Garden simultaneously, imposed a lower salary scale on both companies (blaming the current theatrical depression on the abolition of the maximum wage) and Bow Street became host to a nightly spectacle of actors and musicians, often in costume, running from one house to the other to double up on parts.

The dual role for Bunn did not last. What he called 'the Great Grand Junction' broke up in 1835, because Bunn, despite pulling every promotional trick in the book, could not afford to pay more than a reduced rent for Covent Garden and lost the lease. His efforts were then restricted to the Lane.

After protracted and difficult negotiations, he signed William Charles Macready for the 1835-6 season. With Kean in his grave, Macready was the country's foremost tragedian and although Bunn did not believe in drama as box-office, there was always a chance Macready would pull in the crowds.

More perfect a contrast to Bunn can hardly be imagined. If Kean had been the Byron of the stage, Macready was its Tennyson. Blessed with an acting talent he almost hated, Macready, who became the friend of Dickens and most of the literary figures of his day, felt himself to be well above the unruly clamour and the disreputable vagabonds of the acting profession. An upright, moral man, he was a model husband and father, but he was also morose, petulant, arrogant and despotic.

He had something of an Atlas complex, discontented unless he was propping the problems of the world and the stage on his own shoulders. He disapproved of Kean, he disapproved of the farragos that passed for drama and entertainment, he disapproved of press criticism and he had a strong line in invective for expressing his disapproval. Once, when a fellow player trod on his hand after a death scene, Macready's 'corpse' sat bolt upright and called the offender a 'beast of hell', a favourite Macready expression. Most of all, he disapproved of Bunn.

Bunn was 'destitute of honesty and honour', 'double-tongued' and his line in spiel, the 'froth of a venomed dog'. Unfortunately for Macready, he had either to sign for Bunn at the Lane, or associate with Charles Kemble at Covent Garden, with whom Macready felt himself unable

The theatre converted for an 1841 Conservative dinner shows the auditorium as it looked after an 1836–7 redecoration. *Westminster Local Collection*

to shake hands because that would have been 'tantamount to making alliance with fraud, treachery, falsehood, the meanest and most malignant species of intrigue: in fact, with vileness and profligacy of the most barefaced character'.

Macready proved not to be the the draw at this stage of his career that Bunn had hoped. Consequently Macready was offered the choice of appearing in after-pieces, and if he refused, to play only on the off-nights to Bunn's latest draw, the Spanish *mezzo* Malibran, and that at half-price. A few months of this passed until Macready, whose flash-point was as low as his ideals were lofty, finally exploded. The last straw was to be made to play only three acts of *Richard III* as a filler to a bill comprising the first act of *Chevy Chase*, and one of Bunn's operatic successes, *The Jewess*. At the end of the truncated play, Macready stalked from the stage, burst into Bunn's office and gave the whiskered cheeks a back-hander—'You damned scoundrel! How dare you use me in this manner?' Bunn bit Macready's little finger and called 'Murder! Murder!' and after a violent struggle the two men, Macready still in his hunchback costume, were pulled apart by theatre staff. As a result, Macready departed to Covent Garden, and Bunn successfully sued him for assault. As the damages awarded were only £150, perhaps the provocation was taken into account.

The unexpected windfall swelled the Bunn funds only temporarily. He had odd successes—the première of Michael Balfe's opera *The Maid of Artois* with Malibran, for which he himself wrote the libretto; Ducrow's performing horses; and Van Ambergh's performing animals which drew Queen Victoria along three times—but in 1839, he went bankrupt.

W. H. Hammond of the Strand theatre, and a dealer in music, took up the lease. He proved a convert to the legitimate drama. On 20 January 1840, he presented Macready in *Macbeth*. On 22 January, he presented Macready in a new play *Mary Stuart*. On 28 February, he absconded with the funds and was declared a bankrupt *in absentia*.

The situation needed a new martyr. It found one in the noblest sufferer of them all—Macready. For two seasons from 1841-3, he was the manager of Drury Lane. Taking over on 4 October, he wrote in his journal, 'I humbly implore the blessing of Almighty God upon my efforts'. He needed it. He revived Shakespeare, but caught a cold with a play called *Plighted Troth*★ which lasted one night and finished to hysterical laughter when Macready was involved in the hand-treading episode mentioned earlier. He was recording in his journal on 26 August 1842:

★ *Blighted Broth* as it was known to some.   147

Looked over my Drury Lane expenditure, and calculating how much it has cost me, find that I am minus what I should have possessed—£8,000.

He was swimming against a strong tide.

The following season he upset Browning by his lack of enthusiasm for the poet's *A Blot in the 'Scutcheon*. Browning's reaction then upset Macready—'I could only think Mr Browning a very disagreeable and offensively mannered person'. Anyone who crossed him got similar

The despotic William Charles Macready, tragedian and one-time manager of Drury Lane in the title role of Byron's *Werner*. *Enthoven Collection*

dismissals. Over the season there were 96 Shakespeare performances, but before we herald this triumph over contemporary taste, let it be noted that there were 148 operas and pantomimes to balance the books. One of the operas, *King Arthur*, employed 79 regular performers, a chorus of 100, 116 supers and 25 extra dancers. It was more than a filler—it was a major attraction of the season. Nevertheless, on 7 April 1843, he was writing in his journal:

Our season is not only irredeemable, but more loss must be incurred. . . .

By 2 June, he had relinquished the managership and went to America to recoup his finances. While he was there, the 1843 Act was passed and the whole face of the London theatre was changed. The most unexpected change was hardly a change at all. His successor at Drury Lane was none other than Bunn.

Bunn, rather like the plastic toys with a rounded base that budgerigars play with, had only to be pushed down, to bounce straight back up again. The first major event of his new régime was Balfe's *The Bohemian Girl*. For this Bunn himself wrote the appalling libretto, beside which *La Forza del Destino* looks a masterpiece of dramatic architecture. Quatrains like

A rival's hate you may better tell
By her rage than by her tears;
And it, perchance, may be as well
To set them both by the ears

abound. Bunn had made a major contribution to consigning the most successful British opera of the nineteenth century to the wordless oblivion of the brass band selections of the twentieth. *The Bohemian Girl* ran for a hundred nights and Bunn duly dreamt he dwelt in marble halls. It was not to last. Despite a visit of the Cirque National from Paris, Bunn's mixture of gingerbread and circuses kept him solvent only until his experiment with a French company in 1848. The company gave their version of *Monte Christo* which was spread over two evenings. The combination of xenophobia directed against the French, with a sense of being cheated by having to buy two tickets to see one show, provoked riots. Bunn had to retire to lick his wounds for the last time in his usual refuge of the bankruptcy court.

At least Macready bowed out in a more dignified fashion with a farewell performance in February 1851 in *Macbeth* when his valiant efforts to keep Shakespeare going, often it must be admitted in adaptation, against the current tide of opinion, were belatedly recognized by a cheering, stamping audience and a shout from the gallery of 'the last of the Mohicans'.

James Anderson took up the management in 1849, reduced prices, gave two lavish productions and went bankrupt himself in 1851. In consequence, all the national theatre could offer to the thousands of foreign visitors crowding to London for the Great Exhibition, was an American circus.

Adopting the Bunn opera formula, Frederick Gye tried to extend his management of Covent Garden by making Drury Lane the 'Grand National Opera House'. It was not a success and he retired to Covent Garden exclusively. Sheridan Smith, a Mr De Vere and George Bolton followed in rapid succession, so rapid none of them lasted a week once rent day arrived.

At the end of 1852, at a rental of £3,500, a neo-Bunn in the form of Edward Tyrrell Smith took the house. The son of an admiral, he ran at various times the Marylebone music hall, the Alhambra, Her Majesty's, the Lyceum, Astley's and the Surrey but still found time to be a land agent, a picture dealer, a bill discounter and a newspaper owner. His Drury Lane fare was as varied. Opening on Boxing Day with an adaptation of the current best-seller *Uncle Tom's Cabin*, he kept going for a full decade on a judicious mixture of opera, Shakespeare, circus and vaudeville turns like the Human Fly who walked upside down on the ceiling. He put up Gustavus Brooke, the 'Hibernian Roscius', in a round of Brooke's best parts and the actor scored a surprising success to do something to wipe out the memory of his insobriety in previous and later years.

In 1862, Dion Boucicault, actor and playwright, came to the Lane and staged his own plays *The Colleen Bawn* and *The Relief of Lucknow*. As E. B. Watson has so rightly pointed out, the public at this time were ready to patronize either a showman or a genius, and in the absence of a genius, they preferred the showman. It was not a point which had escaped Boucicault. He knew that the people wanted an extravaganza of melodramatic plots, comic characters and music hall entertainment, so he gave it to them. When he appeared in *The Shaughran* himself, Joseph Knight thought,

Mr Boucicault is probably the best stage Irishman that has been seen. It is impossible to make drollery more unctious, and blarney more attractive, than they appear in his rendering.

But his real success was as a writer. In a letter to Charles Reade, he said,

When our people shall demand the highest class of dramatic entertainment, a Shakespeare and a Garrick will appear. Until then, my
dear friend, the world will rest contented with such poor things as you
and me.

Boucicault was unashamedly commercial. His American success *The Poor
of New York* became successively *The Poor of Liverpool*, and with metro-
politan sensitivity to consider, *The Streets of London*. Of the play's merits,
he was brutally frank:

> I can spin out these rough-and-tumble dramas as a hen lays eggs. It's
> a degrading occupation but more money has been made out of guano
> than out of poetry.

In the 1860s, there was a lot of guano. It was the only thing likely to
succeed.

Edmund Falconer, who became the lessee in December 1862, found
such hard facts difficult to grasp. Engaging Samuel Phelps, Falconer staged
King John, *Henry IV*, *Manfred* and *Comus*. The profits that Falconer had
made in a term at the Lyceum were soon swallowed up, and having
temporarily staved off defeat by taking in F. B. Chatterton as a partner in
1863, he finally went under in 1866. Chatterton, alone, replaced him.

Chatterton began with Shakespeare and Byron. It was a noble gesture
but ineffective in keeping the theatre open. By 1868, he had surrendered
to the most effective of all demonstrations of public opinion, empty
houses; and staged *The Great City*, horse, hansom and all. In 1869, he
gave Boucicault's *Formosa*, as unlikely a title as one could wish for a play
containing a representation of the Oxford and Cambridge Boat Race.
Also in 1869, he engaged the Vokes family in a pantomime which then
became an annual institution.

Chatterton was a sensitive man. When *Formosa* was attacked for
'desecrating the National Theatre', he felt bound to defend himself in
print. He would have preferred to stage more substantial drama but he
would never have lasted until 1879 if he had. Eking out a hand to mouth
existence, and relying on sensation drama and pantomime to pay the
bills, that he lasted thirteen years is not an achievement to be belittled.

CHAPTER ELEVEN

The Dramas of Druriolanus

1879-1900

WHEN Chatterton finally fell by the wayside, all the traditional reasons for failure were put forward. An unidentified cutting in the Enthoven Collection says:

> The last Christmas pantomime, for so many years his sheet anchor, had to fight against the unforeseen odds of an unusually severe winter, depression of trade, corresponding scarcity of cash among the play-going classes, and hard times generally; and the end of it was his management of Old Drury dismally collapsed.

One would hardly think that a severe winter in Britain could have been 'unforeseen odds', and the reasons sound flimsy. Rather, Chatterton, £36,000 to the bad at the end, had most of the correct ideas but lacked the real flair to carry them out and, perhaps, the courage of his convictions. His successor lacked neither.

Sir Augustus Harris—his knighthood came from his services as a Sheriff of the City of London during the visit of the German Emperor in 1891, not as a result of his services to the drama—grew up in an atmosphere of theatre. His father, Augustus Glossop Harris, had taken over from Charles Kean as manager of the Princess's theatre, introduced Fechter to London audiences, and was connected with the opera at Covent Garden for nearly thirty years.

Harris himself as an actor had appeared as Malcolm in *Macbeth* in Manchester in 1873. He was young, slim and had a total faith in his own abilities. The closure of Drury Lane drew him like a magnet. In common with a number of likely and unlikely applicants, he was interviewed by the committee and conveyed an aura of competence and affluence. Considering that his own capital resources amounted to less than £4 at the time, it was no mean achievement. By the time of his death at the

The young Augustus 'Druriolanus' Harris as seen in an *Entracte* cartoon of 1879. The caption reads: 'Master Gussy Harris—What will he do with it?'
Enthoven Collection

early age of 45, he had the rounded waistline of the brilliantly successful businessman he was and looked remarkably like the Prince of Wales. From his father and others (including a rival applicant!) he raised funds to fulfil the bond of £1,000 the committee demanded as a token of good faith, and once at the helm, immediately sublet the theatre to George Rignold. While Rignold indulged himself in *Henry V* by William Shakespeare, known to his nineteenth century colleagues as Ruin, Harris prepared a Christmas pantomime *Bluebeard*. Written by E. L. Blanchard, who turned out such pantomimes by the turbanful, and starring as usual the entire Vokes family in their annual benefit, it could as well have been staged by Chatterton. Harris's unique contribution to Drury Lane was to introduce an annual drama i.e. melodrama, at first in July or August and later in September, and to change the concept of the Christmas pantomime.

In both cases his brilliant success stemmed from his understanding of the basic emotions that working class entertainment of his day catered for, and by dressing them in a cloak of respectability, drawing in an admiring if philistine middle class. The people who would not have dared to be seen in an East End theatre slumming with the working classes

A richer, fatter Harris; master of a profitable Drury Lane theatre.
Enthoven Collection

were able to come to Drury Lane in their evening dress and relish the sentimentality and sensations of melodrama.

Harris, who today would have been a perfect managing director of an Independent Television company, performed a similar service for his patrons with the pantomime. Music hall, which had started in the London public houses in the 1840s, was an aggressively proletarian phenomenon. Surrounded by drunkenness, disorder and sheer gutsiness, the halls catered for the labouring classes with perhaps a sprinkling of aristocrats on a daring night out.

One has only to look at the content of music hall songs—the moving one step ahead of the bailiff of *My old man says 'Follow the Van'*, the slum conditions of *If it wasn't fir the 'ouses in between*, or the lack of family planning of *Don't have any more, Mrs Moore*—to see that the lyrics have a direct hard-hitting relevance to working-class life, and therefore an immediate appeal to those to whom such events were commonplace. A respectable middle-class woman, who could patronize the Savoy operas of Gilbert and Sullivan, would no more have entered a music hall than disrobed at a funeral or sworn in a cathedral.

By scouring the halls for talent, and introducing music hall personalities into his pantomimes, Harris brought the mountain to Mahomet. He provided his audience with major talents like Dan Leno, Marie Lloyd and Vesta Tilley, meanwhile giving these artists an opportunity to extend their talents and to become family entertainers. When one remembers that variety was not really accepted until the first Royal Variety Command Performance in 1912, it was a major achievement.

Occasionally his new stars let him down—he was furious with Marie Lloyd when she knelt by her grandmother's bed and peeped underneath for the chinaware—but generally speaking even the critics relished the humour of a man like Dan Leno who must have been blessed with comic genius. Clement Scott wrote of him:

When we see Dan Leno as a woman and hear his delightful patter it never strikes us that he is a man imitating a woman. It is a woman who stands before us, the veritable Mrs Kelly, not a burlesque of the sex, but the actual thing . . . without suspicion of vulgarity. . . . In brief, a most admirable, versatile, persuasive, volatile and intense comedian and artiste. Whenever he is on the stage . . . he literally holds his audience tight in his power. They cannot get away from him. He is monarch of all he surveys.

Leno and his fellow 'Dames' revived the art of playing women, lost since

Marie Lloyd, one of the many
music hall artists brought to the
Lane by Harris. *Enthoven Collection*

the days of Kynaston. He was not restricted to Dame roles alone. Once
World Champion Clog Dancer, an art lost to the world today with the
limited exception of Bill Tidy's 'The Cloggies' in *Private Eye*, he was a
host of talents in one. A superb clown, yet he had Buster Keaton's
ability to suggest the tears behind the laughter. Ernest Short suggested,
'The essence of Lenoesque humour was the speed with which absurdity
was piled on absurdity, leaving time for nothing save laughter, not too
far removed from tears. When Dan was on the stage, the laughter was

not noisy.' Is there not the infinite sadness of the born philosopher in lines
like

Ah, what is man? Wherefore does he why? Whence did he whence?
Whither is he withering?

Bertrand Russell could hardly have capped that.

His ubiquitous partner Herbert Campbell, the vast extrovert, was the
perfect contrast. No one wrote their pantomime scripts, they were left

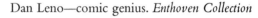

Dan Leno—comic genius. *Enthoven Collection*

to improvise them themselves within the context of a scene. Theirs was not the humour to be reproduced on paper.

Significantly, Harris did not start with Leno and Campbell but with Arthur Roberts, one of the earliest of the music hall comedians, who specialized in immaculate fashion-setting elegance. He appeared in *Mother Goose* in 1880 at Drury Lane and paved the way for the others—Little Tich, whose boots were almost as long as he was, and Vesta Tilley, of male attire and patriotic songs, among them.

After a failure with *La Fille de Madame Angot* in March 1880 (Harris once said when the work was criticized in his presence, 'If you had to pay a thousand pounds for rent, and hadn't got it, and if a friend turned up and offered to find the shekels if you'd produce *Madame Angot*—what would *you* do?'), Harris launched the first of his sensation dramas on an unsuspecting public, and struck gold. Playing in it himself as one of the villains—for good measure the play had seven—this was *The World*. It was the first of many of what have been described as 'nailed up pieces'. Harris was part-author with Paul Merritt but as always his creative contribution was confined to suggesting a few basic situations and scenic disasters, to be filled out with dialogue by his collaborator.

Harris played Harry Huntingford, who gets his brother Sir Clement committed to a lunatic asylum run by two mad doctors. This was particularly bad luck on Sir Clement who had to survive the explosion of the ship he was travelling on, and a mid-ocean fight on a raft, in previous acts. Justice was eventually meted out when the Harris character was trapped and crushed in a lift shaft, and all ended happily at a fancy dress ball. *The World* was a huge financial success.

Harris, who secretly nurtured an ambition to play Shakespeare, a desire he kept under severe control, was probably not much of an actor, a fact which many critics found necessary to point out. His reply, though more self-effacing than usual, was characteristically ebullient.

Let 'em slate away, all their slating won't deter me from making myself eligible for the Drury Lane Dramatic Fund. Chatterton was a clever man, but where is he now? Had he acted for three years, had he only said 'My Lord, the carriage awaits,' he would be on the fund now.

Harris, needless to say, never needed his pension.

The World was the forerunner of many. *Youth* was the first, which included the Battle of Rorke's Drift in the 1879 Zulu War, and *Pluck* the second. *Pluck* had a train smash and practically an avalanche of snow in Piccadilly Circus. Harris had established his formula.

It did not suit everyone. In 1881, an anonymous poet wrote *The New Augustan Age* which summarized the Harris approach.

> Tremendous announcements and empty verbosity,
> Silly postponements to stir curiosity,
> Cuttings from newspaper padding and puff,
> This is the recipe rendered in rough.
> Add to it anything else inexcusable,
> Meet all together—there's nothing refusable.
> Set 'em to simmer and take off the scum,
> And a Drury Lane play is the residuum.

Harris did not care for this sort of attack too much, not that it was likely to change what he well knew was packing Drury Lane. He had no objections to personality cults and he loved to be given the unofficial title of 'Druriolanus'.

When the opera house at Covent Garden was vacant in 1888, Harris put up some of the thousands his dramas had earned him and secured that house as well. It was a defiant gesture—'Confound them, they talk about Art with a big A, I'll show the fellows what art is'—and a bid for recognition as a grand impresario. His intentions were quite clear:

> I mean the name of Augustus Harris to be known all over the world. Mr Gye* was like the Grand Llama of Tibet, unknown, unseen, impenetrable and unapproachable. But now his name is actually forgotten. Ninety-nine people out of a hundred who pass by the statue in Covent Garden don't know that it is the statue of Frederick Gye.

He brought opera in the original language to Covent Garden, imported Melba and the De Reszkes and did a great deal to popularize Wagner. This is outside Drury Lane but it does show that Harris was no Philistine. Neither was he ever unknown, unseen, impenetrable or unapproachable.

An 1882 production of *Macbeth* preceded the natural disasters of *Pluck*, but the traditionally unhappy play brought two mishaps for William Rignold as Macbeth, one comic, one tragic. Contemporary newspaper cuttings tell the story.

When, after an unconceivable pause, he began the famous soliloquy,

---

* Manager of Covent Garden from 1849–77.

'Is that a dagger I see before me?', a cat sedately strolled upon the stage to form his opinion on the subject, and the presence of the harmless, necessary animal as it investigated the stage and the auditorium and peered down to see if there were any mice in the orchestra, was not found to assist the solemnity of the act.

A few evenings later, Dame Fortune frowned again.

Just before the closing of 'Macbeth' at Drury-Lane Theatre on Wednesday night, Mr William Rignold was accidentally stabbed in the chest by Mr J. H. Barnes. While the actors were fencing in the last act, Mr Barnes, instead of thrusting his sword in the side of his opponent, accidently thrust it into his chest. A doctor was immediately called, and it was found the wound was rather serious.

The previous year, Harris brought the Saxe-Meiningen players in their first appearance outside Germany, but whatever influence the ensemble playing of the company and their handling of crowds had on the London theatre, at the Lane it was the mixture as before. Druriodrama and pantomime continued.

Harris and Rowe's *Freedom* in 1883 found *Punch* pleased that despite the Middle Eastern troubles of the government, Harris and Rowe seemed to have solved the difficulties between them; and *Illustrated London News* in 1885 discussing *Human Nature* by Harris and Pettitt, said

We grant that the same talent of stage management might be better employed. The actors from Saxe-Meiningen used it for the glorification of scenes from Shakespeare. But if we cannot get Julius Caesar at Drury Lane, and no actors are forthcoming to do justice to Brutus or Antony, we must be content with crowds at Charing Cross.

A Sailor and his Lass (1883) exploited ship-sinking and street explosions, *A Run of Luck* (1886) was the first of many to feature the sporting attractions of the Turf, and although Eleanora Duse gave a season in 1895, the major attraction of the season was *Cheer, Boys, Cheer!* by Harris, Raleigh and Hamilton, which rambled down Rotten Row and took in polo at Hurlingham as a preamble to the Matabele rising. (One stage direction is classic, the cowardly Boer guides are instructed to 'slink' off.)

Harris's death in June 1896 made no difference to the fare at the Lane. He was succeeded by Arthur Collins his right-hand man, described by the *Pall Mall Gazette* as 'a first lieutenant, a prime minister and a grand vizier all rolled into one ubiquitous individual'.

Collins's talent for stage mechanics had been spotted by Harris while he was an apprentice to the Drury Lane scene-painter Harry Emden, and Harris had made him his stage-manager. Learning all the tricks of the Harris trade from the inside, Collins had also grasped the secrets of filling the house. He raised capital and formed a joint stock company. On 28 May 1897 he became the Managing Director of the Theatre Royal Drury Lane Ltd and having obtained an extended lease from the Duke of Bedford, he, Cecil Raleigh and Henry Hamilton continued to give the public what it so clearly wanted.

The White Heather in 1897 went underwater for a fight to the death between hero and villain in diving suits; *The Great Ruby* in 1898 visited Lord's and the Military Tournament and wrote *finis* to the career of the villain with a fall from a balloon. The last of the nineteenth century dramas was *Hearts are Trumps* in 1899. The villain was satisfactorily dispatched in an Alpine avalanche, but not before there had been a scene which is for me a perfect summary of Victorian melodrama.

The characteristically cretinous hero is unable to prevent the characteristically adoit villain obtaining a nude picture of the characteristically virginal heroine. The painting is hung in the Summer Exhibition of the Royal Academy. The viewers discussing the painting are pushed aside by an elderly lady who slashes the picture to ribbons. The crowd standing aghast at the act, she is asked: By what right have you done this deed? On the classic reply, By the greatest right that God or man ever gave woman. I am . . . her MOTHER! the curtain falls to the relieved cheers of an enthusiastic audience momentarily anxious lest villainy had triumphed over virtue. It was the curtain of the century.

PART IV

*The
Twentieth
Century*

CHAPTER TWELVE

The Whip and Last Appearances
1900–24

THE dawning of a new century was not at Drury Lane the dawning of anything new in the way of drama. The formula for box-office success established by Augustus Harris was followed religiously by Collins and it continued to serve its purpose. Bridging the centuries, was the Christmas pantomine *Jack and the Beanstalk*, which Collins produced in his grand manner and which gave plenty of opportunity for inspired mugging by Dan Leno as Dame Trott, Herbert Campbell as Bobbie and Johnny Danvers as His Imperial Majesty King Rattatat.

That it was 1900 and that there was a Boer War being fought in South Africa had not been entirely forgotten. In the finale, when the slain Giant sprawled lifeless across the stage, the pocket of the 'corpse' was unbuttoned—'He's got the British Army in his pocket!'—and a phalanx of children in military dress poured out, to, we may be sure, rounds of patriotic applause from the audience, anxious if only by proxy to do their bit.

The pantomime gave way eventually to another Collins production which was very much for the benefit of an Edward Vroom, who wrote and starred as Adrian de Marsac in his own *Marsac of Gascony*. A review in the *Sketch* on 25 April makes happy reading.

[It] . . . gives the author opportunity for thrilling combats, daring escapades, wicked abductions, ending with the overthrow of vice and the happy marriage of virtue, for the lovely Louise proved to be the legitimate long-lost daughter of a Duke . . . perhaps the first great outburst of applause was when de Marsac broke from the Cardinal's guard and, rushing upstairs, leaped through a great window into the river, which was presented through the window in a remarkably lifelike manner. After this, events followed fast and furious. . . .

The autumn drama *The Price of Peace* by the indefatigable Welsh master of the melodrama, Cecil Raleigh, offered similarly spectacular feasts for the eye. The fast and furious action of the plot, 'full of startling situations' thought the *Illustrated London News*, took place variously in the accident ward of St Thomas's Hospital, the Terrace of the House of Commons, a skating rink, Westminster Abbey, the seaside, the Chamber of the House of Commons and on board a two level yacht. In Act Four, the steam yacht *Marigold* is involved in a collision while on the top level a baroness and her maid climb panic-stricken up the rat-lines, just as Tom Sin a Chinese servant strangles Marcus Benton the villain at the lower level. Raleigh and Collins believed in giving value for money. This orgy of 'marvellous mechanical effects and scenic beauties', a term which could have been applied equally to the 1900 pantomime *The Sleeping Beauty* with its Enchanted Crystal Garden with 'Stanley's Illuminated Fountains', and two lavish transformation scenes, cannot be dismissed even now.

To look at the 1900 production photographs with a modern eye is to see conclusively that the scenery was indeed magnificent, beautifully painted, solidly built and providing a visual feast. The impact upon an audience who had never seen cinema or television must have been electrifying. Small wonder that people staggered from the Drury Lane in a state of pleasant shell-shock. ('I wonder what time it is,' said Mrs Herman Finck after one pantomime. 'You mean you wonder what day it is,' replied her husband.) For a child from the grimmer greyer areas of East London, one can see that a few hours spent with Collins's enchanted castles and forests, must have been the thrill of a lifetime.

The tradition for spectacle, however, was only one tradition. Also in keeping with the long history of the house as the prestigious home of histrionic talent, was its automatic choice for occasional charity matinées. In these it is easier to count who did not appear than who did. Hardly a late nineteenth century or early twentieth century name, would be missing from a list of actors, actresses and entertainers who at one time or another fleetingly graced the Lane with their presence. We can only dream and regret that we missed, say, the Canadian matinée on 19 June which offered in a long programme (thirty items was by no means unusual at the time), such varied delights as W. S. Gilbert appearing in his own *H.M.S. Pinafore*, Henry Irving in an Arthur Conan Doyle one-acter *Waterloo*, Herbert Beerbohm Tree's first *Othello*, Marie Tempest songs and a comedy turn by Dan Leno.

Few on that bill would, however, have realized the threat to their future presented by Item 28 on the programme—the Derby and the relief of Ladysmith shown in Biograph pictures. Did anyone on that happy

166

(*Opposite*) Two sumptuous scenes from the 1900 pantomime
The Sleeping Beauty. Enthoven Collection

afternoon consider that here was a revolutionary new medium which would render the staple fare of the Lane of stage avalanches, train smashes and faithfully rendered exteriors, completely redundant? Somehow, I doubt it.

The year 1901 came and went, helped on its way by a new Raleigh play *The Great Millionaire* which had a car crash costing alone some £700, fifty-six speaking parts and seventeen different locales including the Guildhall and the Carlton Hotel. And in 1902, the fare was even more aggressively grandiose. From 3 April the stage shook and trembled under the impact of the Roman galley ships and on-stage chariot race of *Ben Hur*. How was it possible to get live horses with real chariots racing on the Drury Lane stage? If you can bear the tortured prose, *The Era* tells all:

> Four great cradles, 20 feet in length and fourteen feet wide, movable back and front on railways supported by a bridge structure capable of supporting twenty tons. The tops of the cradles are two inches below the stage level. Each cradle bears four horses and a chariot. On each are four treadmills covered with rubber, twelve feet long and two and a half feet wide, and on these the horses are secured by invisible steel cable traces, which serve to hold the animals in their places. As the horse gallops the treadmill revolves under his feet, thereby eliminating the forward pressure created by the impact of his hoofs, which would force him ahead on an immovable surface. The wheels of the chariot are worked by rubber rollers, operated upon by electrical motors. An impression of great speed is created by the presence of a panoramic background, thirty five feet high, representing the walls of the arena, with numbers of spectators seated in their places. This is made to revolve rapidly in a direction opposite to that in which the chariots are going. . . .

All quite simple really.

Raleigh was back in September with *The Best of Friends* but even a scenic sortie to South Africa seems old hat after a chariot race. He tried a strong comeback in 1903 with *The Flood Tide*, in which a Boat Train, the Kempton Park Paddock and naturally a flood are featured, but by straying from his usual brief of straight melodrama to what he called 'a new and original melo-farce', he was booed at the opening night for his effrontery in having trifled with the audience's feelings. Whatever one may say about Raleigh's lack of originality, one must also admit that he was not given much encouragement to be different.

Mrs Beerbohm Tree who played the adventuress in *The Flood Tide*—

there was *always* an adventuress!—was not without censure either. *The Referee* thought

> . . . her prunish and prismatic tone was pitched just an octave [*Just an octave?!*] too high . . . and although she looks the part to perfection, there is less of the tigress than of the insinuating domestic puss in her manner. . . .

Perhaps it would be kinder to remember Drury Lane 1903 for the Henry Irving season of April when, as often, he set his magnificent talents to work in a poor part. As the *Illustrated London News* put it of his Dante in Sardou's play of the same name:

> . . . the whole play, mere series as it is of disconnected pictures and melodramatic episodes, was one long triumph—the triumph of an arresting personality.

Alternatively we can marvel at the *Merchant of Venice* cast assembled for the Actors' Association Benefit in June. Henry Irving as Shylock, George Alexander as Bassanio, Oscar Asche as the Moroccan Prince, H. B. Irving as Salerio, Ben Webster as Gratiano, Martin Harvey as Lorenzo, Seymour Hicks as Balthazar and Ellen Terry as Portia. How do you cap that? It took until 1906 but they did. The occasion was the Ellen Terry Jubilee.

In the interim, there were two sad last appearances. In 1904 Dan Leno and Herbert Campbell played their last pantomime and died before the year was out, and in 1905 Sir Henry Irving, who had not had the necessary finance to rebuild his own Lyceum theatre to conform to new safety regulations, played one last season at Drury Lane, giving his admirers his Shylock and another of his greatest parts, Tennyson's Becket. In the latter role he was taken ill at Bradford and died. In a brief space of time, both the greatest actor of Victorian times and the leading figure of the Victorian music hall had disappeared for ever.

On a more prosaic plane, 1904 also saw a Manners English opera season and 1905 a play by Hall Caine, *The Prodigal Son*, notable for a specially trained flock of sheep and not much else.

The recent death of Irving gave an added pathos to the momentous 12 June 1906, when what seemed the entire theatrical profession gathered at the Lane to pay tribute to Ellen Terry. Boxes cost up to 100 guineas but, at Miss Terry's specific request, the pit remained at 5s and the amphitheatre at 2s 6d to give ordinary members of the public an opportunity to share in the feast. And how they responded! A queue started on the *previous* morning and Arthur Collins persuaded a local shop to stay open all night to supply coffee and food to the queuers. When some thirty hours of discomfort was over and they were inside the theatre, they must have thought the sacrifice worthwhile.

Mrs Patrick Campbell recited, Ellaline Terriss sang, as did Gertie Millar and Caruso, Adeline Genée danced, the Coquelins played Molière, W. S. Gilbert appeared himself in *Trial By Jury* with a courtroom crowd that included Conan Doyle, Aubrey Smith, Nigel Playfair, Zena Dare and Arthur Collins. Then George Alexander and Sir Charles Wyndham played a scene from *The School for Scandal* which also featured a youthful A. E. Matthews, a Minstrel Entertainment had Seymour Hicks, Johnny Danvers, Will Bishop and George Grossmith Jnr, and in *Much Ado About Nothing* the great Ellen Terry herself played Beatrice to Beerbohm Tree's Benedick, a scene which also featured a masked dance with Henry Ainley, Gerald du Maurier and Harcourt Williams. The souvenir programme had special plates designed by the most distinguished painters of the day (Alma-Tadema, Nicholson, Orpen and Sargent among them) and, with a true sense of theatre and occasion, Eleanora Duse leaned out of her box and threw a bouquet to Beatrice.

Hall Caine's next offering in September, *The Bondman*, was hardly in the same league, despite real cows milked on the stage. To read the early scenes of the play is to wonder why Michael and Jason the heroes have been sent as convicts to a *Sicilian* sulphur mine. Later it becomes clear why—because it gives an on-stage Etna a chance to erupt. The production also had Henry Ainley as the Governor of Sicily, and a Greeta in Mrs Patrick Campbell, who could be an Etna in her own right. So far as I have been able to trace, she did not do in *The Bondman* what she did in one play when she got bored with the proceedings—enliven a particularly dull part of the dialogue by flicking chocolates up against the backcloth.

In 1907 came *Last of His Race*, a turgid account of the 'Okotchee' tribe of Red Indians, where the programme tried to set the audience's, or possibly Equity's, minds at rest with a note:

> To avoid misconception the management beg to state that all the speaking characters will be played by well-known actors, the REAL SIOUX INDIANS are used only as supernumeraries.

Arthur Collins no speak with forked tongue but play, him last only fourteen nights.

Its successor was another Raleigh play, *The Sins of Society* written with his old collaborator Henry Hamilton, a partnership somewhat hampered by the fact that they could not stand one another. This time it was a plot delicately hinged on pawning lumps of coal and pretending they were diamonds. Perhaps pawnbrokers were pretty stupid in 1907, who knows? The scenes included Longchamps, the Windsor Rhododendron Gardens and a weir, with as a *pièce de résistance*, the sinking of the S.S. *Beachy Head*. Saluting and singing the National Anthem, with the Union Jack fluttering bravely above their heads, the soldiers stood to attention and sank to a watery grave below the surface of the stage. The play did capacity business until it was replaced by *Babes in the Wood*, and plans to revive it in the spring were only cancelled because of a backstage fire.

Instead, 1908 got Raleigh and Hamilton's *The Marriages of Mayfair* which featured so realistic an avalanche that one horse was killed during the run. After a nod towards culture with an Italian Grand Opera season, the Raleigh and Hamilton team was back in the autumn of 1909 with *The Whip*, yet another play with a background of the Turf. Why this play more than any other should be a box-office smash hit is difficult to see. It ran until panto time and was revived in March 1910 for another 277 performances. Its success could hardly be due to the dialogue of which the following is a representative sample:

> *Lord Brancaster* (played by Vincent Clive). It was you who called me back to life and made me want to live again.
> *Lady Diana* (played by Jessie Bateman). I'm—I'm glad to think that.

And what did the gallery make of the line delivered by the adventuress, unrepentant at having caused a train smash?

> Never mind, they were only third class passengers—something is always happening to people of that kind.

Again the success must have been based upon Collins's mastery of stagecraft. Having decided that the public wanted spectacle, he gave it to them. *The Whip* boasted a reconstruction of Madam Tussaud's Chamber of Horrors (yes, you've guessed it, the villain's schemes *are* overheard by a man impersonating a waxwork); a Hunt breakfast; a train smash when The Whip (a racehorse) is lead out of its rail box seconds before the express smashes it to smithereens; and the 2,000 Guineas fought out between The Whip and fifteen other horses before the audience's very eyes.

Unfortunately, the first night found the backstage staff somewhat less

171

Two incidents in *The Whip* of 1909, one of the many equine box office
successes. *Enthoven Collection*

than masters of Collins's scenes and machines. At a crucial stage of the running of the race, The Whip was a bad fifth and the judges' box soared up into the flies. Overnight adjustments were made and The Whip proved its real class by winning the 2,000 Guineas 387 times in succession, and without even a wager on the race, Collins, Raleigh and Hamilton made a small fortune.

In 1911, *The Whip* was at last retired to stud or to pasture, and *The Sins of Society* was revived in its place. There was also a special command performance by an all-star cast in Bulwer Lytton's *Money* as part of the State Visit of the German Emperor and Empress. The orchestra played His Imperial Majesty's own composition 'Song of Aegir' and all was Anglo-German sweetness and light, ironically enough, in view of the fact that a world war was but three years away.

In the autumn, Raleigh and Hamilton were back with *The Hope* which, amazingly, ended Act Four with The Derby. The only change was that the moving treads were placed to run towards the footlights so that the horses pounded head-on at the audience. Their galloping was particularly futile on the first night because a black masking curtain concealing the race preparations was never drawn up and the entire race was run with the audience in pitch darkness and not seeing a thing. It must be the only time that an exhausted bunch of three-year-olds having run twelve frantic furlongs has been asked to go round Epsom again. At this blatant attempt to repeat the success of *The Whip* with little more than a change of title and race, the *Tatler* was sarcastic, pointing out that:

> Most actors and actresses on the stage forgot themselves and called it The Whip . . . if someone or other introduced any originality into a Drury Lane autumn melodrama, the whole of London would collapse like the wonderful earthquake scene at the end of the third act.

The Hope, which of course the heroine has drawn in the great Calcutta Sweep, wins the Derby; and the hero, despite having to conduct his beloved to safety over a perilous arch only to be buried alive himself, gets to Epsom in time to see the race. The earthquake which temporarily holds him up was one of the most successful features of the evening. Even the *Tatler* pretended to be impressed:

> Before this cataclysm sit the audience petrified with fear, clutching each other in the darkness like early Christian martyrs just before the hour of the lions' supper. The whole theatre seemed one great bead of cold perspiration.

173

The following year, 1912, saw a re-run of another famous race for *Ben Hur* was back, and a taste for religion in dramatic form brought a modern morality play called *Everywoman* from America to fill the autumn drama spot. And at the end of the year George Graves laid claim to Leno's vacant pantomime crown with his clowning in *The Sleeping Beauty*.

It was time for another spectacular farewell. In 1913 Drury Lane was taken by Sir Johnston Forbes-Robertson. Together with his American wife Gertrude Elliott, he undertook a final tour of Britain, Canada and America repeating for the last time the roles which had made him famous. In his two month season he played Shaw's Caesar which Shaw had written for him after seeing Forbes-Robertson play Hamlet. He also played The Stranger in *The Passing of the Third Floor Back*, the Christ-like character whose messianic qualities return others to the straight and narrow.

It could have been tailor-made for his classical features, his effortless elegance and his beautifully modulated voice, but in fact he disliked the role intensely. The story is told of him waiting for his entrance behind the scenes muttering, 'Christ, will they never let me give up this bloody part?' then stepping on to the stage with his face and bearing the very epitome of moral rectitude.

And he repeated Hamlet, giving a final farewell performance on 6 June when he made a moving speech saying, 'I bid you farewell, but how can I be sad when at the most dramatic moment of my career my King honours me?' (he had just received a knighthood). But he belied his words by coming down into the audience to shake hands with admirers in the stalls and unashamedly weeping. He played Hamlet only once more—in private before film cameras. The film, which is still extant, compresses Hamlet into ninety minutes (!) although even that drew a sense of wonder from the *Daily Mirror*—'it is about three miles in length'.

Three weeks later there was ample proof that the whole world was changing and that with the passing of Leno and Irving and the retirement of Forbes-Robertson, an era had come to an end. Not only were new political and economic forces gathering to plunge Europe into a disastrous war, but in the arts themselves the modern movement was bursting into life. An astonished London saw the Lane transformed for four weeks from a moribund home of melodrama to an outpost of the *avant-garde*. Sir Joseph Beecham, father of Sir Thomas and a wealthy industrialist and musical amateur, launched a Russian ballet and opera season upon an unsuspecting London public.

Suddenly, ears nurtured to the sweet strains of Balfe and the wit of Sullivan, had to re-adjust to the Eastern splendour of *Boris Godunov* and singing from Chaliapin (or Chaliapine as the programme uncertainly spelt it) that made English basses sound like counter-tenors. *Khovanschina* also received its London première. But if Mussorgsky's music sounded advanced, what was one to make of Stravinsky's *Rite of Spring*? Here was music and ballet to call all one's assumptions about the nature of the arts into question.

The fourteen ballets of the season, Bakst's use of daring colours, Fokine's determination to lift ballet from the realms of the pink slipper to an expression of the most complex emotions, dancing from Nijinsky, Cecchetti and Karsavina that seemed to transcend human capabilities as they had been understood—can we doubt that London sat back dumbfounded and, to be fair, lost in admiration? Incidentally, collectors of such miscellaneous pieces of information may like to know that the programme for 25 June lists a 'Mme Ramberg' as a second dancer, a printers' error that should not disguise the first appearance of Dame Marie Rambert, one of the great founders of modern English ballet.

That there were great changes abroad did not affect Messrs Raleigh and Hamilton who were back on 11 September with *Sealed Orders* which included the Chelsea Flower Show for some botanical titivation, a fall from the bridge of a battleship, an airship brought down by a gun, and a sea rescue to show they were well aware that they had a tradition for action to keep up.

The effect of war can be seen not in a closing of the theatre because, unlike the Second World War, London life continued relatively unaffected. It showed rather in economic measures avoiding the capital outlay on a new production. *Sealed Orders* was revived in both 1914 and 1915, and *The Sleeping Beauty* pantomime became *The Sleeping Beauty Re-awakened* in 1913, and *The Sleeping Beauty Beautified* in 1914. The Russian opera and ballet, with German opera for good measure, returned in 1914 for two months, featuring amongst other highlights Richard Strauss conducting his own ballet score *La Légende de Joseph*, and the first English performance of *Prince Igor*, *Le Coq d'Or* and *Daphnis and Chloe*. When it was possible to see a full eighteen performances in the Balcony for £4 1s, it must have been easy to forget, for a few hours a night, that Europe was on the brink of tearing itself to pieces.

So far as the theatre was concerned the new enemy was not Germany, but the rapidly developing cinema. The new medium captured the citadel in 1916 when Drury Lane was given over to a showing of D. W. Griffith's *The Birth of a Nation*. This was spectacle on a scale that Raleigh and Collins could only have dreamed of. With almost an air of embarrassment, the management issued a programme with a cast list and came very near to claiming credit for the epic.

175

> The Birth of a Nation is a production which, by the aid of the camera is enabled to put on the stage of Drury Lane Theatre, 18,000 people, 15,000 horses and 3,000 scenes. . . .

More traditional replies to this new monster were a 1916 revue *Razzle-Dazzle* which neither razzled nor dazzled; and a new Hamilton, Raleigh and Collins play *The Best of Luck* with an underwater fight, a sunken galleon and, with a half-admiring nod towards the Germans, a submarine moving along the ocean bed. That the country was at war with Germany got further recognition in the Shakespearean Tercentenary. Playwright Henry Arthur Jones brought out a pamphlet expressing his horror at the news that Germany was also celebrating the event with her own performance of *Macbeth*. Showing all the detachment and objectivity of a Coupon Election address, he thundered:

> . . . let them not imagine that if Shakespeare were alive today, his pen would scratch one syllable till he had engraved on their foreheads in characters redder and starker than the sign of the forehead of Cain, the blazon of his uncontrollable hate for the Germany of today. . . .

Plundering the bard's work for Portia's dismissal of the Duke of Saxony's nephew for confirmation, he went on:

> . . . he could scarcely have written it unless he had experienced some unpleasant contact with Germans, or unless their odious habits and natures were so well-known that he could make a general unqualified reference to them before a popular audience.

The event itself on 2 May 1916 was a legitimate opportunity for patriotic pageantry, accompanied by music directed from the podium by Henry Wood, Edward German, Thomas Beecham and Hamilton Harty. It also gave F. R. Benson an opportunity to display his talents as Julius Caesar. Benson had become a national institution, stumping around the country with his own Shakespeare company with all the fervour of a Wesley. His own athleticism, which made stage fights frighteningly acrobatic and once led him to advertise for an actor who could double as a leg-break bowler, was not really matched by his verse-speaking or his acting. When at the end of *Julius Caesar* he was knighted in the theatre itself by King George V (with only a slight delay for a sword to be borrowed from a local military outfitters as a property sword was felt to be out of keeping with the solemnity of the occasion), one hopes the honour was more for his proselytizing and his immense personal good nature than for his performance. According to one of his friends, his delivery was

> . . . largely incomprehensible. He mouthed lines until they were meaningless, sang them till they were indistinguishable, and bawled them till they were deafening.

For all the deference shown in 1916 to the English theatre's greatest name, it was left to D. W. Griffith to keep the box-office window open in 1917 with a revival of *The Birth of a Nation* and a showing of *Intolerance*. Sir Thomas Beecham helped with three seasons of opera in English from 1917 to 1919, but the retirement of Arthur Collins was not far away.

His twenty-first birthday as manager was celebrated with a Pageant of Drury Lane Theatre 1663–1918 which included extracts from highlights of the previous centuries, from *The Humorous Lieutenant* to *The Best of Luck*. To remember the days when Betterton, Garrick, Sheridan and Siddons had lifted the house to its share of the history of the drama, at a time when the regular fare offered was a feeble operetta-cum-panto called *Shanghai*, struck no one as incongruous.

Before Collins's final retirement, he shared the managing-directorship with a new and formidable member of the board, Sir Alfred Butt. The transformation of the Harris and Collins formula however took longer. As if the cinema had never happened, the 1919 autumn drama *The Great Day* by Louis Parker and George Sims relied on such novelties as the furnace of a steel-works and the flooding of a Parisian night refuge by the rising of the Seine. And in 1920, after eight weeks of Anna Pavlova dancing in ballet extracts and *divertissements* the theatre 'packed from floor to ceiling at every performance bears witness to the potency of her genius', said the *Dancing Times*—Collins pulled out all the stops as a stage director.

He not so much staged *The Garden of Allah* by Robert Hichens and Mary Anderson as swamped it. The play itself featured Godfrey Tearle as a young monk torn between his solemn vows and the temptation of making love to Madge Titheradge in the Sahara desert. (No prizes for guessing which triumphed.) It was Raleigh and Hamilton with pretensions, but it ran from June 1920 to April 1921 mostly on the strength of the Collins-inspired scenery and effects. His sandstorm which turned the front row of the stalls into serried ranks of flour-coated ghosts had even the on-stage camels turning their backs. Camels and Collins had triumphed over what the *Daily Telegraph* called 'a great deal of high-falutin [*sic*] twaddle. . . .' Even the pantomime had to make way for the camels, and only an extensive rebuilding of the auditorium which cost Butt and his colleagues some £150,000 brought the run to an end. It was not the final exit of Collins, for he collaborated on plays up until 1924, but it was something of an apotheosis.

The re-opening of the house in April 1922 was another excuse for the vast and the colourful. This time it was *Decameron Nights*, costing some £40,000 and featuring such Eastern delights as the Royal Hanging Gardens of Damascus and a multitude of palaces and piazzas. Unfortunately the improbable does not end there. The Lady Theodora, falsely accused of adultery (it was her own fault actually but stupidity not fornication led to the charge) is sentenced to be stripped in the public square of San Marco (perish the thought) and honour is preserved by the intervention, not of the hero, but, believe it or not, a total black-out caused by an eclipse of the sun. And very convenient too. At least it ran until 1923, a year otherwise notable for not very much.

Angelo, a romance based on the life of Hoffman, and *Ned Kean of Old Drury* about you know who, came and went more with a whimper than a bang, then *Good Luck* settled in for the autumn and ran until the following May. This had a car hold-up, a wreck at sea followed by a rescue by motor life-boat, and, racking the racing calendar for another equine attraction, the Royal Hunt Cup. It was the last Collins production and the only unpredictable element in the whole venture was that it was written by Seymour Hicks and Ian Hay.

It was the end of the partnership between the gregarious Arthur Collins and Sir Alfred Butt which had all the appearances of amicability. This is more than can be said for relations between Butt and the new appointee, Basil Dean.

CHAPTER THIRTEEN

Musicals and National Fervour

1924–39

THE contrast between Butt and Dean is perfectly demonstrated by the ways they interpreted the future role of the refurbished Drury Lane. Butt, as a business man, rightly saw that he had some 2,000-odd seats to be filled nightly or he would not remain a business man for long. If the purists disliked his offerings and the current public taste was bad, that was unfortunate but he did not see why he, any more than Harris or Collins, should be deterred from putting on what he thought would make money. Samuel Johnson was not alone in finding that the drama's laws the drama's patrons give.

Dean as first and foremost a man of the theatre wanted to look more to the history of the great house. He was conscious that he was a manager following in the footsteps of Cibber, Garrick and Sheridan. Because the house was sometimes still referred to as the home of the national drama, he wanted to translate that dream into a reality. If he could form a permanent company of actors with similar dedication to the cause, Drury Lane could become the national theatre.

A national theatre some forty years before it was established is an intriguing thought. That such a theatre, when it came in 1963, would be wholly dependent upon public funds, was anathema to Dean. When the *Illustrated London News* suggested that the government should subsidize a national theatre by buying Drury Lane, Dean was horrified.

'Heaven forbid—Government assistance means Government control, and that means control by a committee which is fatal to artistic success,' he said. He had what the *Evening Standard* called 'a tendency to regard the position of a theatrical manager as akin to that of a schoolmaster, and to dragoon the public with restrictions and admonitions'.

In June 1924 Dean produced *London Life* by Arnold Bennett and Edward Knoblock. The story, of a Five Towns solicitor who enters national politics, was decked out with some impressive scenery—the

Carlton Gardens ballroom and moonlight Scarlatti ballet in a millionaire's grounds included—but it lasted only 39 performances. 'A too thin slice of ham in an otherwise too thick sandwich' was how the *Tatler* put it.

Dean then went to America and the management resorted to another film—*The Thief of Bagdad* starring Douglas Fairbanks and Anna May Wong. When Dean returned, he launched a prestige production of *A Midsummer Night's Dream*. Athene Seyler played Hermia, Gwen Ffrangçon Davies was Titania and Edith Evans, Helena. To a certain extent he was beguiled by the effects possible with the Lane's sophisticated equipment. Consequently, not only was there Mendelssohn music and Fokine ballets, but also a Puck who shot many feet up in the air projected by a trapdoor. 'Scenic over-emphasis,' said *The Times* sourly. *The Dream* started on Boxing Day 1924 and ran until 7 March 1925. On 23 January Dean was claiming that the success of *The Dream* promised a new era of greatness at the Lane, and on 26 January his resignation was accepted.

Dean said that he had resigned because 'I heartily oppose the production of musical comedies at the Lane'. Sir Alfred could see no reason at all why a musical should not be given, and countered that 'since March the only play outside revivals of the classics which Mr Dean has submitted was *London Life* which resulted in appalling financial loss'. Dean replied, 'I am opposed to rank commercialism in the theatre', and pointed out that his *Midsummer Night's Dream* had been done 'only in the teeth of the fiercest opposition'.* Butt answered that Dean now offered nothing to keep the theatre open, and that the resort to *The Thief of Bagdad* had been due to Dean's absence in America.

Butt had logic on his side, however much one admires Dean's idealism. His turn to the musical was both timely and unerringly accurate as a reading of public taste. The idea which had been the final straw to Dean was to import an American musical called *Rose Marie*. Considering *The Belle of New York* had crossed the Atlantic in 1898, this was not a particularly novel idea. On the other hand, although Butt did not know it then, he was formulating a pattern which would serve the house at least as well as the Harris and Collins formula had before him. So successful, indeed, that it continues even today.

Rose Marie, with book and lyrics by Otto Harbach and Oscar Hammerstein II, and music by Friml and Stothart, had already proved its drawing power in New York in 1924. It suited London at least as well. Opening on 20 March 1925, it broke all the Lane's previous records by continuing

---

* In his autobiography *Seven Ages* (1970) Dean gave his account of these events and revealed that Butt demanded Dean's resignation before he would agree to the choice of *The Dream*.

Rose Marie, first of Drury Lane's American imports—the Totem Tom-Tom
dance led by Mira Nirska. *Mander and Mitchenson Collection*

until March 1927, an unprecedented 851 performances in all. It would
be nice to think that this was due to the quality of the work but once
one has granted it two intensely memorable and haunting melodies in
the title song and the 'Indian love call', one has said the lot.

The plot could be from any second-rate melodrama; and the characters
are pure cardboard cut-outs expected to sing, smile and register little
in the way of believable emotion. The humour rested mainly on the
shoulders of Billy Merson, the last of the old school music hall comedians,
and specifically on his personality rather than on any lines he was given
as Hard-boiled Herman. 'Why are you wearing spurs?' 'You never know
when you might meet a horse' is a fair sample.

More on the credit side, the American singer-actress Edith Day scored
a considerable personal success (and started another lasting tradition in
so doing) and the Totem Tom-Tom number with a chorus of redskin
totem girls collapsing in order like a pack of playing cards was cheered
nightly. Meanwhile, Britain, from King George V downwards, hummed
'When I'm calling you-oo-oo-oo, oo-oo-oo' and Butt smiled and sang
'Rose Marie, I love you' all the way to the bank.

Edith Day was back again in the next offering together with Harry
Welchman. 1927 was *The Desert Song* year. It lasted just over twelve
months and 432 performances. Composer Sigmund Romberg himself
conducted the first performance, but the work hardly represented an
artistic advance on either *Rose Marie* or *No, No, Nanette*, which had been
packing the Palace theatre.

The all-night queue which waited patiently outside the theatre to see the £25,000 production, responded rapturously to Romberg's melodies; marvelled at the spectacle of a column of troops marching over the desert; and politely suspended their disbelief in the schizophrenic son of the Governor of a French Moroccan province who, for reasons best known to himself, behaved like an idiot by day and transformed himself into a Riff leader, the Red Shadow, by night.

Because *Rose Marie* and *The Desert Song* represent such uneasy compromises between melodrama and operetta—the comedy in the latter is equally inept ('When I see a spy I want blood.' *Benjamin*. 'Don't look at me, I'm anaemic')—it is a relief to turn to the 3 May 1928 opening of Jerome Kern's *Show Boat*. Of course the book shows evidence of its times and modern revivals have found it necessary to excise lines like 'Gay looks a bit queer today', and discreetly lose 'niggers', but the frequency of contemporary references to 'coons', 'darkies' and 'touches of the tar-brush' show that the twenties sensibilities were not ours. Nevertheless, the heart of the show is in the right place, and it was the only musical before the thirties of which one can say that it tells a coherent story about recognizable people, and that the libretto is not just ineffectual and silly. *Show Boat* was in many ways a genuine breakthrough from both melodrama and cretinous sub-Viennese Prince Charmings.

It had songs which have remained standards, it had Edith Day, it had Paul Robeson to sing 'Old Man River', and it had a distinguished actor in Sir Cedric Hardwicke to clown remarkably effectively as Captain Andy, master of the *Cotton Blossom*. He recorded in his memoirs much later that he himself had serious doubts:

> When the script arrived, my heart sunk like a plumb-line. My part seemed to consist of one line of dialogue to fifty of business. . . . It was unthinkable that anybody in the audience would detect an ounce of humour in my lines, when most of what I had to say was completely pointless to me.

We should not let Sir Cedric's tongue-in-cheek humour (he once said of London's capacity to survive the Blitz that 'anyone who could survive British weather and the British pantomime could endure anything') disguise the fact that he brought the house down nightly. Despite some trials and tribulations at the dress rehearsal when a large troupe of coloured girls engaged especially for authenticity turned up in white make-up, and despite a legal dispute about Paul Robeson's services, *Show Boat* was a hit, a hit seen by 20,000 people a week.

Jerome Kern's *Show Boat* in 1928—the show within the show on the stage of the *Cotton Blossom. Mander and Mitchenson Collection*

Butt was able to conduct the September Annual General Meeting and announce that the success of his musicals had enabled the management to pay out over a million pounds to artists, authors and musicians, give the government £217,000 in entertainment tax and still make a large profit.

Unfortunately, the artistic advance of *Show Boat* was not consolidated by its successors. In April 1929 *The New Moon*, an unlikely series of happenings in late eighteenth century New Orleans, brought Evelyn Laye 'torrents of applause', according to the *Daily Mail*, but for all the popularity of Romberg's 'Softly as in a morning sunrise' and 'Lover come back to me', not even a sea fight and a blazing pirate ship could draw enough people to the theatre. A few months later, *The New Moon* finally waned and was replaced by a special twelve week revival of *Rose Marie*.

The closure of *New Moon* had an added significance if we remember that talking pictures were looming large on the horizon. With *The Jazz Singer* (1927) and its successors, the last advantage the theatre held over its youthful rival had vanished. It was not that *The New Moon* had been doing bad business. Butt was quoted as saying:

The New Moon is playing to what is probably the second best theatre business in London—more than £4,000 a week in box office receipts—but the profits do not justify us in keeping it on. It is not sufficient to make only two hundred and something pounds a week out of a theatre such as Drury Lane.

The fact was that Butt was already beginning to have doubts about the capacity of stage musicals to compete with imports from Hollywood. He may have been a Member of Parliament, and the controller of seven London theatres and thirty-eight music halls all at the same time, but he was well aware of what was happening outside his own particular fields.

For the moment, however, he continued with the musical. 1930 saw *The Three Musketeers* with music by Friml and some all-action sword play that cost Jerry Verno a double dislocation in a dive through a door followed by a tumble down a flight of steps. The following year it was a British musical by Vivian Ellis and Herman Finck, *The Song of the Drum*, with £35,000 worth of Himalayan scenery, Indian bazaars, and even a live dromedary with velvet hoofs (or maybe it was a camel). The fortunes of hero Derek Oldham and heroine Helen Gilliland in British-ruled Huzbaria stretched credulity. One critic outlined the plot thus:

An Anglo-Indian young woman with a diamanté corsage, confessing sojourn in a scoundrel's bedroom to save her pukka lover from being shot as a spy while forty subalterns stand aghast in scarlet regimentals . . . the half-time curtain descended at this point, after which the play degenerated into a fusion of 'Chu Chin Chow' and 'The Green Goddess'.

The two musicals cost the management a loss of nearly £20,000 which suited Butt not at all. On 15 April 1931, he called a special board meeting, resigned and walked out of the theatre. 'I feel very strongly that huge musical plays . . . can no longer compete successfully with the talkies,' he said. In fact he was wrong but we have the advantage of hindsight. Butt did not.

His successor was George Grossmith. Grossmith was not prepared to surrender so easily to the talkies. He announced that he had no objection to using films as fillers, but the musical would continue where possible. Despite the brave words he himself left the next year. But not before London had suffered another musical with a libretto that was a minor masterpiece of banality.

On 8 May the curtain rose on the doings of Prince Sou Chong in

The Land of Smiles. Soothed by the Lehar music, the audience survived the soporific effects of such masterly lyrics as the duet between Sou Chong and Lisa:

Lisa   There's nothing nicer than a cup of China tea!
            And that's a point which, I'm sure, we both agree.
Sou Chong All kinds of tea I might agree to rave about
            If I but knew that I had you to pour it out.

The inanity was irrelevant, what the audience had come to see and hear was Richard Tauber. Reportedly engaged at £1,500 a week, this outstandingly sweet-toned and immaculate tenor had arrived, sporting a large hat and a monocle, to a fanfare of publicity more commonly associated with post-war stars. He sang part of his music in German, and acted in a charmingly broken English. When he proposed to his wife he said, 'I send other women away; finish other women. I buy you mink coat, yes?' His speech on stage was not dissimilar.

Not long after the show opened, he took a short vocal rest in Bavaria and returned in June to even more rapturous acclaim. With him, he brought Lehàr himself who duly conducted three nights of the subsequent weeks. The first night of his return, he had to sing 'You are my heart's delight' six times before the show could continue, and took sixteen curtain calls at the end of the performance. It was, the *Daily Mail* said, 'the greatest personal triumph since Chaliapin'.

So gratifying a reception has some significance in the later years of Drury Lane for it was the first time that the publicity media were used to sell not a show, but a star. One wonders if anyone drew the meaningful conclusion at the time that this was as effective a way as any of filling a vast theatre. The shows over the next few years make one doubt it.

In 1934 came *The Three Sisters*, a Kern and Hammerstein offering that had nothing to do with Chekhov, and despite the presence of Albert Burdon and Stanley Holloway, not much to do with entertainment either. James Agate despairingly asked 'how long Drury Lane is to be the asylum for American inanity?' and to prove the question was not meant rhetorically, he answered it himself—'For ever, dear heart!'

Before that, in 1932, it was *Wild Violets*, an Edwardian fashion parade with music by Robert Stolz and such novelties as plush covered scenery at director Hassard Short's behest, and a chorus mounted on bicycles. And in 1933 it was a Paul Abraham and Oscar Hammerstein offering, *Ball at the Savoy*. With more than a token nod towards *Die Fledermaus* for the plot, and lines like 'I am engaged to marry Mister Mustapha Bei;

he's a Turk, but I'll cure him of that', the ball was soon over. *Wild Violets* saw the exit of George Grossmith when the musical took precedence with the board over a play based on Clive of India which he had wanted to do in its place.

The early thirties had one great success, but the reasons for that lie outside the world of theatre, and beyond the control of any management. It came from a partnership between two of the most striking names in the theatre—Noël Coward and C. B. Cochran. The author, who had shocked West End audiences with *The Vortex*, and sparked them to gales of laughter with comedies like *Hay Fever*, had a yen to stage something on the grand scale. The impresario, Cochran, was a man who understood the grand scale. The son of a Brighton tea-merchant, he had in his time promoted championship professional boxing, Wembley rodeos and Hackenschmidt the wrestler. Coward had a measure of admiration for Cochran's talents. He once said of him and his mania for stage accuracy:

> . . . even if you saw in a Cochran production, a black man dressed in a Highland kilt in a canoe on the Ganges, there would be some very good reason for it.

Before the project had reached even the early stages, Cochran tried to book the Coliseum, but the persistence of *White Horse Inn* stalled him. Instead he booked Drury Lane. The ball was in Coward's court. The writer had been lacking inspiration, but a casual browse through old bound volumes of the *Illustrated London News*, and a glimpse of a photograph of a troop ship departing for the Boer War, stirred his muse from her lethargy. Cochran received a 300-word telegram from America outlining the massive demands Coward would be making on the unparalleled Drury Lane mechanical resources. The idea was no less than a grandiose twenty-two scene epic of thirty years of British history. Undeterred, Cochran began to organize giant liners, troop ships, dockyards, beaches, Victoria Station and Trafalgar Square.

When Coward returned, there was friction between them. A show which gave employment to over 400 actors in 1931, when unemployment was soaring to record heights, drew 'resting' actors like a magnet. Coward had the depressing role of choosing the lucky 400 from over a thousand applicants. They got only 30s a week even then, for although Cochran was always able to offer a grossly inflated salary to a big name, he had very much a take-it-or-leave-it attitude to spear-carriers. When he tactlessly gave three society girls walk-on parts, Coward exploded. He threatened to walk out unless there were two needy girls employed for every one of Cochran's débutantes. Cochran conceded but relations between them were never as cordial again.

Controlling the vast cast superbly as director, Coward brought the original concept to fruition—*Cavalcade* was born. Where he was so fortunate was that his ultra-jingoistic pageant coincided perfectly with the almost hysterical burst of patriotism that swept a Conservative-loaded National Government to an unprecedented General Election victory two weeks after the opening night. Drury Lane became temporarily the home not of a theatrical experience but a focusing point of the nation's traumas. The *Morning Post*'s account of the performance on Election Night when the King and Queen came to see the play gives some idea of the contemporary mood:

. . . there was last night an outburst of loyalty, a welling up of love for England and faith in English destiny such as has rarely moved and quickened the heart of London since the war . . . this pageant of the nation's soul and history, stirred and roused the immense audience to intimate and deep emotion. 'England yet shall stand'—that is the message of 'Cavalcade' and the message of that vaster drama which England has put before the whole world in these last two days.

Scene 2 of *Cavalcade*—Saturday January 29, 1900. Accompanied by a band playing *Soldiers of the Queen*, the troopship leaves for the Boer War. *Mander and Mitchenson Collection*

Cavalcade's closing speech, which ends '. . . and let's drink to the hope that one day this country of ours, which we love so much, will find dignity and greatness and peace again', fading to the chaos of 'Twentieth century blues', only to be superseded by the entire company beneath a Union Jack singing the National Anthem, brought audiences to their feet cheering for the next eleven months. Coward himself closed the proceedings at the first night with a famous curtain speech: 'I hope that this play has made us feel that despite our national troubles it is still a pretty exciting thing to be English.'

With the benefit of hindsight we can see that what brought 2,600 people to their feet nine times a week for nearly a year was the opportunity to cheer not Coward or *Cavalcade* but their projected and idealized picture of themselves. Meanwhile, the *Daily Mail* increased its circulation by serializing *Cavalcade*, and the original £30,000 invested recouped £300,000. *Cavalcade* was a unique phenomenon but no one who has read this far of Drury Lane's glorious theatrical past will be tempted to concur with A. E. Wilson of the *Star* who concluded '. . . this is the best Drury Lane drama ever'.

When the success of *Cavalcade* had been followed by the musical disasters of the next few years, and George Grossmith had been succeeded by a new General Manager, H. M. Tennent, the old problem of filling the house reared its ugly head yet again. As a stop gap, Tennent got Julian Wylie to stage a pantomime, *Cinderella*, and, although Wylie died before the opening performance in December 1934, Phyllis Neilson-Terry as Prince Charming, aided and abetted by Billy Danvers, Dan Leno Jnr, Ethel Revnell and Gracie West for comedy, and some Collins-style scenery and effects—bathing belles in the enchanted lake included—kept the house open until the spring of 1935. It still lost money and the problem was to find an adequate and financially successful replacement.

The answer came from a surprising quarter—the lunch table of the Ivy Restaurant. Tennent was lunching with the matinée idol of the day, the immensely successful Ivor Novello. On impulse, after hearing Tennent's catalogue of woes about the temporary drying up of the American source of musicals, Novello proffered the information that he himself had an idea for a musical. Tennent, clutching at straws over his coffee, asked him to outline it. After a deep breath, Novello launched himself on to an *extempore* outline of a handsome hero involved in a Ruritanian mish-mash of blazing liners, gypsy weddings and world-shaking inventions. Carried away by his own impudence, he made it sound sufficiently plausible to interest Tennent, who asked if he could submit a synopsis to the board next day for their approval. With discreet

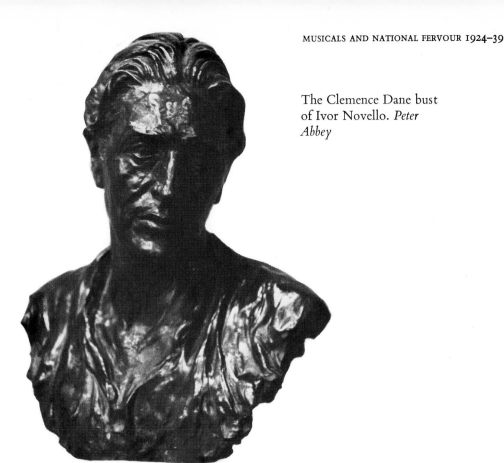

The Clemence Dane bust of Ivor Novello. *Peter Abbey*

changes and developments, Novello handed in next day a story outline on the basis of what he had already said. It was approved and duly became *Glamorous Night*.

Honesty would compel me to say that the plot of *Glamorous Night* sounds remarkably like a story made up over coffee and brandy at the end of a heavy meal, if it were not for the fact that all Novello librettos, even those conjured in less fraught circumstances, follow a broadly similar pattern. As if *Show Boat* had never been, plastic heroes and heroines conduct romances with varying degrees of success in some sub-Ruritanian kingdom or other—Krasnia in the case of *Glamorous Night* where the handsome young Englishman Anthony Allen is decorated for his services with the Most Noble Order of Saint Michael (regrettably the programme does not carry a credit for Ribbons by Marks and Spencer). The *Tatler* sarcastically suggested the liner sunk in *Glamorous Night* must have struck something; 'possibly a small musical-comedy land that has broken loose from the mainland'.

How do we explain that such meanderings in never-never lands as

Glamorous Night and its three successors kept Drury Lane open and prosperous from 1935 to the outbreak of war in 1939? Firstly, Novello was able carefully to tailor his romances to the genteel escapist taste of a middle-class audience trying to ignore Hitler in the hope that he would go away. One can mock the undiluted sentiment, and say, as does Ernest Short, that 'seldom has so slender a vein of artistry produced financial rewards so generous', but inescapably one comes back to the fact that he provided a fodder for which an enormous number of people were hungry.

Secondly, what would be galling in a cynical exploitation of people's emotions, cheap or superficial as they may be, is less so when the perpetrator so manifestly believes it all himself. As Ivor Brown said of *Glamorous Night*, 'I lift my hat to Mr Novello. He can wade through tosh with the straightest face; the tongue never visibly approaches the cheek.' This is an important point. In return for sincerity, one can forgive a great deal.

Speaking on the radio in 1950 about *King's Rhapsody*, although the

Novello in *Glamorous Night*, one of the four musical plays at Drury Lane in which he starred in the triple capacity of actor, writer and composer. *Enthoven Collection*

point could apply to any of the Novello Drury Lane shows, Philip Hope-Wallace put his finger on it precisely:

... merely as a musical play is it good? Has it wit, pithiness, originality, suspense and drive? I think the answer has to be 'No' in each case. But with triumphant assurance it does what it sets out to do—that is to tell a Ruritanian taradiddle with handsome emotion. Now the point is this: I believe it suceeeds because Ivor Novello is completely sincere. No tongue in the cheek about it. He really believes in this romantic tushery. And so as when somebody believes in Cinderella or in fairies, it all comes to life ... a master of the shameless cliché.

Whatever hopes the management held that Novello would prove to be the answer to their dreams in his triple capacities of author, composer and actor, they had already committed themselves to the insurance policy of a pantomime at the end of the year. Consequently, to the rage of

Anthony Tudor's ballet for Novello's *Careless Rapture* with the writer and Dorothy Dickson held aloft. *Mander and Mitchenson Collection*

Novello, *Glamorous Night* doing capacity business had to close, and his leading lady Mary Ellis returned to America. He offered to guarantee £8,000 of his own money to keep his show open, but *Jack and the Beanstalk* slew the Giant and Novello's hopes simultaneously.

As a springtime successor to the panto, Novello submitted another synopsis for a play called *Careless Rapture*. With a unique capacity for looking a gift horse in the mouth and staring it out, the management, despite pleadings from Tennent, turned it down. Instead they raised the curtain on 7 May 1936 to show Binnie Hale in *Rise and Shine*, a Robert Stolz musical produced by Ralph Reader. The show, which cost £15,000, shone wanly and disappeared behind a cloud after five and a half weeks. With almost sickening irony, one of the tunes was called 'I'm building up to an awful let-down' (with music by, surprisingly enough, Fred Astaire) and the whole show was set in Moronia (*sic*).

In desperation, the management turned to Novello to resuscitate *Careless Rapture*. He was now in a powerful position to negotiate and he took advantage of the fact to get complete artistic control, a guarantee that no pantomime would interfere with a successful run and that in return for supplying 75% of the money, he would get 75% of the profits. Then, and only then, did he start to prepare for a September opening. To allay any fears he may have had, the ticket agencies reached agreement on a deal that guaranteed £100,000 and a nine month run.

Careless Rapture was captured by J. C. Trewin in a sentence:

> Dorothy Dickson was leading lady and the night managed to get in Hampstead Heath on August Bank Holiday, an earthquake in a Chinese city at the Feast of the Moon, a Temple Ballet, and an all-white wedding finale.

It was another bedtime fairy story to lull his public gently into dreamland and was, predictably, a smash hit. Novello himself decided against singing, which was perhaps just as well, but in addition to treating the audience to a feast of the theatre's most handsome profile, he did ballet dance after a fashion, and somehow carried off a costume that looked suspiciously like hot pants and wellington boots. Unlike *Glamorous Night*, the ending was happy, which should have pleased King George V, who had praised the actor-writer-composer's previous show but told Novello that the closing scene had made the Queen cry. Happy Endings by Appointment?

At last realizing what a goldmine they had on their hands, the management asked for another, and from 1 September 1937 to 21 February

1938 both they and Novello rode on the *Crest of the Wave*. Not much changed. Dorothy Dickson was back, the earthquake became a train-smash and Novello played two parts instead of one—the noble Duke of Cheviot and the sulky foreign film star Otto Fresch. The Duke duly retrieved the family's fortunes by the sweat of his profile, as one wag put it, and the film star confirmed all current prejudices of Latin fits of temperament.

The boldest line in the evening came from a duchess:

Miss Winter, there are some kennels at Gantry. They used to be full of lady dogs, I was just wondering if you are looking for somewhere to live.

But the Lord Chamberlain raised no objection. Novello, whose extraordinary persona brought *5,000* good luck telegrams on the opening night, had done it again. Or as Ivor Brown thought:

One staggers out sated and a trifle stunned, observing with a bloated species of relief, as one does at the end of a long Christmas dinner with the family, that this occasion is over for another year.

In fact it was over for another two.

June 1938 provided a break from a continuous diet of Novello when *The Sun Never Sets* was launched. Based on Edgar Wallace's famous character Sanders of the River, it was originally designed as a vehicle for Paul Robeson. Unfortunately they could not get Paul Robeson, and the vehicle lurched on to the stage without its driver. That it was a pure resuscitation of the sort of melodrama that Harris would have loved, became glaringly obvious.

Steamboats puffed, aeroplanes flew, temples burst their walls, wicked natives pranced and good natives sang. Hero Leslie Banks sported a cigarette holder with British phlegm as heroine Edna Best escaped narrowly from fates infinitely worse than death. James Agate said, in a phrase that deserved to join any anthology of theatrical *bons mots*, that it was about 'masterful subalterns shooting rude natives spitting where they should have polished'. The play ended with the cast (including Stewart Granger in his first appearance and in training for similar corn to come in his film career), standing to attention in an African outpost listening to the King's Christmas Day message on the radio. (The King was played on a record by the King.)

Relief came in July with a season by the Ballets Russes de Monte Carlo and Léonide Massine. *Noblissima Visione*, a St Francis of Assisi ballet to music by Hindemith, who himself conducted, got its world première; and Alicia Markova and Serge Lifar danced in *Giselle*.

At about this time, Novello for the first time lost his unerring instinct for giving the public what it wanted. Beguiled by a brief appearance as Romeo in the balcony scene at a charity matinée some years before, he was determined to prove that in addition to his other talents, he could be a classical actor. A production financed by Novello himself and Tom Arnold was announced for 16 September 1938: Shakespeare's *Henry V* at Drury Lane. Lewis Casson was called in to mount a spectacular production with gleaming armour and tumultuous clashes of arms.

Within this brightest heaven of invention, Henry the lover wooing Dorothy Dickson as Katharine was predictably effective, but the warlike Henry of the patriotic speeches, alas, was beyond Novello. His voice was too light and he lacked the inner fire. The self-indulgence also cost him a great deal of money for the brief run was, as he described it later, 'a financial disaster'. In fairness, one must concede that it was not entirely his fault. What did a nation cheering Chamberlain's useless scrap of Munich stationery want of a King who urged them to stiffen their sinews and summon up their blood?

Babes in the Wood at Christmas 1938 was the last ever Drury Lane pantomime. It had Fay Compton as Robin Hood, and the whole caboodle of flying ballets and Dresden China spectacles, but it was more of a variety show than a pantomime. One six-year-old child in the audience liked the slapstick—'the best bit of all was when they were throwing the dough about'. The six-year-old grew up to be Senator Edward Kennedy.

Novello regained his magic touch in March 1939. For the fourth time in succession he wrote, composed, and starred in, a Drury Lane musical play. His lyric writer, Christopher Hassall, who had performed the same service for the previous three, worked with his customary despatch—Novello once asked when he was going to get a lyric not covered in tea and Guinness—and *The Dancing Years* was ready. Novello, in leather shorts and Edelweiss braces, played Rudi Kleber, the penniless young composer; Mary Ellis played Maria Zeigler, the Viennese opera star who falls heavily for Rudi and his latest waltz alike; and petite Roma Beaumont played the young girl who loved Rudi for himself. For a touch of topical authenticity, some inefficient Nazis made their appearance but were waltzed to defeat. Unfortunately, in real life, they were less easily deterred.

CHAPTER FOURTEEN

Shows and Stars

1939–71

ON 1 September 1939, the Drury Lane curtain descended on *The Dancing Years* for the last time. There were few people in the house and the total takings for the night were £35. War with Germany was declared on the 3rd and that brought the compulsory closing of cinemas and theatres. So successfully had Novello·captured contemporary taste that the show itself went on tour throughout the country, returned to a blitzed London at the Adelphi later, and then toured again.

A week after the outbreak of war, the theatre had become the headquarters of the Entertainment National Service Association (ENSA) under Sir Seymour Hicks and Basil Dean. The building was bombed more than once during the Blitz but it survived and provided a base for operations that took morale-lifting shows to troops at home and abroad. Drury Lane resumed its functions as a commercial theatre only in December 1946 under the continuing chairmanship of Prince Littler, one of the most powerful men in the entertainment industry.

Hopes were high. A nation starved of theatre for seven years would surely respond to a new show, and one written by Noël Coward at that. This was the ill-fated *Pacific 1860* which was set on the Island of Samolo in the South Pacific. The programme carried a long note explaining Samolo to the audience, but if they grasped the geography, they did not care for the plot. 'Sounds the lower depths of banality,' said *The Times*, finding its 'pseudo-Viennese sentimentalities in waltz-time' worthy of neither author nor house. Even an orchestra playing under Mantovani and a new American star in Mary Martin, who had burst into fame in 1938 with her singing of 'My heart belongs to Daddy' in *Leave it to me*, could do nothing to save the play which finally surrendered, as the nation shivered in the middle of the infamous 1947 fuel crisis. 'This is a changing world' proclaimed one of the songs; the pity was that Coward had not recognized what the changes were.

Oklahoma—Curly (Howard, then Harold, Keel) suggests a future for 'Pore Jud' (Henry Clarke) in the smoke-house. *Angus McBean photograph: Harvard Theatre Collection*

To do full justice to the next major event at the Lane, let us set it into perspective. Because of the startling changes in British society in the fifties and sixties, it is difficult now to recapture the immediate post-war atmosphere. Queues, rationing, austerity, shortage and all the other depressing facets of that drab age seem almost as remote to us as the age of Garrick. It takes a conscious effort to remember that we are talking of a time when television was a rich man's toy, long-playing records a transatlantic pipe-dream, and a visit to a London West End theatre a once-in-a-lifetime experience for the mass of the provincial population. Only against this grey and drab background can one see the full impact of the American musical that burst upon the London scene in April 1947.

Suddenly, with Rodgers and Hammerstein's *Oklahoma*, there was, for the first time in years, life, colour, action and vitality. And I do not think it would be too fanciful to say that the birth of the state of Oklahoma in the story succeeded in reviving the inarticulate hopes of people in this country for a new and exciting post-war Britain. Not all the optimism

which had put a Labour Government in power in 1945 had foundered on
the rock of disillusion by 1947.

In many ways, *Oklahoma* was genuinely new. The lyrics had fresh
arresting images—'the corn is as high as an elephant's eye' has the im-
mediacy and appeal of genuinely popular poetry. Gone was the stock
opening chorus and in its place was a striking solo for the male lead—
'O, what a beautiful morning'. The humour came not from an amiable
buffoon stumbling in and out of the plot, but from the mouths of the
protagonists themselves—suddenly they had become people. Instead of
a stock melodrama villain, there was Jud Fry, pathological perhaps but
curiously human and pathetic.

There was an abundance of good songs but they grew out of the
situation, or illustrated a character's thoughts in a self-communicating
soliloquy. The most striking aspect is that one cannot imagine a song from
Oklahoma transposed to, say, *South Pacific* or *The King and I*. (On the
other hand, did Novello's song 'If this were love' come from *Glamorous
Night*, *Crest of the Wave* or *Careless Rapture*?★) And there was the dancing
—choreography which genuinely furthered and pointed the story.

The first night had to be a triumph. The critical reception was enthusiastic—J. C. Trewin in the *Observer* hailed:

> . . . a musical play without the lumber, one that—for a miracle—has
> been conceived as a unity . . . the sunrise score that dawns so freshly
> after the stuffy night of the mammoth musical.

and Lionel Hale in the *Daily Mail* thought:

> . . . it is colour, plus music, plus wit, plus dancing put together with
> a sort of inspired single-mindedness to recreate on stage the young
> people of a youthful part of the earth.

The effect of unity had been achieved by the three main creators of the
show, Rodgers, Hammerstein and choreographer Agnes de Mille, working
as a team from the outset. As a result they were the first to bring drama,
music and dance together in a satisfying mould. The effort had been
worthwhile. The £42,740 it cost to put on dwindled in comparison
with the takings—£220,000 by November—and the subsequent profits
£1,583,000 excluding the film rights.

If you think I am overstating the impact of *Oklahoma*, consider the

★ From *King's Rhapsody* actually but you see what I mean?

evidence of Beverley Baxter, the Conservative M.P. Looking back in 1950, he wrote:

> As a fairly hardened critic I must confess that it was one of the most emotional evenings I ever experienced in the theatre. You must remember how weary and disillusioned we were at the time. We had passed from the war of the scorched earth to a parched peace. We were under-nourished, over-taxed, ill-clad, badgered and bothered by endless regulations; and we were tired. Then suddenly on the stage we saw vibrant youth, and felt the thrill of open plains. From our old-world garden of England we watched the tempestuous birth of a state. . . .

Oscar Hammerstein must have been particularly gratified. Once told by Mae West to 'get out of the theatre . . . you got too much class', he had five flops in a row before *Oklahoma*. After its original success in America, he took a full page advertisement in *Variety* listing the unhappy five and adding the slogan 'I've done it before and I can do it again!'

Oklahoma was not a show dependent upon stars, although one must mention Harold Keel as Curly. The programme was not inaccurate—he used the now so familiar *Howard* Keel only later. It left Drury Lane to make way for *Carousel* from the same stable in 1950, and even then it got another six months' life at the Stoll theatre before finally closing on 21 October 1950. (During its run, it is pleasant to record that the 83-year-old Richard Strauss attended an October 1947 Sunday concert of his own music conducted by Sir Thomas Beecham at the Lane.)

The four musicals from Rodgers and Hammerstein which occupied the Lane from 1947 until 1956 were superior examples of the *genre*. None of the three successors to *Oklahoma* were quite as artistically successful, but they had compensating virtues of their own. *Carousel* had a host of good songs—'June is bustin' out all over', 'When the children are asleep', 'When I marry Mr Snow', 'If I loved you', and 'You'll never walk alone' among them—and a hero in Billy Bigelow (played by Stephen Douglass) who was considerably less than shining-white. With his death and redemption 'Up there', the borderline to the maudlin was dangerously skirted but within the limits of fantasy was acceptable. Curiously enough, Molnar's *Liliom*, the starting point of Hammerstein's book, had failed in London despite Fay Compton, Ivor Novello and Charles Laughton. *Carousel* ran for sixteen months and coined £327,685.

On 1 November 1951 *Carousel* was succeeded by *South Pacific*. Based on two of James Michener's *Tales of the South Pacific*, it had no fantasy

Carousel—the Rodgers and Hammerstein adaptation of *Liliom* which succeeded *Oklahoma* at Drury Lane in 1950. *Mander and Mitchenson Collection*

Mary Martin as Ensign Nellie Forbush in *South Pacific*, the third of the four Rodgers and Hammerstein musicals to sustain Drury Lane from 1947 until 1956. *Angus McBean photograph: Harvard Theatre Collection*

element at all; some memorable songs—'Some enchanted evening', 'Bali Hai', 'I'm gonna wash that man right out of my hair' and 'There is nothing like a dame' included—and most important of all, it had a recognizable star. It was the return of Mary Martin, who, undaunted by her previous sojourn in the South Seas with Mr Coward, was back to play Ensign Nellie Forbush.

For the first time since the arrival of Tauber, there was a surge of pre-publicity for the show and particularly for her. Some critics reacted with hostility to what they saw as an attempt to form their opinions for them. 'South Soporific between songs' said one, but most had to concede some merit to the work. With Wilbur Evans as Emile and Muriel Smith as Bloody Mary, one could hardly dismiss the show as merely a star vehicle. Star vehicles were to come later.

South Pacific got 792 performances, took £743,202 at the box-office windows, and for those who collect bizarre statistics, Mary Martin, in America and Britain, washed her hair over 3,000 times without ever getting Emile out. Her exertions in the cause of health and beauty brought her an undeniably justified rapturous reception. Her less than classical features moved Harold Hobson to quote Bacon:

> . . . there is no excellent beauty without some strangeness in the proportion . . . perhaps there should also be some proportion in the strangeness. The proportion in Miss Martin's strangeness could not be finer, and it gave her . . . that rare, that heart-warming thing, an immense personal triumph.

I hope she took it as a compliment. On her return to America before the end of the run, she was replaced by Julie Wilson.

For the next Rodgers and Hammerstein transfer, *The King and I*, it was rumoured that Gertrude Lawrence would repeat her New York performance in London. Instead Anna Leonowens was given to an English actress Valerie Hobson, who scored a gratifyingly huge success at a theatre where she had once been romantically enough an unknown extra. The King of Siam, the arrogant monarch unable for three-quarters of the story to see the patently obvious attractions of Miss Hobson's governess, was played by Herbert Lom. Directed by John van Druten, better known perhaps as a playwright, the two of them brought the show to life and, despite sarcastic references to Drury Lane as the forty-ninth State of the U.S.A., proved that Britain too had something to offer.

The show did not suit everybody. The *Daily Express* thought it a 'treacle-bin *Mikado*' and it sent Gilbert Harding to sleep. His contribution did not end there. An angry letter in the *Evening Standard* next day complained that he 'snored and snored throughout the whole of the first act . . . making the most disgusting noises in the most objectionable manner'. I doubt that he meant it as a critical comment. The songs alone should have kept an auditor awake. 'Hello, young lovers', 'I whistle a happy tune', 'We kiss in a shadow', 'Something wonderful' and 'Shall we dance?' are small masterpieces of their kind, and kept the show going until January 1956.

It provoked correspondence in *The Times* about the inaccuracy of the story with regard to the original King Mongkut. Apparently he signed his nineteenth century treaties before Anna Leonowens ever arrived in Siam. Personally I prefer the Hammerstein version, but everyone to their taste.

No one would have felt like writing to *The Times* about the authenticity or otherwise of *Plain and Fancy* which eventually replaced *The King and I* at Drury Lane. It lacked the magic of Rodgers and Hammerstein and was, said the *Sunday Express*, 'as musical as a yawn and laced with a morphia-like charm', a charm which for J. C. Trewin and others soon wore off. The book by Joseph Stein and Will Glickman started with the promise of a setting in Bird-in-Hand in the Amish country of Pennsylvania. Bird-in-Hand, I am reliably informed, is half-way between two other townships—Intercourse and Paradise. The impact made on the local inhabitants, followers of Jacob Amman, Mennonite Bishop of Switzerland, by two visiting New Yorkers, gave rise to one memorable song 'Young and foolish' but the rest has disappeared into oblivion, the very state from which I must temporarily rescue the other 1956 Drury Lane musical *Fanny*. As a sidelight on the economics of failure, *Plain and Fancy* lost £40,215 and there was no Drury Lane dividend in 1956, but it was kept going for eight months because it would have been more expensive to take it off!

Based on the Marcel Pagnol trilogy and set in Marseilles, *Fanny* deals with Panisse who desperately wants to be a father. It lasted until August 1957, presumably because the novelty of Robert Morley as Panisse singing for the first time in his twenty-eight years on the stage, and a genuine singer in Ian Wallace, counter-balanced the defects catalogued by the *Sunday Express* as 'indifferent music, indifferent acting and the sticky gloss of American sentimentality'.

What the Lane and its public were waiting for was an opportunity to judge for themselves the musical which had taken New York by storm in 1956, Lerner and Loewe's *My Fair Lady*. They had to be patient. The rest of 1957 was occupied with brief seasons by the Formosan Chinese

Julie Andrews and Rex Harrison (centre) in *Pygmalion* Lerner and Loewe style. Oliver Smith's set and Cecil Beaton's costumes for the Ascot scene in *My Fair Lady. Sir Cecil Beaton*

Classical Theatre, Inbal—the National Ballet and Dance Theatre of Israel—and the Urals Ensemble, who sang that well known Russian ballad 'On Ilkley Moor baht at'.

In December, for a seven week season, Peter Brook's Stratford production of *The Tempest* arrived with John Gielgud as Prospero, Alec Clunes as Caliban, Richard Johnson as Ferdinand and Patrick Wymark as Stephano. This delighted Londoners unable to travel to Stratford, pleased those with a sense of history as the first *Tempest* at the Lane since Macready and Helen Faucit, and annoyed Peter Brook who claimed that his actors were being used as guinea pigs for the lighting equipment installed ready for *My Fair Lady*.

Another filler, a relatively undistinguished Italian opera season, lasted the first three months of 1958 and at last, on 30 April, *My Fair Lady* was on show; that is, if one could get tickets. Fantastic stories of the New York shortage of tickets, snobs hovering like vultures outside the theatre waiting to pick up stubs to lend authenticity to their claims to have seen the show, began to look credible.

Stanley Holloway had a nice story in the same vein. At an American performance, with the house packed to the rafters, an attractive middle-aged lady had a seat vacant at her side. Someone asked her why. She told them she was a recent widow and that she had planned to come with her husband. The questioner sympathized, but said surely she could have found an escort for the most popular show in history. 'Normally, yes,' she said, 'but they're all at the funeral!'

Did the show itself live up to the promise of a boom in fashion, acres of newspaper space and the ten million dollars it made in the U.S. in the first two years? I suppose the answer has to be yes. Shaw's *Pygmalion*, whatever he might have thought about the process, did provide the starting point for a musical that had a fine score, plenty of wit and a coherent unity. One may regret the absence of Shaw's most famous exit line which was bowdlerized to 'move your ruddy arse', but enough remained to justify its popularity.

Dressed in Cecil Beaton's elegant costumes, its three stars, Julie Andrews, Rex Harrison and Stanley Holloway repeated the performances that they had given in New York to even more rapturous applause. Julie Andrews struggled with the difficulty of reproducing an authentic Cockney accent before a London audience, or as Kenneth Tynan said at the time, 'nothing in Julie Andrews's cockney became her like the leaving it . . . she blossoms once she has shed her fraudulent accent'. Stanley Holloway stopped the show with his 'Get me to the church on time', and Rex Harrison found a *Sprechgesang* of his own invention to bring Higgins's music within his compass. Despite the rumours of Harrison's 'tremendous rages and stalkings off during rehearsals' as *John Bull* put it, and that he was never bosom friends with the other two, enough genuine warmth came over the footlights to keep the show going (with, if only for the sake of their own sanity, cast changes) for a phenomenal five and a half years and 2,281 performances. In August 1961, it passed *Oklahoma*'s previous record of 1,375 performances. In November 1961, the film rights were sold for nearly two million pounds. In May 1963, it was given a special Gala performance to celebrate the tercentenary of the theatre itself, and it finally closed on 19 October 1963. It was, one might say, something of a hit.

Hoping that Lerner and Loewe could take up where they had just left off, *Camelot*, which had Richard Burton and Julie Andrews in its American cast, was originally scheduled to replace *My Fair Lady*. It was not ready and was postponed for a year. In its place a Rodgers and Hart show of 1938, *The Boys from Syracuse*, was given a revival, or in the words of *The Times* 'less a revival than an exhumation'. After Shakespeare's *Comedy of Errors*, and so far after that the programme omitted to mention the fact, it was less than kindly treated. Other critics reached for their hatchets, Bernard Levin for his sickle.

> What finally scuttles the whole enterprise is the production, the loudest, crudest, hammiest parade of mugging, grimacing, camping, nudging, yelling and falling down (with, in the manner of Mr Charlie Drake, a crash on the cymbals as buttocks meet floor) that has been seen at Drury Lane since Sweet Nell was an orange-seller.

The Queen notice began, 'To speak first of the living dead . . .', and the *Sunday Times* weighed in with '. . . endless banality, the infantile stupidity of the interminable series of sexual jokes which it lamely and pathetically parades before the audience'. One anonymous exchange in the stalls at the end of the first night bears repetition. 'What an attractive curtain.' 'Yes, and so welcome!' For the record, I cannot spare their blushes by failing to mention that the principals were Bob Monkhouse as Antipholus of Syracuse, Denis Quilley as Antipholus of Ephesus, and Maggie Fitzgibbon as Luce.

The resounding failure of *The Boys from Syracuse* left an empty theatre with *Camelot* still hanging fire. Three foreign dance companies (Antonio, Ballet Folklorico of Mexico, and the Polish State Song and Dance Company 'Slask') filled in for short seasons at a time, and the closing of the Royal Opera House for amphitheatre rebuilding brought the Royal Ballet to a temporary home at Drury Lane from 9 June to 18 July. They included Margot Fonteyn and Rudolf Nureyev; Nureyev, by the way, made his first London appearance at Drury Lane at a Gala matinée of ballet on 3 November 1961, *not* at Covent Garden.

On 19 August, presented by Jack Hylton, *Camelot* at last appeared. Although technically a transfer from America, it was actually given a new cast, a new director in Robert Helpmann, new choreography and an extensively rewritten book. John Truscott, who was responsible for the designs, re-read T. H. White's *The Once and Future King*, one of his favourite books and the basis of Lerner's libretto, and conjured one superb Arthurian picture after another—a shimmering cobweb palace for Morgan le Fey (or Fay as in T. H. White), a glowing amber chapel for Arthur and a stunning sunset backdrop for the finale.

The unkind joke of the time was that *Camelot* was the only show anyone ever left whistling the scenery. Somewhere, somehow, all the magic in White's masterpiece got lost in adaptation. The lovable Merlyn, promisingly cast to Miles Malleson, got severely reduced in the writing.

One of the many brilliant John Truscott sets for *Camelot*. *Tom Hustler*

(Originally there were suggestions that Helpmann himself might play Merlyn but his interest varied in inverse proportion to the size of the role when it began to shrink.) The score could not boast a memorable song and the strong cast was left to struggle with what remained.

Laurence Harvey as Arthur proved a far better singer and dancer than anyone had expected, and he extracted the utmost from the speech he was given to provide an unconventional Act One curtain. Elizabeth Larner, previously the Kate of *Kiss Me Kate*, as Guenevere; and Barry Kent as Lancelot, gave no hint that they lacked faith in their roles if indeed they did, but played them up to the hilt. Sadly, there was nothing they could do to dispel the general air of disappointment. The long awaited mountain had proved to be a mouse.

In February 1965, Paul Daneman took over from Laurence Harvey and *Camelot* ran until 13 November of the same year. It closed to make way for *Hello Dolly*! This Michael Stewart book, with lyrics and music by Jerry Herman, was based on Thornton Wilder's *The Matchmaker*—a sentimental farce that promised little. It was unashamedly a star vehicle, and by the time twelve songs had been interpolated, there were no genuine characters left. Jokes that might have been funny rising from believable situations were tacked on and fell flat. Horace Vandergelder the miser was played by Loring Smith who had had the distinction of creating the role of Yonkers in the original play, but the role, like the others, was pared to a functional minimum. This 'real old show-business hokum at its loudest and brightest' (*Daily Telegraph*) displeased Milton Shulman considerably. He thundered in the *Evening Standard*: 'The arch squirming, the naive slapstick, the gauche lines that are proffered as comedy in this situation makes our weariest Whitehall farce a master-piece of intellectual wit by comparison.'

One can grant the justice of most of the harsh words, but the show had compensating virtues. With Gower Champion directing his own choreography, the dancers moved with the precision lost to the London stage with the demise of *West Side Story*. Oliver Smith supplied elegant backdrops and Freddy Wittop colourful period costumes. And *Hello Dolly!* had a genuine eighteen-carat star. This was Mary Martin. Now fifty-two, and in her first London appearance for thirteen years, she came, she saw, she sang, she danced and she conquered. The audience ate from the palm of her hand. As the *Queen* put it: 'Mary Martin can

Jak's December 1965 view of the craze for the title song from *Hello Dolly!*
Evening Standard

" I'll spear the next one who sings Hello Dolly !"
London Express Service.

turn them from roaring laughter to foot-stamping applause to pin-dropping silence with one flick of a ginger eyebrow. . . . It isn't art, it isn't theatre; it's mass surrender and at least half the joy of it is in being part of an audience so euphorically overcome.' With the title, and some would say only, song in the evening, an amusing Gower Champion dance for waiters ended, and Miss Martin appeared at the top of a stairway (where else?) to belt it out with gusto. It was, conceded Hugh Leonard, 'the show-stopper of all time'. For those who like that sort of thing, it was precisely the sort of thing they like.

In May 1966, Mary Martin was succeeded by Dora Bryan who had the courage to bend the role to her own well-known idiosyncrasies, and scored something of a minor triumph in so doing. By transforming the show to Hello, Dora! she also restored some semblance of balance. No mean achievement when one realizes that that other well-known Dolly Levi, Barbra Streisand, had just opened elsewhere in London with *Funny Girl*.

An interesting example of the hard sell was adopted by David Merrick, the presenter of *Hello Dolly!* Shortly after the first night and the generally hostile critical reaction, he launched a television commercial which included selective quotations from reviews which made the show sound the greatest American import since air-conditioning. This is common managerial practice, but what drew complaints from the London Critics' Circle was that he quoted the master of invective, Bernard Levin, who had reviewed only the New York production. The Independent Television Authority were rightly displeased.

I tell the story because it demonstrates how the big musical has become not just a show but a vast financial gamble resting not on artistic merits alone but upon the power of publicity. When he who pays the piper calls the tune, we are not always going to like the melodies.

We now come to December 1967 and the unhappy *The Four Musketeers*. I say unhappy advisedly, because of the trials and tribulations that attended the frantic rewrites in the last week before the opening. Bill Owen, Jan Brinker and opera singer Joyce Blackham left during the preview week when their roles were curtailed, and it was revealed in January that the three musketeers, Jeremy Lloyd, Glyn Owen and John Junkin had already given notice for the same reason, but had agreed to continue until March to give the show a chance of opening on time.

All this was doubly tragic in view of the considerable talent involved. There was Peter Coe, a talented and imaginative producer, a book by Michael Pertwee, music by Laurie Johnson, lyrics by Herbert Kretzmer, costumes by Loudun Sainthill and one of Sean Kenny's giant transmogrifying sets. On paper it looked to be the Great British Musical. In the event it was a sub-standard British panto.

When the dust had settled on the back-stage disputes, all that was left was Kenneth Connor to camp it up as King Louis XIII, Elizabeth Larner to play, at three days' notice, Joyce Blackham's Milady, and, in as unlikely a casting as Charlie Drake as Hamlet, Harry Secombe as D'Artagnan. I love Secombe dearly, but even I would doubt his ability to sustain a two and a half hour musical with rubber eyebrows and squeaky Goon voices. Apart from his genuine tenor, that was about the sum total and without one memorable song, it showed.

The year 1968 saw the start of the London Opera Society's annual feasts for canary fanciers, seasons that have brought the greatest singers in the world to the Lane—Joan Sutherland, Elena Suliotis, Renata Tebaldi, Placido Domingo and Boris Christoff among them. Meanwhile *The Four Musketeers* died a lingering death and the publicity machine began working towards the next major event—February 1969 and *Mame*.

Milton Shulman suggested that the real stars of *Mame* were Bernard Delfont and Harold Fielding, and when one considers the publicity build-up to the arrival of Ginger Rogers and the opening of *Mame*, he was absolutely correct. If a latter-day Messiah got one quarter of the column inches devoted to Miss Rogers, he would have done well.

Ginger Rogers in *Mame*—a triumph for artistry or for publicity? *Roger Clifford Ltd*

Ginger Rogers smiles for the Press in the Drury Lane dressing room specially decorated in silk and glass for her sojourn in *Mame*. *Syndication International*

Compared with her, Tauber, Mary Martin and Julie Andrews crept in *incognito*.

She docked at Southampton with fifty-seven years of her life and seventy-three films behind her, to be greeted by a 52-piece band playing the title song of *Mame*. After a few waves to the waiting press photographers, she stepped into a private train—'The Ginger Rogers Mame Express'—and arrived to a similar fanfare at Waterloo Station. Later she was shown her dressing room which had had a face-lift of 194 yards of pale pink raw silk and 6,000 pieces of mirrored glass at a cost of £2,000. Of the £100,000 spent on *Mame*, £15,000 went on her costumes. Her salary, the highest ever paid in the English theatre, was £5,000 a week, that is, about a quarter of a million a year. If star treatment made a star, Miss Rogers was super-stellar. Even her opinions became important—'I'll tell you what's wrong with this country. Socialism, yeah, socialism. That's what's wrong with you.'

There was only one thing lacking in all this, a performance which could match the bally-hoo. *Mame* has been unfairly dismissed as a one song show, because Jerry Herman produced music and lyrics which, without being brilliant, are acceptable and pleasant. Where the tedium crept in was in a muddled book by Jerome Lawrence and Robert E. Lee which gave no hint of the gloriously eccentric Mame whom Patrick Dennis had created in his original novel. And what they left out, Ginger Rogers was unable to put in.

When the evening begged for the zany and the wacky, she was only able to supply Ginger Rogers. It was not enough. If it had been the dazzling Ginger Rogers of 1935 and *Top Hat*, there might have been compensations. As it was, the only sense of wonder came not from what she did, but that she was able to do it as well as she did.

Mame duly took £100,000 in the first month, so the gamble and the expense paid off financially. Artistically, even allowing for an amusing cameo by Ann Beach as the pregnant Gooch, it did not. It ended in March 1970 when Ginger Rogers's contract ran out. Harold Fielding said that there was no point in continuing without her. Let, however, the final word rest with another American super-star Carol Channing who gave thirty-seven one-woman shows at the Lane when *Mame* ended. She opened by recalling the stars who had preceded her on the

The closing scene from *The Great Waltz. Roger Clifford Ltd*

The Royal retiring room behind the Royal Box. *Peter Abbey*

august Drury boards. 'Betterton, Cibber, Garrick . . .' with a pause for a
hint of a wicked smile '. . . and Ginger Rogers?'

If *Mame* represented a look back to the Hollywood of the thirties,
The Great Waltz, known to its enemies as *The Great Schmaltz*, might
have emerged from a search in a Viennese discard pile of old operettas.
It opened on 9 July 1970, and continued doing good business into 1972.
In 'B' movie dialogue, it purported to tell the story of the relationship
between Johann Strauss Snr and his son Johann Strauss Jnr (known for
the purposes of easy identification as Schani), as Strauss Jnr battled for the
old man's crown as the Viennese Waltz King. The conflict was not
allowed to get out of hand and all ended happily with Strauss Snr, who
had been waylaid by a subterfuge which would not fool an intelligent
three-year-old, grabbing the baton from his son to lead the entire company in *The Blue Danube* with all the appearance of belated paternal
admiration.

The décor and costumes are derivative of the once popular chocolate
box school, and the evening is as overlaid with icing sugar and double

The Saloon. *Peter Abbey*

cream as a rich Viennese pastry. Adapted from the music of Strauss by Robert Wright and George Forrest, who proved with *Kismet* and *Kean* that they are capable of better things, even the melodies could not rescue the tedium engendered by an excess of Viennese V's—'Vell, I vill be on my vay now, Herr Shtrauss'. Peter Graves, who joined the cast as Harthopf in 1971, was returning to the house where he had played in *Glamorous Night*, *Careless Rapture* and *Crest of the Wave*. He must have thought the clock had stood still in the interim.

The singing, at least at the performance I saw, was below par, despite the presence of Sari Barabas of the Munich State Opera and Walter Cassel of the New York Met.

It can be argued that if this is what people want, what is wrong with that? The whole history of the Lane proves that poor quality fare, if it is in accord with the mood of the times, can make money. Shakespeare, even in so dazzlingly original a form as Peter Brook's *Midsummer Night's Dream*, is not going to fill Drury Lane nightly for twelve months or so. A big musical in all probability will.

Today's exterior. *Peter Abbey*

So long as there are such vast profits to be reaped from the lavish musical, not only at the box office, but from the sales of gramophone records and film rights, hopeful investment in the *genre* is likely to continue. What worries me is that as the costs of launching a new musical increase, the writers, composers and others who bring creativity, originality and wit to the proceedings, will increasingly lose control over their product. There are already signs that the men who put up the money tend to rely on the adoption of a computerized proven formula; to play safe.

If the trend continues, we may see the musical become a moribund museum piece as out of touch with its time and its audience as the melodrama. Its decline and fall could parallel the demise of Hollywood where ultimately the accountancy mind brought disaster. In the short term, safe formulas can bring life; in the long term, an inevitable lingering death.

If this happens, it will be fascinating to see what new theatrical phenomenon will sustain a Drury Lane faced with yet another vicissitude. With three hundred years of resilience and a tradition unique in world theatre behind it, who could be arrogant enough to assert that the Theatre Royal, Drury Lane will not find an answer? If any lessons from the past emerge from this account of its history to help find that answer, the labour of the writing will have been well worth while.

Books Consulted

NB: Plays are included only if the edition carries a useful introduction.

ADOLPHUS, JOHN. *Memoirs of John Bannister, Comedian* (2 volumes), 1839.
AITKEN, GEORGE A. *Life of Richard Steele* (2 volumes), 1889.
APPLETON, WILLIAM W. *Charles Macklin*, 1961.
ARCHER, WILLIAM. *William Charles Macready*, 1890.
ASHLEY, MAURICE. *England in the Seventeenth Century*, 1952.
ASTON, ANTHONY. *A Brief Supplement* to Apology for the Life of Colley Cibber, Esq. (see under Colley Cibber), 1889.
BAKER, DAVID ERSKINE. *Biographia Dramatica* (6 volumes), 1812.
BAKER, H. BARTON. *The London Stage 1576-1888* (2 volumes), 1889.
BAKER, HERSCHEL. *John Philip Kemble*, 1942.
BAKER, ROGER. *Drag*, 1968.
BARKER, RICHARD HINDRY. *Mr Cibber of Drury Lane*, 1939.
BARTON, MARGARET. *Garrick*, 1948.
BEHN, APHRA (edited M. Summers). *The Works of Aphra Behn*, 1915.
BELLAMY, GEORGE ANNE. *An Apology for the life of George Anne Bellamy by herself* (6 volumes), 1785.
BETTERTON, THOMAS (Collected Oldys & Curll). *History of the English Stage*, 1741.
BOADEN, JAMES (edited). *The Private Correspondence of David Garrick* (2 volumes), 1831.
   Life of Mrs Jordan (2 volumes), 1831.
   Memoirs of John Philip Kemble (2 volumes), 1825.
BOOTH, MICHAEL. *English Melodrama*, 1965.
BORGMAN, ALBERT S. *Life and Death of William Mountfort*, 1935.
BOSWELL, ELEANORE. *The Restoration Court Stage 1660-1702*, 1932.
BROWN, JOHN RUSSELL. *Shakespeare's Plays in Performance*, 1966.
BROWN, TOM (edited Hayward). *Amusements Serious and Comical* etc., 1927.
BUNN, ALFRED. *The Stage, Both Before and Behind the Curtain* (3 volumes), 1840.
BURNIM, KALMAN A. *David Garrick, Director*, 1961.
BUSS, R. W. *Charles Fleetwood*, 1915.
BUTLER, E. M. *Sheridan: A Ghost Story*, 1931.
BYRON, GEORGE GORDON, LORD. *Letters*, Everyman, 1962.
CAMPBELL, LILY BESS. *Scenes & Machines on the English Stage during the Renaissance*, 1923.
CHALMERS, GEORGE. *An Apology*, 1797.
CHATTERTON, FREDERICK BELSIR AND KENNEY, CHARLES. *Poets and Profits at Drury Lane*, 1875.
CHESHIRE, DAVID. *Theatre, History, Criticism and Reference*, 1967.
CHETWOOD, WILLIAM RUFUS. *The British Theatre*, 1750.
   The Dramatic Congress, 1743.
   General History of the Stage, 1749.
CIBBER, COLLEY. *Apology for the life of Colley Cibber, Esq.*, 1740.
   New edition with *Historia Histrionica* and Aston's *Supplement* (2 volumes), 1889.
   The Laureat: The Right Side of Colley Cibber Esq., 1740.

CIBBER, THEOPHILUS. *Letter to John Highmore*, 1733.
　　Lives and Characters of Actors (2 volumes), 1753.
COLLIER, JEREMY. *A Short View* etc. (5th edition) with answers to Congreve, Drake etc., 1730.
CONGREVE, FRANCIS. *Authentic Memoirs of the late Charles Macklin*, 1798.
COOKE, WILLIAM. *Memoirs of Charles Macklin, Comedian*, 1804.
　　Memoirs of Samuel Foote (3 volumes), 1805.
'CORNWALL, BARRY'. (PROCTOR, B. W.). *Life of Edmund Kean*, 1835.
CUMBERLAND, RICHARD. *Memoirs*, 1806.
CURLL, EDMUND. *Faithful Memoirs of Mrs Oldfield*, 1731.
　　Life of Robert Wilks, 1733.
DARBYSHIRE, ALFRED. *The Art of the Victorian Stage*, 1907.
DARLINGTON, WILLIAM. *Sheridan 1751–1816*, 1951.
DASENT, ARTHUR. *Private Life of Charles II*, 1927.
DAVIES, THOMAS. *Dramatic Miscellanies* (3 volumes), 1783.
　　Memoirs of the Life of David Garrick (2 volumes), 1780.
DEAN, BASIL. *The Theatre at War*, 1956.
　　Seven Ages: an Autobiography 1888–1927, 1970.
DICKENS, CHARLES (edited Richard Findlater). *Memoirs of Joseph Grimaldi*, 1968.
Dictionary of National Biography
DISHER, MAURICE WILLIAM. *Blood and Thunder (Victorian Melodrama)*, 1949.
　　Mad Genius: A Biography of Edmund Kean, 1950.
　　Melodrama: Plots that Thrilled, 1954.
DOBREE, BONAMY. *Restoration Comedy 1660–1720*, 1924.
　　Restoration Tragedy 1660–1720, 1929.
　　English Literature in the Early Eighteenth Century 1700–40, 1959.
DORAN, JOHN. *Their Majesties Servants: Annals of the English Stage* (3 volumes), 1864
　　In and about Drury Lane, 1881.
DOWNER, ALAN S. *The Eminent Tragedian William Charles Macready*, 1966.
DOWNES, JOHN. *Roscius Anglicanus*, 1708.
　　(Edited F. G. Waldron and additions by Thomas Davies), 1789.
Dramatic Censor, 1811.
DRURY, GEORGE THORN (editor). *A Little Ark*, 1921.
　　Covent Garden Drollery, 1928.
DRYDEN, JOHN. *The Poems* (edited James Kingsley) (4 volumes), 1958.
DUNBAR, JANET. *Peg Woffington and Her World*, 1968.
EGERTON, WILLIAM (Edmund Curll). *Faithful Memoirs of Mrs Oldfield*, 1731.
ELLIS, STEWART. *Life of Michael Kelly*, 1930.
ENGEL, LEHMAN. *The American Musical Theater*, 1967.
FEASEY, L. *On the Boards of Old Dury*, 1951.
FFRENCH, YVONNE. *Mrs Siddons, Tragic Actress*, 1954.
FILON, AUGUSTINE. *The English Stage*, 1897.
FITZGERALD, PERCY. *Life of David Garrick*, 1899.
　　A New History of the English Stage (2 volumes), 1882.
　　Books of Theatrical Anecdotes, 1874.
FLECKNOE, RICHARD. *Life of Tomaso the Wanderer*, (orig. 1667), 1925.
FORSTER, JOHN AND LEWES, G. H. *Dramatic Essays*, 1896.
FOTHERGILL, A. B. *Mrs Jordan*, 1965.

FOWELL, F. AND PALMER F., *Censorship in England*, 1913.

FULFORD, ROGER. *Samuel Whitbread 1764–1815*, 1967.

GALT, JOHN. *The Lives of the Players*, 1831.

GARRICK, DAVID. *The Letters of David Garrick* (edited David M. Little and George M. Kahrl) (3 volumes), 1963.
    The Poetical Works of David Garrick, 1785.

GASCOIGNE, BAMBER. *World Theatre*, 1968.

GENEST, JOHN. *Some Account of the English Stage 1660–1830* (10 volumes), 1832.

GENTLEMAN, FRANCIS. *The Dramatic Censor*, 1770, (2 volumes reprint), 1969

GEORGE, MARY DOROTHY. *London Life in the Eighteenth Century*, 1925.

GIBBS, LEWIS. *Sheridan*, 1947.

GILDON, CHARLES. *Life of Betterton.*
    (edited) *The Postboy Robbed of His Mails*, 1706.
    Memoirs of Life of William Wycherley, 1718.

GOLDSMITH, OLIVER. *Enquiry into the Present State of Learning in Europe*, 1774.

GOSSE, SIR EDMUND. (introduction) *Restoration Plays*, 1912.

GOULD, ROBERT. *The Playhouse: a Satyr* in
    The Works (Volume 2), 1709.

GRAVES, CHARLES. *The Cochran Story*, 1951.

Grove's Dictionary of Music and Musicians (ed. Maitland), 1904–10.

HAMILTON, ANTHONY. (translated Quennell). *Memoirs of Count Grammant*, 1930.

HARBAGE, ALFRED. *Annals of English Drama*, 1964.
    Sir William Davenant: Poet, Venturer, 1935.
    Thomas Killigrew: Cavalier Dramatist, 1930.

HARDWICKE, CEDRIC, SIR. *A Victorian in Orbit*, 1961.

HARTNOLL, PHYLLIS (editor), *The Oxford Companion to the Theatre*, 1951.

HASLEWOOD, J. *Green Room Gossip*, 1809.

HAYMAN, RONALD. *Techniques of Acting*, 1970.

HAZLITT, WILLIAM. *A View of the English Stage*, 1818.

HEPPNER, SAM. *Cockie*, 1969.

HERBERT, SIR HENRY. (edited Joseph Q. Adams). *Dramatic Records*, 1917.

HOLLAR, WENCESLAUS. *Portrait of Thomas Killigrew with Verses* (Thomason Tracts) 1642.

HOTSON, JOHN LESLIE. *The Commonwealth and Restoration Stage*, 1928.

HOWARD, DIANA. *London Theatres and Music Halls 1850–1950*, 1970.

HUNT, LEIGH (edited L. H. and C. W. Houtchens). *Dramatic Criticism 1808–1831*, 1950.

JOHNSON, SAMUEL. *Prologue Spoken at the Opening of the Theatre in Drury Lane in 1747*, 1902 (Facsimile of 1st Edition).

JONES, HENRY ARTHUR. *The Renaissence of the English Drama*, 1895.

KELLY, JOHN ALEXANDER. *German Visitors to English Theatres in the Eighteenth Century*, 1936.

KELLY, MICHAEL (actually written Theodore Hook). *Reminiscences* (2 volumes), 1826.

KIRKMAN, JAMES THOMAS. *Life of Macklin* (2 volumes), 1799.

KNIGHT, G. WILSON. *The Golden Labyrinth: A Study of British Drama*, 1962.

KNIGHT, JOSEPH. *David Garrick*, 1894.
    Dramatic Criticism, 1893.

KRAUSE, DAVID (edited and introduction). *The Dolmen Boucicault*, 1964.

KRUTCH, J. W. *Comedy and Conscience after the Restoration*, 1924.
    Eighteenth Century English Drama, 1967.

LAMB, CHARLES. *Essays of Elia*, 1820–33.

LANGBAINE, GERARD. *An Account of the English Dramatick Poets*, 1691.

LEGOUIS, EMILE AND CAZAMIAN, LOUIS. *A History of English Literature*, 1928.

LEWES, GEORGE HENRY. *On Actors and the Art of Acting*, 1875,

LOFTIS, JOHN. *Comedy and Society from Congreve to Fielding*, 1959.
    The Politics of Drama in Augustan England, 1963.
    Steele at Drury Lane, 1952.

London Stage, The, 1660–1800.
  Part I   1660–1700, edited William Van Lennep, 1965.
  Part II 1700–1729, edited Emmett L. Avery, (2 volumes) 1960.
  Part III 1729–1747, edited Arthur Scouten, (2 volumes) 1961.
  Part IV 1747–1776, edited G. W. Stone, Jnr., (3 volumes) 1962.
  Part V 1776–1800, edited C. B. Hogan, (3 volumes), 1967.

LOWE, R. W. *Bibliographical Account of English Theatrical Literature*, 1888.
    Thomas Betterton, 1890.

LUBBOCK, MARK. *Complete Book of Light Opera*, 1962.

MACAFEE, HELEN. *Pepys on the Restoration Stage*, 1916.

MACINNES, COLIN. *Sweet Saturday Night*, 1967.

MACKLIN, CHARLES. *An Apology for his Conduct* (trial for murder of Hallam), 1773.
    The Case of Macklin v Garrick, 1743.
    Mr Macklin's Reply to Mr Garrick's Answer (including previous papers), 1743.

MACMANAWAY, JAMES (edited). *Joseph Quincy Adams Memorial Studies*, 1948.

MACMILLAN, DOUGALD. *Drury Lane Calendar, 1747–76*, 1938.

MACQUEEN-POPE, W. *Ivor*, 1954.
    Pillars of Drury Lane, 1955.
    Theatre Royal, Drury Lane, 1945.

MACREADY, W. C. (edited J. C. Trewin). *Journal 1832–51*, 1967.

MALCOLM, JAMES, P. *Anecdotes of the Manners and Customs of London in the Eighteenth Century* (2nd edition), 1810.

MANDER, RAYMOND AND MITCHENSON, JOE. *Musical Comedy*, 1969.
    The Theatres of London, 1961.

MANTZIUS, KARL. *History of Theatrical Art in Ancient and Modern Times*, volume V, 1909.

MANVELL, ROGER. *Sarah Siddons*, 1970.

MARSTON, WESTLAND. *Our Recent Actors*, 1888.

MORLEY, SHERIDAN. *A Talent to Amuse* (Noël Coward), 1970.

MURPHY, ARTHUR. *Life of David Garrick*, 1801.

NETTLETON, G. H. *The Drama and the Stage*, 1913.
    English Drama of the Restoration and Eighteenth Century 1642–1780, 1914.

NICOLL, ALLARDYCE. *A History of Restoration Drama 1660–1700*, 1923.
    A History of Early Eighteenth Century Drama 1700–50, 1925.
    A History of Late Eighteenth Century Drama 1750–1800, 1927.
    A History of Early Nineteenth Century Drama 1800–50, 1930.
    A History of Late Nineteenth Century Drama 1850–1900 (2 volumes), 1946.

ODELL, G. C. D. *Shakespeare from Betterton to Irving* (2 volumes), 1921.

OMAN, CAROLA. *David Garrick*, 1958.

On the Unhappy Conflagration of the Theatre Royal, 1672.

OSBORN, JAMES M. *John Dryden: Some Biographical Facts and Problems*, 1940.

OTWAY, THOMAS (edited Montague Summers). *The Complete Works of Thomas Otway* (3 volumes), 1926.

OULTON, W. C. *History of the Theatres of London* (2 volumes), 1818.

PALLAVICINO, F. (edited Gildon). *The Postboy Robbed of His Mails*, 1706.

PEARSON, HESKETH. *The Last Actor-Managers*, 1956.

PEDICORD, H. W. *The Theatrical Public in the Time of Garrick*, 1954.

PEPYS, SAMUEL (edited Latham and Matthews). *Diary* (volumes I, II, III), 1970.

PLAYFAIR, GILES. *Kean*, 1939.
   The Strange Life of Master Betty, 1967.

Playhouse Scuffle, The, 1710.

PLUMB, J. H. *England in the Eighteenth Century 1714–1815*, 1950.

POLLOCK, SIR FREDERICK, BART. (edited). *Macready's Reminiscences* and *Selections from his Diaries and Letters* (2 volumes), 1875.

PRICE, CECIL (editor). *The Letters of Richard Brinsley Sheridan* (3 volumes), 1966.

QUIN, JAMES. *Life of James Quin*, 1887.
   Quin's Jests, 1766.

RAE, W. F. *Sheridan* (2 volumes), 1896.

RAYMOND, GEORGE. *Life of R. W. Elliston*, 1857.

REYNOLDS, ERNEST. *Early Victorian Drama 1830–70*, 1936.

REYNOLDS, FREDERIC. *Life and Times of Frederic Reynolds by himself*, 1827.

RHODES, RAYMOND CROMPTON. *Harlequin Sheridan*, 1933.

RICE, CHARLES (edited Arthur Colby Sprague and Bertram Shuttleworth). *The London Theatre in the 1830s*, 1950.

RICHARDS, DICK. *Ginger: A Salute to a Star*, 1969.

ROBINSON, HENRY CRABB. *The London Theatre 1811–66*, 1966.

ROSENTHAL, HAROLD AND WARRACK, JOHN. *Concise Oxford Dictionary of Opera*, 1964.

ROWELL, GEORGE. *The Victorian Theatre*, 1956.

RUSSELL, WILLIAM CLARK. *Representative Actors*, 1869.

SAXE WYNDHAM, HENRY. *The Annals of Covent Garden Theatre from 1732–1897* (2 volumes), 1906.

SCOTT, CLEMENT. *The Drama of Yesterday*, 1899.

SENIOR, FRANCESCA D. P. *Life and Times of Colley Cibber*, 1928.

SHAKESPEARE, WILLIAM. *Plays and Poems* (Malone edition) (volumes II and III), 1821.

Shakespeare Society's Papers (Volume IV), 1844–9.

SHELDON, ESTHER. *Thomas Sheridan*, 1967.

SHERIDAN, RICHARD BRINSLEY. *The Letters* (edited Cecil Price) (3 volumes), 1966.
   The Works (edited by F. Stainforth), 1874.

SHERWIN, OSCAR. *Uncorking Old Sherry*, 1960.

SHORT, ERNEST. *Fifty Years of Vaudeville*, 1946.
   Sixty Years of Theatre, 1951.

SICHEL, WALTER. *Sheridan* (2 volumes), 1909.

SISSONS, MICHAEL AND FRENCH, PHILIP (edited). *The Age of Austerity 1945–51*, 1963.

SKIPWITH, FULWAR. *A Brief Account of the Skipwiths of Newbold, Metheringham and Prestwould*, 1867.

SMYTH, WILLIAM. *Memoir of Mr Sheridan*, 1840.

SPENCER, HAZELTON. *Shakespeare Improved*, 1927.

State Papers, Domestic: Charles II 1660–66 (7 volumes), 1860–64.

STEELE, SIR RICHARD (edited John Loftis). *The Theatre, 1720*, 1962.

STIRLING, EDWARD. *Old Drury Lane: Fifty Years Recollections of Author, Actor and Manager* (2 volumes), 1881.

STOCHHOLM, JOHANNE M. *Garrick's Folly*, 1964.

SUMMERS, MONTAGUE. *The Playhouse of Pepys*, 1935.

    The Restoration Theatre, 1934.

    Shakespeare Adaptations, 1932.

Survey of London (volume XXXV), 1970.

SUTHERLAND, JAMES. *English Literature in the Late Seventeenth Century*, 1969.

TAYLOR, DEEMS. *Some Enchanted Evenings*, 1955.

TAYLOR, W. D. (edited and introduction). *Eighteenth Century Comedy*, 1929.

THALER, ALWIN. *Shakspere to Sheridan*, 1922.

THOMAS, TOBYAS. *The Life of the Famous Comedian Joe Haines*, 1701.

THOMSON, DAVID. *England in the Nineteenth Century 1815–1914*, 1950.

TREWIN, J. C. *The Gay Twenties*, 1958.

    Mr Macready, 1955.

    The Night has been Unruly, 1957.

    The Pomping Folk in the Nineteenth Century Theatre, 1968.

    Shakespeare on the English Stage 1900–64, 1964.

    The Turbulent Thirties, 1960.

TURBERVILLE, A. S. (edited). *Johnson's England* (2 volumes), 1933.

VICTOR, BENJAMIN. *History of the Theatres of London and Dublin* (3 volumes), 1761–71.

VILLIERS, G., DUKE OF BUCKINGHAM (edited M. Summers). *The Rehearsal*, 1914.

WATSON, E. B. *Sheridan to Robertson, a Study of the Nineteenth Century London Stage*, 1926.

WELLS, STARING B. (editor). *A Comparison Between the Two Stages*, 1942.

WHINCOP, THOMAS. *Scanderbeg*, 1747.

WILEY, AUTREY NEIL. *Rare Prologues and Epilogues 1642–1700*, 1940.

WILKINSON, TATE. *Memoirs of his own Life* (4 volumes), 1790.

WILSON, G. B. L. *A Dictionary of Ballet*, 1961.

WILSON, JOHN H. *All the Kings' Ladies*, 1958.

    Mr Goodman the Player, 1964.

    Nell Gwynn, 1952.

    A Rake and his Times, 1954.

WOODDESSON, W. T. *A Slight Sketch of the Performances at Drury Lane*, 1828.

WRIGHT, JAMES. *Historia Histrionica* (in Cibber's Apology for the Life), 1889.

WRIGHT, THOMAS. *Caricature History of the Georges*, 1868.

OTHER SOURCES

PUBLIC RECORD OFFICE: Lord Chamberlain's Papers, Correspondence and Warrant Books.

BRITISH MUSEUM: Collection of Memoranda relating to the Drury Lane Theatre arranged by James Winston (23 volumes).

Collection of Newspaper Cuttings.

R. J. Smith Collection of Dramatic Materials (collected 1825–40).

Miscellaneous Harleian and Additional MSS.

ENTHOVEN COLLECTION, VICTORIA AND ALBERT MUSEUM:

Drury Lane boxes.

Miscellaneous files and cuttings books.

Journals, Newspapers etc. including: *Annual Register, Daily Post, European Magazine, Grub Street Journal, Illustrated London News, Modern Philology, Notes and Queries, Plays and Players, Pall Mall Gazette, Play Pictorial, Plays and Players, Review of English Studies, The Sketch, Stage Year Books, The Tatler, The Times, Theatre Notebook, Theatre World.*

Index

© Cassell & Co. Ltd., 1972

Siege of Rhodes, The (D'Avenant), 11
Silent Woman, The (Jonson), 27
Sims, George R., 177
Sins of Society, The (Raleigh and Hamilton), 170–1, 173
Skipworth, Sir Thomas, 62, 80
Sleeping Beauty, The (pantomime), 166, 174, 175
Smith, C. Aubrey, 170
Smith, Edward Tyrrell, 150
Smith, Loring, 206
Smith, Muriel, 200
Smith, Oliver, 206
Smith, Sheridan, 150
Smith, William, 60
Song of the Drum, The (Ellis and Finck), 184
South Pacific (Rodgers and Hammerstein), 198–200
Steele, Sir Richard, 69, 86–7
Stein, Joseph, 201
Stewart, Michael, 205
Stolz, Robert, 185, 192
Strauss, Richard, 175, 198
Streets of London, The (Boucicault), 151
Summers, Montague, 24
Sun Never Sets, The, 193
Swiney, Owen, 78–9, 81, 82, 83–4

Tate, Nahum, 57, 70
Tatham, John, 6
Tauber, Richard, 185
Tearle, Godfrey, 177
Tempest, Marie, 166
Tempest, The, 202; Shadwell's version, 51
Tennent, H. M., 188, 192
Terriss, Ellaline, 170
Terry, Ellen, 169, 170
Thief of Bagdad, The (film), 180
Three Musketeers, The (musical), 184
Three Sisters, The (Kern and Hammerstein), 185
Tilley, Vesta, 155, 158
Titheradge, Madge, 177
Tree, Herbert Beerbohm, 166, 170
Tree, Mrs Beerbohm, 168–9
Trewin, J. C., 124, 192, 197, 201
Trial by Jury (Gilbert and Sullivan), 170
Truscott, John, 204
Tynan, Kenneth, 203
Tyrannick Love (Dryden), 40, 44, 46, 50

Underhill, Cave, 20, 63
Urals Ensemble, 202

Van Druten, John, 200
Van Lennep, William, 17
Vanbrugh, Sir John, 63, 74, 78, 111
Venice Preserved (Otway), 61
Verno, Jerry, 184
Vestris, Madame, 124, 143
Victor, Benjamin, 88, 95
Virtuoso, The (Shadwell), 42
Vokes family, 151, 154
Vortigern and Rowena (Ireland), 117
Vroom, Edward, 165

Wallace, Ian, 201
Walpole, Horace, 116
Waterloo (Doyle), 166
Way of the World, The (Congreve), 70
Welchman, Harry, 181
West, Gracie, 188
Whincop, Thomas, 35
Whip, The (Raleigh and Hamilton), 171–3
Whitbread, Samuel, 133, 134
White Heather, The (Raleigh and Hamilton), 161
Whitehead, Charles, 91
Wild Gallant, The (Dryden), 38–9, 49
Wild Violets (Stolz), 185, 186
Wilks, Robert, 75–6, 79, 80, 82, 83–5, 87, 88, 89
Williams, Harcourt, 170
Wilson, Julie, 200
Winter's Tale, The, 104, 116
Wintershall, William, 17, 19, 20, 26, 29, 52
Witts, The (D'Avenant), 15
Woffington, Peg, 92, 98, 101, 102, 114
Wonder, The (Centlivre), 107
Wood, Sir Henry, 176
Woodward, Henry, 71, 101, 103
World, The (Merritt and Harris), 158
Wren, Sir Christopher, 31, 52
Wright, Robert, 212
Wyatt, Benjamin, 133
Wycherley, William, 38, 42
Wymark, Patrick, 202
Wyndham, Sir Charles, 170

Yate, Richard, 101, 103
Younge, Elizabeth, 103
Youth, 158